TRADITIONAL MALAYSIAN CUISINE

Berita
Publishing Sdn Bhd (15654-K)

ISBN 967-969-139-X

BERITA PUBLISHING SDN. BHD. (15654-K)
No. 16-20, Jalan 4/109E
Desa Business Park
Taman Desa
Off Jalan Klang Lama
58100 KUALA LUMPUR

Tel: (603) 76208111
Fax: (603) 76208018

A Member of Malaysian Book Publishers Association
Membership No: 198105

© Berita Publishing Sdn. Bhd. 1983

ISBN 978-967-969-139-9

First published 1983
Twentieth reprint 1998
Twenty first reprint 1999
Twenty second reprint 2001
Twenty third reprint 2003
Twenty fourth reprint 2007
Twenty fifth reprint 2010

Distributed by:
Cresent News (K.L) Sdn. Bhd.
No. 19, Jalan SBC 3
Taman Sri Batu Caves
68100 BATU CAVES
SELANGOR DARUL EHSAN

Tel: (603)-61842448   Fax: (603)-61842418
E-mail: crescent@tm.net.my
Website: www.crescentbook.com

Printed by:
Percetakan Jiwa Baru Sdn. Bhd. (18264-U)
Lot 14, No. 2, Jalan P/8
Kawasan MIEL Fasa 2
Bandar Baru Bangi
Cheras Jaya
43000 BANGI
SELANGOR DARUL EHSAN

CONTENTS

Edited by AYESHA HARBEN

Compiled by Faizah Omar, Hannah Abisheganaden, Ellina Majid

Photographed by Jenhor Siow

Photography Co-ordinator: Latifah Idris

Art Director: Tony Chong

Artists: Samad Karim, Hassim Ahmad

INTRODUCTION

Think Malaysia and think the heady eternal green of the jungle, the fragrance of wild flowers, the steamy warmth of the tropics punctuated by refreshing downpours of monsoon rain, the languid, meandering rivers teeming with fish, the leafy, tropical trees hanging heavy with exotic fruits.... a meeting of cultures, a mingling of races... And a wealth of culinary delights.

Malaysia's gastronomic heritage goes back more than half a dozen centuries to the age of discovery and exploration. Stately brigantines resplendent with cargoes of ebony, sandalwood, opium and perfume from as far-flung places as India and Arabia, scanned the Malay archipelago on missions of trade. Magnificent Chinese junks on goodwill missions by royal command, arrived on Malay shores bearing precious chests of porcelain, ivory, silk, brocade and even a genuine Chinese princess — gifts from the Chinese emperor to the Malay sultan.

And the Portuguese came too, the first European fleet whose keels had ever cleaved Malay waters. The commercial supremacy of the Malay empire housed in Malacca, a city that lay on waters so smooth the white invaders termed them the Ladies' Sea, is thus described,

"Here dwell up to now great wholesale merchants of every kind, both Moors and Heathen, men of great estates and owning many great ships which they call *juncos*. They trade everywhere in goods of all kinds. Numbers of ships also come hither to take cargoes of sugar, very fine four-masted ships; they bring great store of silk, very fine raw silk, porcelain in abundance, damasks, brocades, coloured satins, musk, rhubarb, sewing silk in many colours, salt-petre, great store of fine silver, pearls in abundance, sorted seed-pearls, gilded coffers, fans, and many other baubles; and all this they sell at good prices to the dealers of the country, and in exchange therefore they take away pepper, incense, Cambay cloths dyed in grain, saffron, coral-shaped and strung and ready for shaping, printed and white cotton cloths which come from Bengala, vermilion, quicksilver, opium.....

"From the city of Malacca ships sail also to the Isles of Maluco there to take in cargoes of cloves, taking thither for sale much Cambaya cloth, cotton and silk of all kinds, other cloths from Paleacate and Bengala, quicksilver, wrought copper, bells and basins, pepper, porcelain, garlic, onions and other Cambaya goods of diverse kinds.

"These ships sail also from Malacca to the islands which they call Bandan to get cargoes of nutmeg and mace, taking thither for sale Cambaya goods. They also go to the Island of Camatra, whence they bring pepper, silk, raw silk, benzoin and gold, and to other islands bringing thence camphor and aloes-wood; they go to Tanacary, Peeguu, Bengala, Paleacate, Charamandel, Malabar and Cambaya, so much so that this city of Malacca is the richest seaport with the greatest number of wholesale merchants and abundance of shipping and trade that can be found in the whole world."

Duarte Barbosa, 16th century Portuguese government official. And then the tin rush began and thousands of Chinese coolies arrived to work the mines, having come direct from China in search of a new life and profits. They came from different provinces in southern China, and brought with them a fascinating diversity of languages, traditions, food and eating habits. Most were Hokkiens from Amoy, but there were also the Teochews from east Kwangtung, Cantonese from South Kwangtung; Hailamese and groups of Hakkas, Hokchius and Hokchias.

The migrants were all men and at that time, there were hardly any Chinese women in the Malay peninsula. The Chinese men ended up marrying Malay women, and this amalgamation of Chinese and Malay evolved a separate ethnic group known as the Straits Chinese or Peranakans.

When the rubber plantations were opened, large numbers of labourers were contracted from India to work as tappers — slender, fine-boned Tamils from Madras and long-limbed Malayalees from Kerala. The Indian commercial community also comprised a sizeable number of Pakistanis, Hindustanis, Punjabis, Bengalis, Sri Lankans , each adding their individual characteristics, traditions, customs, lifestyles, religious beliefs to the rich tapestry of Malaysia's cultural heritage.

And so began the merging of lifestyles and culinary methods. The original settlers, the easy-going Malays with their staple diet of rice and fish, the ubiquitous Chinese and their imaginative blend of cuisine, the conservative Indians and their piquant traditional fare, the Peranakans and their exquisite nyonya specialities, the exotic Portuguese Eurasians and their delightful melange of east-west cooking methods — all this individual culinary expertise has now been brought together in one volume, Traditional Malaysian Cuisine, the very best of authentic Malaysian recipes.

MALAY

Variety is the spice in Malay food. The traditional culinary style has been greatly influenced by long-ago traders from neighbouring countries — Indonesia, India, the Middle-East, China. Many of the spices and ingredients essential in Malay cooking were introduced by the Indians and Arabs.... spices such as pepper, ginger, cardamom.

Malay food also varies quite significantly across the country. Each of the 13 Malaysian states has its native specialties. Even the best-known Malay 'satay' — cubes of meat, poultry and even seafood, marinated in a deliciously spiced sauce and then skewered on bamboo sticks, roasted over glowing charcoals, and eaten dipped in a peanut sauce — differs in flavour from state to state.

The basic pattern of Malay cooking lies in the preparation of 'wet' and 'dry' spices used to flavour the dish. The 'wet' spices include shallots, ginger, garlic, fresh chillies, fresh turmeric and are usually pounded in mortar and pestle or *batu lesong* if used in small amounts. The 'dry' spices are coriander, cummin, aniseed, cloves, cinnamon, cardamom.

Malay curries are delicately flavoured with various herbs and leaves — *serai* or lemongrass, *lengkuas* or galangal, *daun limau purut* or fragrant lime leaf, *daun ketumbar* or coriander leaf and the *karuvapillai* or curry leaf.

The mainstay of every meal is rice, a generous, steaming helping of it, accompanied by a selection of *lauk* or dishes, including fish, vegetables, poultry and sambal.

SOUPS

Sup Kepah *(Mussel Soup)*

Ingredients:

500 gms fresh mussels
4 small red onions — quartered
1 stalk lemon grass
1 clove garlic — crushed

Serves 4 — 6

Method:

1. Wash the mussels well and place in a pan with enough water to cover the mussels.
2. Put in the onions, lemon grass and garlic and salt to taste.
3. Place on a medium fire until the mussels are well-cooked.
4. Serve as a soup.

Sup Daging Lembu

(Beef Soup)

Ingredients:

500 gms beef steak
4 potatoes
1 large onion — quartered
½ tsp aniseed
1 tsp coriander seeds
1 piece cinnamon stick
4 small red onions — sliced
Spring onions for garnishing
Salt to taste

Serves 6 — 8

Method:

1. Cut the beef into bite-sized pieces and wash well.
2. Boil the beef in sufficient water until tender.
3. Pound the aniseed and coriander seeds finely and wrap in muslin coth. Put into the soup together with the cinnamon stick and onion.
4. When the beef is already tender put in the peeled and quartered potatoes.
5. Add in salt and continue boiling until the potatoes are tender.
6. Fry the sliced onions and use as garnishing, together with the spring onions.

> *Young, unmarried girls are forbidden to sing in the kitchen while cooking. The old folk say that if they do, they will get married to old men.*

Sup Ikan dengan So Hoon

(Fish with So Hoon Soup)

Ingredients:

2 pieces white fish
15 gms so hoon
4 small red onions
1 clove garlic
Salt and pepper to taste
1 tbsp oil

Serves 4 — 6

Method:

1. Slice the red onions and garlic.
2. Soak the so hoon in a cup of water.
3. Heat the oil and fry the sliced onions and garlic until golden brown.
4. Put in 3 cups of water, salt and a dash of pepper.
5. When the soup boils, put in the fish and when the fish is almost cooked, add in the so hoon.
6. Carry on boiling until the so hoon softens.
7. Serve hot garnished with chopped spring onions.

Sup Sayur Campuran

(Mixed Vegetable Soup)

Ingredients:

½ head of cabbage
300 gms mustard greens (sawi)
250 gms fresh beans
1 carrot
4 small red onions — sliced
1 clove garlic — sliced
3 cups water
Salt and pepper to taste
1 tsp oil

Serves 4 — 6

Method:

1. Clean the vegetables, cut them and drain them.
2. Heat the oil and fry the sliced onions and garlic until golden brown.
3. Add in the water and salt and pepper. Bring to the boil.
4. Add in the carrot first, followed by the french beans, cabbage and lastly the greens.
5. When the vegetables are done, switch off the fire and serve hot.

Sup Kepah (Mussel Soup)

Sup Ekor Lembu *(Ox-tail Soup)*

Ingredients:

600 gms ox tail
4 potatoes
1 tsp cummin seeds
½ tsp aniseed
1 tsp coriander seeds
1 piece cinammon stick
1 large onion — quartered
Salt to taste

Serves 6 — 8

Method:

1. Clean the ox tail well and cut into small pieces. It is advisable to get the ready cut ox tail as it is quite difficult to cut.
2. Pound the aniseed and coriander finely and wrap in muslin cloth.
3. Peel the potatoes and quarter them.
4. Boil the ox-tail in enough water until almost done with the quartered onion, wrapped spices and cinnamon stick.
5. Add in the potatoes and continue cooking until tender.
6. Serve garnished with chopped spring onions and fried onion slices.
   Can be served with either bread or rice.

Sup Bebola Daging *(Meat Ball Soup)*

Ingredients:

400 gms minced meat
2 cloves garlic — chopped finely
2 carrots — sliced
1 cm piece ginger — sliced finely
1 tin button mushrooms
1 tsp salt
2 tbsps white pepper
1 tbsp cornflour
1 tbsp vegetable oil

Serves 4 — 6

Method:

1. Place the minced meat, onions, garlic, salt and pepper in a pot. Sprinkle in the cornflour and oil.
2. Knead the mixture and shape into small meat balls 2 cm in diameter.
3. Boil the carrots, mushrooms and ginger in vegetable or meat stock. Bring to boil.
4. Add in the meatballs and cook for 5 minutes.
5. Serve hot, garnished with fried shallots.

Sup Bebola Udang *(Prawn Ball Soup)*

Ingredients:

250 gms fresh prawns — shelled and minced
2 chicken breasts
1 tbsp cornflour
1 egg white — beaten
1 litre chicken stock
1 small tin button mushrooms — sliced
1 tin bamboo shoots — sliced
4 shallots — chopped
Salt and pepper to taste

Serves 4 — 6

Method:

1. Season the minced prawns with salt and pepper.
2. Add in the cornflour and beaten egg white.
3. Mix well and shape into tiny balls, using a teaspoon.
4. Boil the breasts in the chicken stock. Reduce heat and simmer.
5. Put the prawn balls into the simmering stock a few at a time and cook for 5 minutes.
6. Add in the sliced mushrooms and bamboo shoots. Simmer for another 5 minutes.
7. Serve hot garnished with chopped shallots.

Sup Makaroni *(Macaroni Soup)*

Ingredients:

500 gms beef — cut into small cubes
5 cups water ⎫
4 potatoes ⎬ Cut into cubes
2 carrots ⎭
2 large onions
500 gms macaroni
1 tbsp coriander seeds ⎫
1 tsp cummins ⎬ Ground together
1 tsp aniseed ⎪
4 shallots ⎭
4 stalks spring onions — chopped
8 shallots — sliced and fried in 1 tbsp ghee

Serves 6 — 8

Method:

1. Boil the beef with water until tender.
2. Add in the ground ingredients.
3. Add in the potatoes, carrots and large onions.
4. Put in the ghee used in frying the sliced shallots. Season to taste and bring to boil.
5. Blanch the macaroni with water and a pinch of salt. Lift and drain.
6. To serve, put macaroni in individual bowls and pour the soup over. Garnish with chopped spring onions and fried shallots.

Soto Mi Hun *(Mee Hoon Soto)*

Ingredients:

For Soto:

1 chicken

2 stalks lemon grass

1 cup thick coconut milk to be obtained from ½ coconut

6 cloves garlic and small onions — pound together

1 tsp aniseeds
1 tsp coriander seeds
1 tsp cummin seeds
1 piece cinnamon stick } Ground together

Salt to taste

Accompaniments:

1 packet Mee Hoon — scalded

500 gms scalded bean sprouts

2 tbsps cili padi

4 tbsps thick soy sauce

10 small red onions — sliced and fried

Spring onions

Serves 4 — 6

Method:

1. Boil chicken in 5 bowls of water with ground spices, cinnamon stick, pounded onions and garlic and lemon grass.
2. When the chicken is tender, take it out and drain. Shred the chicken.
3. Pound the cili padi and mix with the soy sauce to get a thick sauce. Add more soy sauce if necessary.
4. When serving, put the scalded mee hoon in individual bowls, add the bean sprouts, the shredded chicken and pour the soup over.
5. Garnish with the fried onion slices and spring onions and top with the chilli sauce.

For variation, you can also add in quails' eggs or you can use beef instead of chicken.

Soto is usually served on special occasions like Hari Raya.

Mi Sup *(Mee Soup)*

Ingredients:

600 gms yellow noodles

300 gms fresh prawns

2 tomatoes — cut into 6

1 tbsp black peppercorns

2 pieces beancurd — fried and cubed

125 gms mustard greens — cut into 3 cm lengths

350 gms bean sprouts

3 cabbage leaves
4 shallots
2 cloves garlic } Sliced finely

4 tbsps oil

Salt to taste

For Sauce:

6 cili padi — sliced thinly

1 large onion — sliced

2 tbsps thick soy sauce

Serves 4 — 6

Method:

1. Heat oil and fry the sliced shallots and garlic until fragrant.
2. Add in the prawns and pepper. Mix well.
3. Add in 6 cups water and bring to boil. Season to taste.
4. Add in the cabbage, bean sprouts, mustard greens and fried beancurd.
5. Put in the noodles and tomatoes. Cook for 1 minute.
6. Prepare the sauce by mixing all the ingredients together.
7. Serve the Mee Soup with the sauce.

Sup Timun Eropah *(Winter Melon Soup)*

Ingredients:

1 winter melon — sliced coarsely

1 bunch so hoon — soaked and cut into 3 cm lengths

6 cm piece young ginger

2 cloves garlic — crushed

200 gms fresh prawns — shelled

Salt and pepper to taste

1 tbsp oil

Serves 4 — 6

Method:

1. Heat 1 tbsp oil and fry the ginger and garlic until fragrant.
2. Add in 2 cups water and bring to boil.
3. Add in the prawns and simmer for 30 minutes.
4. Add in the so hoon and season well with salt and pepper.
5. Put in the winter melon and simmer over low heat until the melon is cooked.

Acar Timun *(Cucumber Pickle)*

Ingredients:

2 cucumbers
1 carrot
1 red chilli
1 large onion
2 tbsps salt
8 dried chillies
8 shallots
4 cloves garlic
2 cm piece ginger
3 candlenuts
½ cup dried prawns
½ cup oil
½ tsp mustard seeds
½ tsp turmeric powder
¾ cup vinegar
3½ tbsps sugar

Serves 6 — 8

Method:

1. Cut cucumbers and carrot into 2.5 cm strips. Cut the red chilli into .5 cm strips and the large onion into .5 cm wedges.
2. Sprinkle salt over the cut vegetables and let them stand for at least 2 hours.
3. When the vegetables are limp, wash away the salt and spread them on a clean tea towel in a cool place to dry.
4. Grind together the chillies, shallots, garlic, ginger and candlenuts. Pound the dried prawns.
5. Heat the oil and fry mustard seeds for ½ minute before adding in the ground ingredients and turmeric powder. Fry for another 5 minutes.
6. When the oil separates, add in the dried prawns and continue cooking for another 3 minutes before adding in the vinegar and sugar.
7. Cook slowly until the mixture is fairly thick. Add in more salt and sugar if necessary.
8. Stir in the prepared vegetables and toss quickly to mix well. When the vegetables are well mixed with the spices, remove the pan from the heat.
9. Cool slightly before storing in clean, dry jars.

> *This is one of the dishes usually served at a wedding feast.*

Acar Mangga *(Mango Chutney)*

Ingredients:

5 black peppercorns
A small piece of belacan (Optional)
1 dsp granulated sugar
1 ripe mango
Salt to taste

Serves 4 — 6

Method:

1. Toast the shrimp paste until it is fragrant.
2. Pound or blend the black pepper, salt and prawn paste until fine.
3. Pare the mango and slice thinly. Mix the mango with the ground ingredients and slightly mash the mango.

Masak Lodeh

Ingredients:

¼ cup fresh shrimps
120 gms cabbage
120 gms long beans
4 brinjals
2 pieces tempe (soya bean cake)
1 coconut — grated
1 tbsp oil
2 cloves garlic — sliced
6 shallots — sliced
2 slices galangal
4 red chillies — sliced
1 tsp salt
1 tbsp oil

Serves 4 — 6

Method:

1. Shell and devein the shrimps.
2. Cut the cabbage into 1 cm strips and long beans into 4 cm lengths. Cut brinjals into 4 cm pieces, then quarter each piece. Cut the tempe into 1 cm piece.
3. Extract 2 cups coconut milk from the grated coconut.
4. Heat oil in a pan over a medium flame and fry the garlic and shallots until fragrant.
5. Add in the shrimps and galangal and fry for 1 minute. Add in coconut milk and salt.
6. When the coconut milk boils, add in the chillies, vegetables and tempe. Cover the pan and allow the coconut milk to come to the boil again.
7. As soon as the coconut milk boils, remove the cover, stir continuously and cook further until the vegetables are cooked.
8. Add in salt to taste.

Acar Rempah *(Spicy Chutney)*

Ingredients:

3 tbsps raisins
4 preserved limes
5 red chillies — deseeded
2 tbsps cloves ⎞
2 tbsps aniseed ⎟ **Ground together**
2 tbsps cardamom ⎟
2 tbsps cummin ⎠
5 cloves garlic
1 cucumber — sliced
1 tbsp granulated sugar
6 prunes
5 dried preserved mangoes
5 green chillies — deseeded
20 shallots
1 bowl thick coconut milk — extracted from 1 coconut
1 carrot — sliced
Salt
Some cooking oil

Serves 6 — 8

Method:

1. Mix raisins, prunes, preserved limes and mangoes in a bowl.
2. Mix cucumber, carrot, red chillies and green chillies in another bowl and then add them to the mixed fruit.
3. Pound or blend 10 shallots and 5 cloves garlic. Add the remainder of the shallots to the other ingredients.
4. Heat oil in a pan and fry the freshly ground spices and also the pounded shallots and garlic.
5. Put in half a bowl of the coconut milk and stir until the milk is cooked.
6. When the gravy boils, add in the remainder of the coconut milk.
7. Add in 1 dsp of sugar and salt to taste. Simmer.
8. Store chutney in a bottle when it is cooled and store in a cool and dry place.

> *Aniseeds come from the star anise. The plant is a herb of the parsley family, but is usually grown for the oil-bearing seeds. They are used in most Malaysian dishes and tea laced with aniseeds can help relieve indigestion.*

Sambal Belacan

Ingredients:

4 red chillies
Thumb sized piece shrimp paste
Salt to taste

Serves 4 — 6

Method:

1. Wash the chillies and deseed them to reduce the hotness.
2. Pound these chillies in a pestle and mortar.
3. Meanwhile, roast the shrimp paste over a flame until fragrant.
4. Pound it while still hot with the chillies and mix well. Add in salt.
5. Serve with sliced cucumbers.

Pecal *(Mixed Salad with Peanut Sauce)*

Ingredients:

1 yam bean
1 cucumber
180 gms kangkung
6 cabbage leaves
5 long beans
Sauce:
15 dried red chillies
6 shallots
½ cup peanuts:
1 tbsp tamarind
Thumb sized piece shrimp paste

Serves 4 — 6

Method:

1. Peel the skin of the yam bean and cut into strips. Also cut the cucumber into strips. Cut kangkung and long beans into 6 cm lengths and cabbage into bite size pieces. Boil all these vegetables with a little salt until cooked, drain and set aside.
2. Clean the chillies and shallots and dry thoroughly.
3. Roast the peanuts and remove the skins. Pound.
4. Heat some oil in a pan and fry the dried chillies until browned. Also fry the shallots and the shrimp paste.
5. Pound together until fine all the fried ingredients and the peanuts. Strain the tamarind juice and mix well with the pounded stuff.
6. To make the sauce, add water to this mixture, the thickness of which depends on individual taste.
7. To serve, arrange the vegetables in a platter and put the sauce in a separate bowl.

Kari Terung (Brinjal Curry)

Ingredients:

4 brinjals — sliced thickly
5 shallots — sliced
2 cloves garlic — sliced
2 tbsps curry powder — blended with 2 tbsps water
2 cups thick coconut milk) Extracted
4 cups thin coconut milk ∫ from 1 coconut
1 sprig curry leaves
2 tbsps oil
3 pieces asam gelugur
Salt to taste

Serves 4 — 6

Method:

1. Heat oil and fry shallots and garlic until fragrant.
2. Add in curry powder and fry until fragrant, making sure it does not burn.
3. Add in the thin coconut milk, asam gelugur and curry leaves. Season to taste and bring to boil.
4. Add in the brinjals and boil until almost tender.
5. Add in the thick coconut milk and bring to boil.
6. Serve hot with plain boiled rice.

Pacri Nanas (Pineapple Pachri)

Ingredients:

1 almost ripe pineapple
2 cloves garlic
3 cloves
1½ tbsps sugar
1 shallot — sliced
5 cm piece cinnamon
3 cardamoms
2 red chillies — deseeded
Salt to taste

Serves 6 — 8

Method:

1. Slice the pineapple in rings and remove the core. Boil it for 5 minutes with 1 tsp turmeric powder.
2. Drain the pineapple slices and put aside.
3. Heat 2 tbsps oil and fry the sliced shallots and crushed garlic until fragrant.
4. Add in 1½ cups of water. Add in also pineapple slices and red chillies. Cook over a low flame and bring to boil.
5. When boiling add salt and sugar to taste. You can also add 2 tbsps vinegar if you desire.

Kangkung Goreng (Fried Kangkung)

Ingredients:

600 gms kangkung
300 gms dried prawns
6 shallots
2 cloves garlic
2 red chillies
1 tbsp oil
Salt to taste

Serves 6 — 8

Method:

1. Peel the onions and garlic. Deseed the red chillies. Pound all these ingredients.
2. Wash the kangkung and cut into 5 cm lengths.
3. Soak the dried prawns and pound coarsely.
4. Heat oil in a pan and fry the pounded ingredients until fragrant.
5. Add in the kangkung and mix well. Add in salt and stir for 1 minute.
6. Serve hot with rice.

> *It is told that the famous Malay warrior, Hang Tuah, once had an audience with a Chinese emperor. It was forbidden to look at the emperor's face and his audience had to look down while talking. However, Hang Tuah requested that he be served kangkung which was not cut. So to eat the kangkung, he had to lift his head and so could see the Emperor's face. He was commended for his ingenuity.*

> *Pineapple pachri is one of the dishes usually served at Malay weddings.*

Rebung Masak Lemak Kuning
(Preserved Bamboo Shoots in Yellow Gravy)

Ingredients:

600 gms preserved bamboo shoots — washed and drained
1 fish head — preferably mackerel
2 cups thick coconut milk ⎱ Extracted
4 cups thin coconut milk ⎰ from 1 coconut
10 stalks cili padi — finely pounded
2 stalks lemon grass — crushed
2 cm piece fresh turmeric — finely pounded
Salt to taste

Serves 6 — 8

Method:

1. Put the preserved bamboo shoots, fish head, pounded ingredients, lemon grass and thin coconut milk in a pan. The thin coconut milk must cover the ingredients.
2. Bring to boil, stirring continously. Add salt.
3. Add thick coconut milk and bring to boil once again.
4. Remove from fire and serve hot with plain boiled rice.

Rojak *(Vegetable Salad)*

Ingredients:

½ pineapple ⎫
1 small yam bean ⎬ Sliced as you please
1 cucumber ⎭
3 tbsps chopped palm sugar
3 fresh red chillies
¼ cup tamarind juice
Thumb sized piece shrimp paste — toasted

Serves 4 — 6

Method:

1. Prepare sauce. Pound chillies with toasted shrimp paste.
2. Mix in palm sugar and tamarind juice.
3. Mix with sliced vegetables and serve as a salad.

> *If your hands smart from handling too much chilli, rub some cooking oil into them and then wash with soap and water.*

Kacang Bendi Sumbat
(Stuffed Ladies' Fingers)

Ingredients:

300 gms ladies' fingers — cleaned and slit on one side
1 piece mackerel — minced
2 cups thick coconut milk ⎱ Extracted
4 cups thin coconut milk ⎰ from 1 coconut
4 fresh red chillies
6 dried chillies
2 stalks lemon grass
3 cm piece galangal ⎬ Ground together
3 candlenuts
4 cloves garlic
10 shallots
Thumb size piece shrimp paste
3½ tbsps oil

Serves 4 — 6

Method:

1. Stuff the minced fish into the ladies' fingers. Arrange on a plate and pour 1½ tbsps oil over them.
2. Steam until half-cooked and remove.
3. Heat oil and fry the ground ingredients until golden and fragrant.
4. Add 2 tbsps thick coconut milk and stir.
5. When oil separates, pour in the thin coconut milk and bring to boil.
6. Pour in the remaining thick coconut milk and the ladies' fingers.
7. Bring to boil, add salt and remove.

Acar Ikan Bilis *(Anchovy Chutney)*

Ingredients:

300 gms anchovies
300 gms peanuts
1 tbsp granulated sugar
1 lime
1 bombay onion
1 tsp oil
Salt to taste

Serves 4 — 6

Method:

1. Roast the peanuts and mix with the anchovies. The anchovies should have been cleaned earlier by removing the heads and the intestines.
2. Pound chillies and slice the bombay onion coarsely.
3. Heat oil in frying pan and stir-fry until fragrant. Add in lime juice and salt and sugar. Stir well.
4. When the gravy has thickened, put in the roasted peanuts and anchovies.
5. Stir well and remove from the fire.

Kubis Masak Lemak
(Cabbage in Coconut Gravy)

Ingredients:

2 red chillies	
4 shallots	
2 cups water	
1 cup shelled prawns	
300 gms cabbage	
2 cups coconut milk	Extracted from
4 cups thin coconut milk	1 grated coconut
1 tsp turmeric powder	
Salt to taste	

Serves 4 — 6

Method:

1. Pound the red chillies and shallots. Place in a pan with thin coconut milk and bring to boil.
2. Add in the prawns and sliced cabbage.
3. When the cabbage is tender add in the thick coconut milk.
4. Let the gravy boil once and lift from fire.

Rebung Masak Lemak
(Bamboo Shoots in Coconut Milk)

Ingredients:

600 gms preserved bamboo shoots	
1 slice of dried fish	
2 stalks lemon grass	
1 cup thick coconut milk	Extracted from
2 cups thin coconut milk	1 grated coconut
10 red chillies	
3 cm fresh turmeric	

Serves 6 — 8

Method:

1. Clean the bamboo shoot and drain.
2. Grind finely the chillies and turmeric. Put in a pan together with the bamboo shoot and dried fish.
3. Put in crushed lemon grass and salt to taste.
4. Add the thin coconut milk to the pan and cook mixture over a medium flame.
5. Stir continuously until the gravy thickens and add in the thick milk.
6. Serve hot with plain boiled rice.

> *If you prefer the gravy to be mild you can reduce the amount of chillies. Deseeding the chillies will also reduce the hotness.*

Kacang Panjang Goreng dengan Telur
(Long Beans Fried with Egg)

Ingredients:

300 gms long beans	
1 egg	
½ cup medium-sized prawns — shelled and deveined	
4 shallots — sliced	
1 red chilli — sliced	
2 tbsps oil	
Salt to taste	

Serves 4 — 6

Method:

1. Wash the long beans well and dice them.
2. Heat the oil and fry the shallots, garlic and chilli until fragrant.
3. Add in the prawns and fry until the prawns are cooked.
4. Add in the diced long beans and stir to mix well.
5. Meanwhile, beat the egg with a fork and pour it over the long beans, mixing well.
6. Season with salt to taste.

Sambal Belimbing
(Belimbing Sambal)

Ingredients:

3 red chillies	
3 ripe belimbing	
A small piece of belacan (shrimp paste)	
Salt and sugar to taste	

Serves 4 — 6

Method:

1. Grill the shrimp paste until fragrant.
2. Pound the chillies, salt, sugar and prawn paste until fine.
3. Slice the belimbing and mix well with the ground ingredients, mashing it slightly.

> *If you have eaten too much hot food, to get rid of the sting in your mouth, turn your plate several times until the sting is gone. This is an old Malay folk belief.*

Nasi Lemak *(Rice in Coconut Milk)*

Ingredients:

1 cup rice

1 grated coconut

3 screwpine leaves

Salt to taste

Serves 4 — 6

Method:

1. Clean the rice and drain.
2. Squeeze out 2 cups of thick coconut milk from the grated coconut.
3. Cook the rice in the coconut milk with screwpine leaves. Add in salt.
4. If you desire, you can also add in some sliced shallots and ginger.
5. Serve this rice with sliced hard-boiled eggs, cucumber and Sambal Ikan Bilis. (Next recipe).

Sambal Ikan Bilis

(Anchovies in Hot Sauce)

Ingredients:

½ cup dried ikan bilis (anchovies)

1 bombay onion

4 shallots

2 tbsps tamarind juice

Prawn paste (belacan) (Optional)

8 dried chillies

1 clove garlic

Salt and sugar to taste

Method:

1. Fry the ikan bilis until crisp and put aside.
2. Grind the prawn paste together with shallots, garlic, deseeded dried chillies. Slice the bombay onion into rings.
3. Heat 2 tbsps oil in a pan and fry the ground ingredients until fragrant. Add in the onion rings.
4. Add tamarind juice, salt and sugar.
5. Cook, stirring occasionally until the gravy thickens.
6. Add in the ikan bilis and mix well.
7. Serve with steaming hot Nasi Lemak.

> *Nasi Lemak is a typical Malay breakfast. Individual portions wrapped in banana leaves, are often taken along on picnics.*
>
> *The typical accompaniments are fried peanuts and sliced cucumber.*

Nasi Tomato *(Tomato Rice)*

Ingredients:

2 tbsps ghee

10 shallots

1 cup water

2 star anise

4 cm piece cinnamon

2 cups long-grain rice

2 cloves

1 tin evaporated milk

Serves 4 — 6

Method:

1. Clean the rice well, drain and put aside.
2. Heat ghee in a pan and fry the ground candlenuts, cinnamon, cloves and star anise.
3. Add in water and bring to boil.
4. Add evaporated milk, tomato sauce and rice Stir well before covering the pan. Cook over a low flame.
5. Serve garnished with fried shallots, spring onions or celery.

Nasi Minyak (1) *(Rice in Ghee)*

Ingredients:

1 cup long grained rice

2 cups water

3 tbsps ghee

5 cm piece ginger — sliced

2 cm cinnamon stick

5 shallots

1 clove garlic

3 cloves

Salt to taste

Serves 6 — 8

Method:

1. Wash the rice well and drain.
2. Slice shallots and garlic finely.
3. Heat ghee and fry the sliced shallots, garlic and ginger until fragrant. Add in the cloves.
4. Put in water and salt, cover the pot and bring to boil.
5. Stir slowly and lower the flame to cook the rice thoroughly.
6. To serve, you can garnish with fried sliced shallots or raisins.

> *When cleaning rice before cooking, the Malays believe that you should put back into the container a handful of rice. This is to ensure that there will be a continous supply.*

Nasi Lemak (Rice in Coconut Milk)

Nasi Impit *(Compressed Rice Cake)*

Ingredients:

2 cups fine rice
3 screwpine leaves (Pandan.)
3½ cups water
Salt to taste

Serves 6 — 8

Method:

1. Clean the rice and cook in water and screwpine leaves. Add in salt.
2. Stir constantly to break up the grains.
3. When the rice is cooked, remove from the pot and put in a tray.
4. Cover the rice with a muslin cloth and compress it with a heavy object. Leave aside for half a day.
5. Cut the rice into neat cubes and serve with satay gravy or beef floss.

> *Compressed rice is very popular during the Hari Raya festival and is also served on other festive days. The trick in cutting the rice is to constantly wet the knife with a damp cloth so that the rice cubes will be smooth.*

Lontong *(Rice in Banana Leaves)*

Ingredients:

2 cups rice
Banana leaves or aluminium foil

Serves 6 — 8

Method:

1. Soften banana leaves by scalding them. Clean and dry the leaves.
2. Wash rice and drain.
3. Wrap rice in banana leaves loosely to get cylindrical packets about 15 cms long and about 5 cms in diameter. Fasten with toothpicks or staple together.
4. If using aluminium foil, just wrap the rice in the foil. Remember to give room for the rice to expand while cooking. The packets should be no more than ¾ full.
5. Place the rice packets in a large pan filled with water and boil for 2 — 3 hours. If necessary, add more water to the pan.
6. Cool and slice into 5 cm sections and serve.

> *Lontong is usually served with Masak Lodeh for Hari Raya or other festivities. The banana leaves give the rice an interesting flavour.*

Nasi Kunyit *(Yellow Rice)*

Ingredients:

7 cm piece turmeric
450 gms glutinous rice
1 piece asam gelugur
10 — 15 peppercorns
2 screwpine leaves
½ coconut — grated
1 tsp salt

Serves 6 — 8

Method:

1. Clean turmeric and pound till fine. Wrap in a piece of muslin and tie it up firmly.
2. Wash the rice and soak in a bowl of water with the turmeric bag and tamarind for at least 3 hours. Preferably, soak the rice overnight.
3. Rinse the soaked rice under running water and drain.
4. Place the rice in a steamer with peppercorns and screwpine leaves and steam over boiling water for 20-30 minutes.
5. Meanwhile, extract 1 — 1½ cups thick coconut milk. Add in salt.
6. When the rice is cooked, dish it into a large bowl and mix it with the thick coconut milk so that the rice grains are loosened.
7. Return the rice to the steamer and steam for another 10 minutes.
8. Serve with chicken curry, beef curry or rendang.

Plain Boiled Rice

Ingredients:

1 cup rice
1 cup water

Serves 4 — 6

Method:

1. Wash the rice well and drain.
2. Put in a pan with the water and cook over a low flame.
3. When the water has dried up, lower the flame to the minimum and cook covered until the rice is soft and fluffy.

> *The Malays believe that to prevent weevils from attacking the rice grains, a few stalks of dried red chillies should be put into the rice bin.*

Nasi Goreng *(Fried Rice)*

Ingredients:

1 bowl cold, cooked rice
4 shallots
2 cloves garlic
25 gms ikan bilis
2 red chillies
2 long beans
Salt to taste
1 tbsp oil

Serves 4 — 6

Method:

1. Clean and wash the ikan bilis. Pound together with the shallots, garlic and red chillies.
2. Clean the long beans and dice them.
3. Heat the oil in a frying pan and fry the pounded ingredients until fragrant.
4. Add in the long beans, stir well and cook over a medium flame.
5. Add in the rice, mix well and season with salt to taste.

> *This is a favourite breakfast item, especially when there is left-over rice from the previous night's meal.*

Nasi Dagang *(Traveller's Rice)*

Ingredients:

3.6 kg Siamese rice	Washed and soaked
900 gms glutinous rice	for about 7 hours
4 cups thick coconut milk	Extracted
9 cups thin coconut milk	from 2 coconuts
25 shallots — sliced thinly	
1 tbsp fenugreek seeds	
8 cm piece ginger — sliced thinly	
Salt to taste	

Serves 6 — 8

Method:

1. Steam the rice over rapidly boiling water until the rice is half-cooked.
2. Pour in the thin coconut milk and steam again until the rice is cooked.
3. Pour in the thick coconut milk and salt and steam until all the coconut milk is absorbed.
4. Mix thoroughly into the rice the sliced shallots, ginger and fenugreek seeds.
5. Serve with Kari Ikan Tongkol. (Next recipe)

> *This dish is a specialty of the east coast states of Malaysia.*

Kari Ikan Tongkol *(Tunny Curry)*

Ingredients:

4 pieces ikan tongkol (Tunny)	
2 tbsps kormah powder	
8 shallots	
3 cloves garlic	Pounded together
3 cm piece ginger	
2 tbsps chilli paste	
2 cups thick coconut milk	Extracted
4 cups thin coconut milk	from 1 coconut
3 pieces asam gelugur	
Salt to taste	

Method:

1. Boil the fish with salt and 1 piece asam gelugur.
2. Mix the kormah powder with the pounded ingredients.
3. Heat oil and fry the chilli paste until fragrant.
4. Add in the kormah powder mixture.
5. Pour in the thin coconut milk and bring to boil. Season to taste.
6. Add in the water used to boil the fish and also the asam gelugur.
7. Put in the fish and bring to boil.
8. Pour in the thick coconut milk, bring to boil and turn off the heat immediately.

Bubur Kanji *(Simple Broth)*

Ingredients:

1 cup rice
3 cups water
½ cup peanuts
½ cup ikan bilis
Salt to taste

Serves 4 — 6

Method:

1. Cook the rice and water into a thick broth. Season with salt to taste.
2. Fry the peanuts and ikan bilis in deep oil separately.
3. To serve, put the broth in small bowls and top with fried peanuts and ikan bilis.
4. If the broth is not salty enough, you can also mix in soy sauce.

> *This is a very simple breakfast dish.*

Nasi Sayuran *(Vegetable Rice)*

Ingredients:

2 cloves garlic — ground
1 tsp cummin
2 star anise
80 gms tinned corn
80 gms diced carrots
6 cups rice
6 cups water
5 small red onions — ground
3 cm piece cinnamon
2 tsps ghee
Salt to taste

Serves 6 — 8

Method:

1. Grind onions, garlic and cummin.
2. In a saucepan, heat ghee, and fry ground ingredients together with cinnamon and star anise until fragrant.
3. Add water and bring to boil.
4. Mix in the rice and stir until almost dry.
5. Add in the vegetables.
6. Cover the pan, reduce heat to a minimum until the rice is cooked.
7. Serve garnished with fried onions.

Nasi Minyak (2) *(Rice in Ghee)*

Ingredients:

3.5 kg rice
3.4 kg water
400 gms ghee
1 tin evaporated milk
6 cm piece ginger — pounded
1 screwpine leaf
Salt to taste

To fry:

3 large onions — sliced
15 shallots — sliced
1 pod garlic — pounded
3 cloves
5 cardamoms
1 star anise
5 cm piece cinnamon stick

Serves 6 — 8

Method:

1. Heat ghee in a large pot and put in the screwpine leaf, sliced large onions and fry until golden brown.
2. Put in the rest of the ingredients to be fried.
3. Add in water, salt and milk and bring to boil.
4. Add in the rice and mix well but do not break the rice grains.
5. Cook as for the plain boiled rice.
6. Garnish with fried shallots when serving.

Biryani Ayam
(Spiced Rice with Chicken)

Ingredients:

1 chicken, about 900 gms
1 clove garlic
5 cm piece ginger
2 chillies
1 tbsp poppy seeds
10 cashew nuts
10 almonds
4 tbsps ghee
5 cloves
5 cm cinnamon stick
1 cup shallots — sliced
2 — 3 tsps salt
1 tsp curry powder
½ coconut — grated
450 gms long-grain rice

Serves 6 — 8

Method:

1. Cut chicken into 4 pieces.
2. Grind together garlic, ginger, chillies, poppy seeds, cashew nuts and almonds.
3. Heat ghee and fry cloves, cinnamon, shallots. Add in the chicken pieces, 1 tsp salt, ground ingredients and curry powder. Stir to mix and cook covered for 10 minutes.
4. Extract 1-2 cups coconut milk from coconut. Add in salt. Mix with the washed rice and cook it.
5. When the rice has absorbed all the milk, make a well in the centre and put in the chicken mixture. Cover and allow rice to cook over very low fire.

This Biryani Ayam is usually served at weddings. You can also garnish the rice with fried raisins.

Udang Goreng Berempah
(Spicy Fried Prawns)

Ingredients:

500 gms medium sized prawns — shelled and deveined	
4 shallots	
2 cloves garlic	Pounded
3 cm piece ginger	together
1 cm piece turmeric	
1 large onion — sliced	
1 cup thick coconut milk — extracted from ½ grated coconut	
1 tbsp curry powder — blended with 1 tbsp water	
1 sprig curry leaves	
1 tbsp oil	
Salt to taste	

Serves 6 — 8

Method:

1. Heat oil and fry the pounded ingredients until fragrant. Add in curry leaves.
2. Add in the blended curry powder and stir until fragrant. Do not let it burn.
3. Add in the sliced onion and coconut milk. Bring to boil.
4. Add in the prawns and cook until done.
5. Dish out and serve with plain boiled rice.

Gulai Lada Hidup
(Fish in Hot Fresh Chilli Gravy)

Ingredients:

2 ikan kembung (Spanish mackerel)	
4 fresh red chillies	
6 shallots	Pounded together
2 cm piece ginger	
2 shallots — sliced	
2 pieces asam gelugur	
2 cups water	
Salt to taste	
2 tsps oil	

Serves 4 — 6

Method:

1. Place the pounded ingredients with water in a pan and bring to boil.
2. Add in the fish and asam gelugur. Season to taste with salt.
3. In a separate pan, heat the oil and fry the sliced shallots. Pour into the gravy.
4. Serve hot with plain boiled rice.

Acar Ikan Bawal
(Pomfret Chutney)

Ingredients:

2 medium sized pomfret
½ bottle white vinegar
1 cucumber
1 carrot
1 onion
1 tbsp sesame seed
2.5 cm piece ginger
4 red chillies
4 green chillies
5 cloves garlic
8 shallots
Mustard seed
Salt and sugar to taste

Serves 6 — 8

Method:

1. Clean the fish and rub on turmeric powder and salt. Deep fry until it is half-cooked.
2. Chop onion, garlic and shallots. Soak in lime water for 10 minutes.
3. Slice the ginger thinly. Remove core of cucumber and carrot and slice about 1.5 cms lengthwise.
4. Heat oil in frying pan and stir-fry onion, sesame seed and mustard seed until golden brown.
6. Add in vinegar and 1 cup hot water. Add in radish, sliced ginger and fried fish.
6. When the carrot is tender, add in cucumber. Remove from fire.
7. When serving, garnish with chillies.

Ikan Masak Lemak Cili Padi
(Fish in Hot Coconut Gravy)

Ingredients:

2 ikan kembung (Spanish mackerel)	
10 stalks cili padi	
2 cups thick coconut milk	Extracted
4 cups thin coconut milk	from 1 coconut
4 shallots — sliced	
1 turmeric leaf	
3 pieces asam gelugur	
Salt to taste	

Serves 4 — 6

Method:

1. Place the pounded ingredients with water in a pan and bring to boil.
2. Add in the fish and asam gelugur. Season to taste with salt.
3. In a separate pan, heat the oil and fry the sliced shallots. Pour into the gravy.
4. Serve hot with plain boiled rice.

Udang Goreng Berempah (Spicy Fried Prawns)

Ikan Goreng *(Fried Fish)*

Ingredients:

3 pieces tenggiri (Horse mackerel)
2 tsps turmeric powder
1 tsp salt
Oil for deep frying

Serves 4 — 6

Method:

1. Rub the slices of fish with salt and turmeric powder.
2. Heat oil in a deep pan and fry the fish until cooked.
3. Drain and serve with rice.

Bawal Goreng Berkuah

(Fried Pomfret in Gravy)

Ingredients:

1 pomfret
2 dsps tomato sauce
1 piece galangal
2 stalks celery leaves
1 tsp salt
4 tbsps cooking oil
1 tsp turmeric powder
2 tomatoes
2.5 cm piece ginger — sliced
4 green chillies
Juice from ½ lemon
½ pint milk from 1 grated coconut
2 stalks lemon grass — crushed
1 bombay onion — sliced

To pound:

8 dried chillies
5 cloves garlic
10 shallots

Serves 4 — 6

Method:

1. Clean fish and drain. Season with salt and turmeric powder.
2. Heat oil in frying pan and deep fry the fish until crispy. Remove from pan.
3. Using the same oil, fry the pounded ingredients until fragrant.
4. Add in the sliced tomatoes and cook until the gravy thickens over a low fire.
5. Simmer for 10 minutes. Add in tomato sauce, fried pomfret and cook until gravy thickens.
6. Add in lemon juice, onion rings, sliced green chillies, sliced celery leaves, ginger and galangal. Turn fish over and simmer for 5 minutes.
7. Remove from fire and serve.

Sotong Sumbat *(Stuffed Cuttlefish)*

Ingredients:

30 cuttlefish, medium size
1 coconut — extract 2 cups thick milk
3 cloves garlic
1 cup glutinous rice
4 pieces palm sugar (or 100 gms brown sugar)
Toothpicks

Serves 6 — 8

Method:

1. Clean the cuttlefish and remove the black liquid. Separate the head from the body.
2. Clean the rice and soak for 20 minutes. Drain.
3. Stuff the cuttlefish with this rice and replace the head using a toothpick so that the rice filling will not spill out.
4. Arrange the stuffed cuttlefish in a deep pot and pour 2 cups thick coconut milk into the pot.
5. Add in palm sugar and sliced garlic.
6. Cook over a medium fire until the gravy is thick and the glutinous rice cooked.
7. Remove from fire and serve hot.

Ikan Sumbat Goreng

(Fried Stuffed Fish)

Ingredients:

3 white fish — cleaned
2 cm piece fresh turmeric (or ½ tsp powdered turmeric)
4 cloves garlic
1 stalk lemon grass
2 cups grated coconut
4 red chillies
1 tsp white pepper
½ cup tamarind juice
Oil for deep frying
Turmeric leaves for wrapping the fish

Serves 4 — 6

Method:

1. Marinate fish with salt and turmeric powder.
2. Grind finely chillies, lemon grass and turmeric until fine. Also grind some of the coconut.
3. Slice thinly shallots and garlic. Mix with the coconut and spice mixture.
4. Add in tamarind juice, pepper and salt to taste.
5. Place coconut filling into the opening in the fish.
6. Wrap the fish with the turmeric leaf and tie with a piece of thread to prevent the filling from bursting out.
7. Fry the fish until slightly brown and turn over. Fry until the fish is cooked.

Sambal Tumis Udang

(Prawns in Spicy Gravy)

Ingredients:

600 gms medium sized prawns — shelled
4 cloves garlic
2 stalks lemon grass — crushed
6 shallots
1.5 cm piece ginger
1.5 cm piece turmeric
1 bombay onion — sliced thickly
3 tbsps ground chillies
Some prawn paste (optional)
Some tamarind juice

Serves 6 — 8

Method:

1. Pound or blend together shallots, garlic, ginger, fresh turmeric and prawn paste until fine.
2. Add the pounded chillies.
3. Heat some oil in a frying pan and fry the pounded ingredients until fragrant. Add the lemon grass and sliced bombay onions.
4. Put in the tamarind juice, sugar and salt.
5. Lastly put in the prawns and cook for 10 minutes or until the prawns are cooked.
6. Serve hot with rice.

Acar Sotong Kering

(Dried Cuttlefish Chutney)

Ingredients:

600 gms cuttlefish
1 tsp prawn paste (optional)
10 dried chillies
1 tbsp oil
2 shallots
2 cloves garlic
½ cup tamarind juice
1 stalk lemon grass
Salt and sugar to taste

Serves 4 — 6

Method:

1. Clean the cuttlefish, cut into pieces and drain.
2. Pound the chillies, shallots, garlic and prawn paste.
3. Heat oil in a pan and stir fry the ingredients until fragrant.
4. Add in lemon grass, sugar and salt. Stir further and add in the cuttlefish.
5. Cook until the cuttlefish is tender.

Bawal Panggang

(Grilled Pomfret)

Ingredients:

1 pomfret
1 whole coconut — grated
10 cili padi
3 cloves garlic
10 shallots
1.5 cm piece fresh turmeric (or ½ tsp powdered turmeric)
1 turmeric leaf
1.5 cm piece ginger
1 stalk lemon grass

Serves 4 — 6

Method:

1. Blend together the chillies, shallots, garlic, fresh turmeric, lemon grass, ginger and turmeric leaf.
2. Meanwhile, add salt and seasoning into the grated coconut.
3. Clean the pomfret and baste it. Put it aside.
4. Clean one banana leaf. If you cannot find banana leaves, use aluminium foil.
5. Sprinkle some coconut mixture on the leaf and put the fish on it.
6. Stuff half of the mixture into the fish. Spread the rest of the mixture on the fish.
7. Wrap the fish in the banana leaf and grill it over a charcoal fire.

Sambal Tumis Sotong Kering

(Dried Cuttlefish in Hot Peanut Sauce)

Ingredients:

1 piece dried cuttlefish — soaked until soft
1 cup anchovies — cleaned
1 tbsp tamarind — juice extracted
½ cup peanuts

4 shallots	
A small piece of belacan	Ground together
15 dried chillies	
1 clove garlic	

Serves 4 — 6

Method:

1. Roast the peanuts and pound coarsely.
2. Heat oil in a pan and stir-fry the ground ingredients until fragrant. Add in the dried cuttlefish and anchovies. Stir once again.
3. Put the pounded peanuts into the pan and add in tamarind juice and salt. Bring it to a boil and when the gravy thickens, add in 1 tsp salt.
4. Remove from the fire and serve with rice.

Kari Ketam *(Crab Curry)*

Ingredients:

600 gms crabs
10 shallots — sliced
5 cloves garlic — sliced
3 tbsps fish curry powder
2 stalks curry leaves
300 gms grated coconut
Salt and seasoning
Oil for cooking

Serves 4 — 6

Method:

1. Clean the crabs and cut into two if the crabs are too big.
2. Blend the curry powder with a bit of water to form a thick paste.
3. Heat 2 tbsps oil in a frying pan and fry the sliced shallots and garlic until fragrant.
4. Add in the blended curry powder and stir fry until the curry powder is fragrant.
5. Squeeze out 2 cups of coconut milk, ½ cup thick and 1½ cups diluted.
6. Add the diluted milk and let the mixture boil.
7. When it boils, put in the crabs, salt, seasoning and curry leaves.
8. When the crabs are cooked, add the thick milk and lower the fire.
9. Simmer until the gravy thickens.
10. The crabs will turn slightly reddish when cooked.
11. Serve this dish with rice.

Singgang Serani

(Fish in a Pungent Gravy)

Ingredients:

3 pieces white fish (threadfin, tuna)
3 large onions — sliced
1 stalk lemon grass — crushed
2 cloves garlic — sliced
2 bowls water
2.5 cm piece fresh turmeric — pounded
2 tbsps tamarind — extract juice
Salt to taste

Serves 4 — 6

Method:

1. Put all the ingredients in a pot and put to boil until fish is cooked.
2. Remove from fire and serve hot with plain boiled rice.

> *The Malays believe that when you are peeling shallots and do not want your eyes to water, you should stick one shallot onto the knife-point.*

Sotong Masak Hitam

(Cuttlefish in Black Gravy)

Ingredients:

600 gms fresh cuttlefish
10 shallots
1 tbsp curry powder
4 cloves garlic
6 red chillies
2 tbsps tamarind juice
Salt and seasoning

Serves 4 — 6

Method:

1. Clean the cuttlefish but do not remove the black liquid bag.
2. Pound the shallots, garlic and red chillies until fine.
3. Put in a pan with curry powder, tamarind juice and cuttlefish.
4. Cook over a medium fire.
5. Add in salt and leave it on the fire until the cuttlefish is cooked.

Kari Ikan Kering *(Salt Fish Curry)*

Ingredients:

4 pieces salt fish
4 potatoes — peeled and quartered
1 brinjal — cut into 2 lengthwise
3 tomatoes — cut into 2
4 shallots — sliced
1 tbsp curry powder — blended with 1 tbsp water
2 cups thick coconut milk — extracted from ½ grated coconut
1 sprig curry leaves
2 tbsps tamarind juice
2 tbsps oil
Salt to taste

Serves 4 — 6

Method:

1. Heat oil and fry shallots until golden. Add the blended curry powder and fry until fragrant.
2. Add sufficient water and season with salt. Bring to boil.
3. Put in the potatoes and cook until tender.
4. Add in the coconut milk and bring to boil.
5. Add the brinjal and when it is almost cooked, add in the salt fish pieces.
6. Dish out and serve hot with rice.

Kari Ketam (Crab Curry)

Kari Ikan *(Fish Curry)*

Ingredients:

4 pieces tenggiri fish (mackerel)
2 tomatoes — quartered
5 ladies' fingers
4 shallots — sliced
2 cloves garlic — sliced
2 green chillies
2 tbsps curry powder — blended with 2 tbsps water
2 cups thick coconut milk ⎱ Extracted
4 cups thin coconut milk ⎰ from 1 coconut
½ cup tamarind juice
1 sprig curry leaves
2 tbsps oil
Salt to taste

Serves 4 — 6

Method:

1. Heat oil and fry the shallots and garlic until fragrant.
2. Add in the blended curry powder and stir until fragrant without letting it burn. Add in the curry leaves.
3. Add the thin coconut milk and bring to boil.
4. Add the tomatoes, ladies' fingers and tamarind juice. Cook for 10 minutes.
5. Put in the fish and bring to boil again.
6. Add the thick coconut milk and as soon as it boils, switch off the heat.
7. Serve hot with plain boiled rice.

Singgang Asam Pedas

(Fish in a Hot Gravy)

Ingredients:

2 pieces white fish (threadfin, tuna)
10 dried chillies
1 bowl water
3 shallots
3 cloves garlic
A little prawn paste (optional)
2 tbsps tamarind juice
A little turmeric and ginger
Salt to taste

Serves 4 — 6

Method:

1. Grill the fish over a charcoal fire until cooked on both sides.
2. Prepare the sauce. Mix together all the ingredients and season to taste with salt.
3. Serve the fish hot with the sauce either with rice or by itself.
4. Remove and serve hot with rice.

Ikan Sumbat Kukus

(Steamed Stuffed White Fish)

Ingredients:

5 white fish (Threadfin, tuna)
2.5 cm piece ginger
A small piece of galangal
5 stalks mint leaves
5 red chillies
1 tsp salt
1 tsp cummin
½ cup tamarind juice
10 shallots
1 coconut
4 stalks lemon grass
1 tsp black pepper
1 tsp monosodium glutamate
1 tsp coriander seeds
½ tsp aniseed

Serves 6 — 8

Method:

1. Clean the fish and remove the flesh very carefully, leaving the skin intact.
2. Grate the coconut and pound half of it with the fish flesh. Extract one cup of thick milk from the remaining half, by adding half a cup of water.
3. Pound the shallots, ginger, lemon grass, galangal, black pepper, salt, coriander, aniseed, cummin and red chillies until fine.
4. Stuff into the fish skin and put in a deep bowl.
5. Pour in 1 cup coconut milk and steam for 25 minutes.

Ikan Asam Rebus

(Fish in a Hot Sour Gravy)

Ingredients:

½ ikan parang (Dorab) — the head part
4 dried chillies ⎫
4 shallots ⎪ Ground together
2 cloves garlic ⎬
2 cm piece ginger ⎭
1 lemon grass — crushed
4 ladies' fingers
2 pieces asam gelugur
4 cups water
Salt to taste

Serves 4 — 6

Method:

1. Bring water to boil together with the ground ingredients, assam gelugur, lemon grass and salt.
2. Add in the fish and ladies' fingers.
3. Continue boiling over a moderate flame until the ladies' fingers are cooked.
4. Serve hot with rice.

Kari Ikan (Fish Curry)

Ikan Panggang *(Grilled Fish)*

Ingredients:

4 Spanish Mackerels — cleaned of intestines

Sauce:

2 red chillies
2 green chillies } Sliced thinly
3 shallots

Thumb size piece shrimp paste — toasted and crumbled

½ cup tamarind juice

Salt to taste

Serves 4 — 6

Method:

1. Grill the fish over a charcoal fire until cooked on both sides.
2. Prepare the sauce. Mix together all the ingredients and season to taste with salt.
3. Serve the fish hot with the sauce either with rice or by itself.

> *The traditional way to grill fish is by using a pair of bamboo holders. The fish is put in between the bamboo and grilled over a charcoal fire.*

Udang Masak dengan Tempoyak *(Prawns Cooked with Tempoyak)*

Ingredients:

500 gms medium sized prawns — shelled

3 cups thin coconut milk } Extracted
1 cup thick coconut milk } from 1 coconut

1 cup tempoyak (fermented durian flesh)

2 turmeric leaves

10 cili padi
3 cm piece fresh turmeric } Ground together
4 cloves garlic

Salt to taste

Serves 6 — 8

Method:

1. Place the ground ingredients, thin coconut milk, tempoyak and prawns in a pot.
2. Stir well so that the tempoyak is well mixed. Cook over a low flame.
3. When the gravy boils, add in the thick coconut milk and turmeric leaves. Season well with salt.
4. Cook until the turmeric leaves are limp.
5. Serve with rice.

Gulai Udang *(Prawn Curry)*

Ingredients:

600 gms fresh prawns

6 dried chillies

2 shallots
2 cloves garlic
2 cm piece ginger } Ground finely
1 sprig curry leaves

1 tsp turmeric powder

1 tsp coriander seeds

1 tsp cummin

2½ cups thick coconut milk — extracted from 1 grated coconut

Salt to taste

4 tbsps oil

1 lime

Serves 6 — 8

Method:

1. Heat oil and fry the curry leaves for 1-2 minutes.
2. Add in the ground ingredients and fry for 5 minutes or until fragrant, stirring constantly.
3. Add in the spices and fry for 1 minute.
4. Add in the coconut milk and simmer for 10 minutes.
5. Squeeze in the lime juice and turn off the heat.
6. Serve hot with rice.

Sambal Terubuk Goreng *(Hot Fried Shad)*

Ingredients:

1 ikan terubuk (shad) — cleaned and seasoned with 1 tsp salt and ½ tsp turmeric powder

½ grated coconut
4 shallots
1 clove garlic
3 cm piece ginger } Ground together
1 tbsp dried shrimps
Thumb sized piece shrimp paste

Salt to taste

1 lemon grass — sliced and pounded finely

Oil for deep frying

Serves 4 — 6

Method:

1. Mix the ground ingredients well with the pounded lemon grass and season to taste with salt.
2. Stuff the mixed ingredients into the fish.
3. Heat oil and deep fry the fish until cooked on both sides.
4. Serve with plain boiled rice.

Ikan Bakar (Grilled Fish)

MEAT

Daging Masak Kicap
(Beef in Soy Sauce)

Ingredients:

400 gms beef
8 large onions ⎫ Sliced
8 cloves garlic ⎭
5 cm piece ginger — pounded
3 tbsps curry powder
1 tbsp pepper
2 tbsps tamarind juice
2 carrots — cut into 3 cm lengths
5 tbsps corn oil
½ cup thick soy sauce
8 cups water
1 tbsp vinegar
1 tsp tomato puree

Serves 4 — 6

Method:

1. Cut the beef into bite sized pieces, wash and drain well.
2. Mix the beef with the curry powder, pepper, tamarind juice, salt, tomato puree and let it stand for 30 minutes.
3. Heat oil in a pan and fry the ginger, garlic, and large onions until golden brown.
4. Add in the beef and mix well. Pour in the soy sauce and carrots.
5. Pour in the water and let it boil until the beef is tender.
6. Serve hot with plain rice.

Beef Serunding *(Spicy Sliced Beef)*

Ingredients:

150 gms beef sliced thinly against the grain
1 cup grated coconut
3 cm piece ginger
1 tsp roasted coriander seeds
3 shallots
1 tsp cummin
1 tsp dried prawns
2 tbsps tamarind juice
Salt to taste
2 tbsps oil

Serves 4 — 6

Method:

1. Grind the shallots, garlic, coriander seeds, cummin, ginger and dried prawns.
2. Heat pan, add oil and when smoking, add ground ingredients and fry till fragrant.
3. Add meat and stir thoroughly. If the gravy dries before the meat is tender add cooled boiled water. Put in salt to taste.
4. Cook over a low flame until it is dry and the meat is tender.
5. Add in tamarind juice and mix well.

Daging Kambing Masak Merah *(Mutton in Tomato Sauce)*

Ingredients:

400 gms mutton
7 large onions — 6 to be sliced
3 cm piece ginger — 2 cm pounded
7 cloves garlic — 6 to be sliced
5 almonds — deskinned
4 tbsps curry powder
8 tomatoes — quartered
1 medium tin tomato puree
1 cup evaporated milk
3 tbsps corn oil
Salt and sugar to taste

Serves 4 — 6

Method:

1. Cut and wash the mutton.
2. Boil in water with the sliced onions, shallots, ginger and garlic.
3. Pound the rest of the onions, shallots and garlic with almonds until fine. Mix well with curry powder and add in water.
4. Heat oil in a pan and fry the cinnamon stick and cloves.
5. Add in the curry powder and mix well. Add in the tomato puree and fry until fragrant.
6. Pour this mixture into the beef and mix well.
7. Add in the tomato quarters and simmer until cooked.
8. Add in the milk, salt and sugar and let it continue boiling until the gravy is thick.

It is taboo for the Malays to plant the low, yellow coconut palm in front of the house. It is supposed to bring bad luck and also strange diseases that could prove fatal. It is also said that when it bears its first fruit one of the house occupants will die. When its first root appears, one of the house occupants will lose a loved one.

Daging Masak Kicap (Beef in Soy Sauce)

Gulai Daging *(Beef Curry)*

Ingredients:

600 gms beef

1 cup water

½ cup oil

300 gms potatoes

5 tbsps meat curry powder

6 shallots

4 cloves garlic

3 cm piece ginger

4 cups coconut milk — extracted from ¾ coconut

3 cm piece cinnamon stick

2 cloves

1 star anise

25 gms grated coconut — fried until golden and pounded

Salt to taste

Serves 4 — 6

Method:

1. Wash the meat well and cut into bite sized pieces and drain.
2. Blend the curry powder with 1 cup water.
3. Pound the shallots, garlic and ginger.
4. Heat oil and fry the pounded ingredients until fragrant. Add in the curry powder and fry further until fragrant.
5. Add the beef with a little bit of water.
6. Add the pounded fried coconut, star anise, cloves and cinnamon stick.
7. Stir slowly and add the coconut milk, potatoes and salt.
8. Simmer until the potatoes are cooked.

Ros Daging *(Roast Beef)*

Ingredients:

3 kg beef

200 gms ghee

1 tin evaporated milk

6 cm piece ginger

4 shallots

1 tsp pepper

4 cardamoms

5 cm piece cinnamon stick

Coriander leaves — chopped finely

Serves 6 — 8

Method:

1. Cut the beef and wash well.
2. Pound the ginger and extract its juice.
3. Pound the shallots and garlic finely and mix with the beef. Let it stand for 45 minutes.
4. Heat ghee and add in the meat. Lower the flame and stir continuously until the beef is almost tender.
5. Add in the spices, salt and coriander leaves.
6. Simmer until oil separates and the beef is tender.

Daging Masak Merah

(Beef in Red Sauce)

Ingredients:

600 gms tender meat — sliced

5 bowls water

1 bowl thin coconut milk
½ cup thick coconut milk } From 1 coconut

2 turmeric leaves

2 stalks lemon grass

20 red chillies

Serves 4 — 6

Method:

1. Slice beef as desired, clean and drain it.
2. Take ¼ of the grated coconut and fry until golden. Pound or grind this coconut until its oil comes out. Leave aside.
3. Squeeze the rest of the coconut to get the milk. Boil it.
4. Grind finally all the other ingredients and mix together with the beef. Put beef into the boiled coconut milk. Simmer until the gravy thickens.
5. Add in the fried coconut, salt and sugar to taste. Simmer until the gravy is slightly dry and remove from fire.

Bergedil Daging *(Meatballs)*

Ingredients:

600 gms minced beef

2 cm piece ginger

2 large onions — diced

12 shallots — chopped

8 cloves garlic — chopped

4 green chillies — sliced

1 tbsp flour

2 tbsps milk powder

150 gms potatoes — boiled and mashed

2 egg yolks — beaten

6 stalks mint leaves

2 stalks spring onions

200 gms bread crumbs

Salt and pepper to taste

1 tbsp oil

Serves 6 — 8

Method:

1. Mix well together minced meat, ginger, onions, shallots, garlic, green chillies, salt and pepper.
2. Heat oil and fry mixed ingredients for 7-8 minutes. Cool it.
3. Mix in flour, milk powder, mashed potatoes, spring onions, mint leaves and egg yolks.
4. Make into balls and roll into bread crumbs before deep frying.

Gulai Daging (Beef Curry)

Rendang Berkicap
(Beef Rendang in Soy Sauce)

Ingredients:

600 gms beef
20 dried red chillies
1 pod garlic
10 shallots
3 cm piece ginger
3 cm piece galangal
3 tbsps vinegar
¼ cup thick soy sauce
1 tsp sugar
Salt to taste

To fry:

4 shallots
5 cloves garlic
3 cm piece cinnamon stick
½ cup coconut oil

Serves 4 — 6

Method:

1. Cut the beef into broad pieces and boil in some water. When the beef is tender, drain it. Set stock aside.
2. Grind together the dried chillies, garlic, shallots, ginger, galangal and sugar.
3. Mix the pounded ingredients with the beef and the soy sauce.
4. Slice the shallots and garlic for frying. Heat the oil and fry them with the cinnamon stick until fragrant.
5. Add in the beef and continue frying. Add in the water from the beef. Add also vinegar.
6. When it is almost dry, season with salt to taste and continue frying until fragrant and oily.
7. Remove from fire and serve hot.

Daging Daun Kunyit
(Roast Beef in Turmeric Leaf)

Ingredients:

300 gms beef — cut into large pieces 5 cm thick
Salt and pepper to taste
2 tsps turmeric powder
Turmeric leaves

Serves 4 — 6

Method:

1. Mix the beef thoroughly with salt, pepper and turmeric powder.
2. Wrap each piece of meat in a turmeric leaf, roll tightly and tie with a piece of string.
3. Roast the beef in a medium oven, turning the pieces of beef so that both sides are cooked.

Kurmah Daging *(Beef Kurmah)*

Ingredients:

600 gms beef	
4 tbsps kurmah powder	
1 cup thick coconut milk	Extracted from
2 cups thin coconut milk	1 grated coconut
6 shallots	
4 cloves garlic	
3 cm piece ginger	
2 cardamoms	
2 star anise	
3 cm piece cinnamon stick	
3 cloves	
2 red chillies	
½ cup oil	

Serves 4 — 6

Method:

1. Pound 3 shallots and 2 cloves garlic together. Mix with the kurmah powder and 1 tsp water. Blend well into a paste.
2. Slice finely the remaining shallots and garlic.
3. Heat oil and fry the sliced shallots and garlic with the spices until fragrant.
4. Add in the blended kurmah powder and fry further until oil separates.
5. Add in the meat and 1 cup water. Cook until the beef is tender.
6. Pour in the thick coconut milk, bring to boil and pour in the thin milk.
7. Season with salt to taste and cook further over a low flame until the gravy is thick.
8. Add in the large onion and red chillies.
9. Stir once and remove from fire.

Daging Goreng Sate *(Fried Satay)*

Ingredients:

600 gms beef — cut into bite sized pieces	
3 cloves garlic	
2 stalks lemon grass	Ground finely
2 cm piece ginger	
2 cm piece galangal	
1 tsp turmeric powder	
3 tsps sugar	
Salt to taste	
2 cups oil	

Serves 4 — 6

Method:

1. Marinate the beef with the ground ingredients, turmeric powder, salt and sugar. Leave aside for 4 hours.
2. Heat oil and fry the meat until cooked.
3. Serve immediately with chilli sauce.

Daging Asam *(Tamarind Beef)*

Ingredients:

650 gms topside steak

6 dried chillies — soaked

10 shallots — chopped

3 cm piece ginger

4 candlenuts

1 tsp dried shrimp paste

½ tsp turmeric powder

2 tbsps oil

3 cups water

2 tbsps tamarind

Sugar and salt to taste

1 fresh red chilli — finely sliced

1 green chilli — finely sliced

Serves 4 — 6

Method:

1. Cut beef into small pieces.
2. Chop or mince dried chillies, shallots and grind to a paste with candlenuts, dried shrimp paste and turmeric.
3. Heat oil in a large pan and fry seasonings for 5 minutes, stirring constantly.
4. Put in the beef and turn several times to thoroughly coat the meat pieces with the seasoning.
5. Fry until well-browned.
6. Soak tamarind in water, squeeze out the juice and strain into the meat.
7. Bring to the boil and add salt and sugar to taste. Turn the heat down and simmer until beef is very tender and the gravy slightly reduced.
8. Remove beef and arrange on a platter. Pour on a little of the sauce.
9. To serve, garnish with sliced red and green chillies.

Daging Bakar *(Roast Beef)*

Ingredients:

600 gms beef — cut into large pieces

Salt and pepper to taste

1 tsp turmeric powder

Serves 4 — 6

Method:

1. Marinate beef with seasoning and keep aside for 10 minutes.
2. Roast over a charcoal fire until evenly cooked.
3. Serve hot with a sauce.

Serunding Daging *(Beef Floss)*

Ingredients:

1 grated coconut

250 gms beef — cut into 1 cm squares

1 lemon

6 dried red chillies	
4 shallots	
2 cloves garlic	Ground finely together
½ tsp cummin	
1 tsp coriander seeds	
3 cm piece turmeric	

½ cup oil

2 tbsps sugar

Serves 4 — 6

Method:

1. Heat oil and fry the ground ingredients until golden and fragrant.
2. Add in the grated coconut and mix well.
3. Add in the beef, salt and pepper and squeeze out the lemon juice.
4. Stir well until dry and the coconut appears golden.
5. Serve with plain boiled rice.

Daging Kambing Goreng
(Fried Mutton)

Ingredients:

850 gms mutton

9 cups coconut milk — extracted from 1½ coconuts

1 tbsp coriander seeds and cummin — pounded coarsely

3 cm piece ginger — pounded

4 cloves garlic — pounded

1 tbsp tamarind

7 tbsps oil

Salt to taste

Serves 6 — 8

Method:

1. Place mutton in a pan with coconut milk.
2. Add in sugar, salt, ginger, garlic, coriander seeds and cummin. Bring to boil.
3. Add in tamarind juice. Reduce heat and simmer until the meat is tender.
4. Remove mutton, drain and cut into thick slices.
5. Heat oil and fry the meat over a charcoal fire for 3 minutes on each side.
6. Cut into smaller pieces and serve with chilli sauce.

POULTRY

Soto Ayam *(Chicken Soto)*

Ingredients:

1 chicken — jointed
1 large onion
1 litre water
1 tbsp salt
2 tsps minced ginger
3 tbsps oil
3 hard-boiled eggs — sliced
1 cup bean sprouts — scalded
1½ cups thinly sliced shallots
1 lemon — sliced

Serves 6 — 8

Method:

1. Combine the chicken, onion, water and salt in a pan. Bring to boil, cover and cook over low heat for 1½ hours until chicken is tender.
2. Remove chicken, strain and add ginger. Cut the chicken into thin strips.
3. Heat oil and saute onions until golden brown. Stir in the bean sprouts and cook over low heat for 5 minutes.
4. To serve, arrange the chicken, vegetables and eggs on a platter. Each individual will make his selection and pour the soup over the ingredients.
5. Serve also with potato cakes and a sauce of chopped cili padi and thick soy sauce.

Ayam Goreng Berempah
(Spicy Fried Chicken)

Ingredients:

1 chicken
8 shallots
2 cloves garlic
1 stalk lemon grass
3 cm piece galangal
2 cm piece fresh turmeric
1 tbsp coriander seeds
1 tsp cummin and aniseed mixed together
Salt and sugar to taste

Serves 6 — 8

Method:

1. Clean the chicken and cut into small pieces.
2. Grind all the other ingredients and rub all over the chicken.
3. Place the seasoned chicken in a pot with 1 cup water and cook over a medium flame until half cooked.
4. Remove the chicken and deep fry until golden.
5. Dish out to serve garnished with lettuce leaves and tomatoes.

Serunding Ayam *(Shredded Chicken)*

Ingredients:

1 chicken — deboned and the flesh minced
20 dried chillies — soaked and ground
2 cups grated coconut — fried brown and pounded
4 cups thick coconut milk — from 1 grated coconut
2 stalks lemon grass
1 turmeric leaf
1 piece dried tamarind
3 cm piece galangal — grated
1 large onion — grated
3 cm piece ginger — grated
1 tsp black pepper
½ tsp turmeric powder
½ tsp aniseed and cummin mixed

Serves 6 — 8

Method:

1. Put the ground chillies, grated onion, ginger and galangal into a pan. Add in the coconut milk and chicken flesh. Bring to boil.
2. Add in the black pepper, spices, lemon grass, pounded coconut and tamarind.
3. Cook over a slow flame until the gravy thickens and is almost dry. Season well with salt.

Rendang Ayam *(Chicken Rendang)*

Ingredients:

1 chicken	
16 cups coconut milk from 4 coconuts	
2 tbsps chilli paste	
8 cm piece galangal	
4 screwpine leaves	
4 lime leaves	
4 turmeric leaves	
20 shallots	
6 cloves garlic	Pounded together
8 cm piece ginger	
Salt to taste	

Serves 6 — 8

Method:

1. Wash the chicken and cut into bite sized pieces.
2. Mix the pounded ingredients with the chilli paste.
3. Extract coconut milk from the coconut.
4. Put the chicken, coconut milk, chilli paste mixture and the rest of the ingredients in a pan and cook over very low flame until the gravy is dry and chicken is tender.

> *Rendang is a favourite during Hari Raya and is best eaten with Nasi Impit.*

Soto Ayam (Chicken Soto)

Sambal Ayam *(Chicken Sambal)*

Ingredients:

1 chicken
10 dried red chillies
10 shallots
5 cloves garlic
3 cm piece ginger } To pound half
2 cm piece galangal
1 tbsp flour
1 piece tamarind (asam keping)
Salt and pepper to taste
Oil for deep frying

Serves 6 — 8

Method:

1. Clean the chicken and cut into 8. Mix with the flour to rid of the smell. Wash and drain well.
2. Season the chicken with the pounded ginger and galangal.
3. Heat the oil and fry the chicken pieces until slightly golden.
4. Pound finely the chillies, shallots, galangal, garlic and the remaining ginger.
5. Remove half of the oil and fry the pounded ingredients until fragrant.
6. Add the tamarind and salt.
7. Put in 1 cup water and bring to boil. Stir constantly for a few minutes then add the chicken pieces. Mix well. Simmer till chicken is tender.
8. Serve with plain boiled rice or Nasi Impit.

Ayam Selera *(Fried Chicken with Sauce)*

Ingredients:

1 chicken
6 cm piece ginger — pounded
For sauce:
2 cloves garlic
3 tbsps vinegar
2 red chillies
Salt to taste
6 lettuce leaves
1 cucumber
Oil for deep frying

Serves 6 — 8

Method:

1. Clean the chicken and season with the pounded ginger and salt.
2. Steam the chicken until tender. Remove and fry until the skin is crispy.
3. Cut the chicken into bite-sized pieces.
4. Make the sauce. Pound the red chillies and garlic together. Mix with vinegar, salt and sugar. Mix in 1 cup water.
5. Serve chicken garnished with lettuce leaves and sliced cucumber. Use the sauce as a dip.

Gulai Ayam Minang
(Chicken Curry Minang Style)

Ingredients:

1 medium-sized chicken
10 red chillies
10 cili padi
3 shallots
2 cloves garlic
2 stalks lemon grass
3 cm piece ginger
3 cm piece fresh turmeric
2 turmeric leaves } Shredded
4 lime leaves
3 tomatoes
Oil for frying
Salt to taste

Serves 6 — 8

Method:

1. Clean the chicken and cut into bite-sized pieces.
2. Grind together red chillies, small chillies, garlic, ginger, lemon grass and turmeric.
3. Heat oil in a pan and fry the ground ingredients until fragrant.
4. Add 1 cup water and cover the pot. Bring to boil.
5. Add in the shredded leaves and salt to taste.
6. When the chicken is cooked, put in the tomatoes.

Ayam Goreng dengan Bawang
(Fried Chicken with Onions)

Ingredients:

1 chicken
2 tsps turmeric powder
1 tsp salt
1 large onions — ringed thickly
2 red chillies — sliced
Oil for deep frying

Serves 6 — 8

Method:

1. Clean the chicken and cut into 8. Wash and dry well.
2. Mix the chicken with salt and turmeric powder.
3. Heat oil in a deep pan and fry the chicken pieces until crisp.
4. Using 2 tbsps of the same oil, in a separate pan fry the onion rings and chilli slices until limp. Turn off the heat and mix with the chicken pieces.

Ayam Kukus (Steamed Chicken)

Ingredients:

1 chicken
1 cm piece fresh turmeric
1 cm piece ginger
2 cm piece galangal — crushed
1 stalk lemon grass
2 tsps coriander seeds
1 tsp cummin
3 cloves garlic
6 shallots
1 tsp sugar
Salt to taste

Serves 6 — 8

Method:

1. Clean the chicken and cut into 4. Wash well and drain.
2. Grind all the ingredients together except the galangal.
3. Rub the galangal and ground ingredients all over the chicken. Set aside for 30 minutes.
4. Place in a steaming tray and steam until the chicken is tender.

Ayam Masak Merah
(Chicken in Thick Red Sauce)

Ingredients:

400 gms chicken drumsticks
7 shallots — slice 3
3 cm piece ginger — pounded
7 cloves garlic — slice 4
2 cm piece ginger — sliced
5 almonds — blanched and skinned
8 tbsps curry powder
1 medium-sized tin tomato puree
1 cup evaporated milk
3 tbsps corn oil
Salt and sugar to taste

Serves 6 — 8

Method:

1. Put the chicken drumsticks into a pan with enough water to cover and add sliced shallots, ginger and garlic. Cook till chicken is nearly done.
2. Pound the remaining shallots, garlic and ginger with almonds. Mix in curry powder blended with 4 tsps water. Mix well.
3. Heat oil and fry the cinnamon and cloves until fragrant. Add the curry powder mixture and tomato puree. Fry until fragrant.
4. Pour the fried ingredients into the chicken mixture. Add in the tomato slices and cook until chicken is tender and tomato is done.
5. Add in milk, salt and sugar. Simmer until the gravy thickens.

Ayam Goreng Berlada
(Fried Chillied Chicken

Ingredients:

1 chicken
60 gms red chillies
4 cloves garlic
2 shallots
3 cm piece ginger
3 cm piece fresh turmeric
Salt to taste
Oil for deep-frying

Serves 6 — 8

Method:

1. Wash the chicken and cut into bite-sized pieces.
2. Heat oil and deep fry the chicken until half cooked.
3. Grind all the ingredients and set aside. Mix in the salt.
4. Heat 4 tbsps oil and fry the ground ingredients until fragrant.
5. Add in the chicken pieces and mix well. Cook until the chicken is tender. If the dish tends to be too dry add some water but simmer till the gravy is thick before dishing out.

Ayam Masak Kicap
(Chicken in Black Sauce)

Ingredients:

1 chicken
5 shallots ⎫
3 cloves garlic ⎬ Pound together
2 cm piece ginger ⎭
2 red chillies — sliced lengthwise
4 tbsps thick soy sauce
1 large onion — sliced into thick rings
1 lime
2 tsps turmeric powder
1 tsp salt

Serves 6 — 8

Method:

1. Clean the chicken and cut into bite-sized pieces. Mix with salt and turmeric powder.
2. Heat oil in a deep pan and fry the chicken pieces until crispy. Drain off the oil but leave 2 tbsps in the pan. Fry the pounded ingredients until fragrant.
3. Add the soy sauce and chicken pieces and mix well.
4. Add in the onion rings and chillies and just before dishing out, squeeze the lime juice over.
5. If you want more gravy you can add ½ cup water and bring to boil before adding in the chicken pieces. Soy sauce is already quite salty so be careful not to add too much salt.

Satay Kajang

Ingredients:

1.5 kg chicken — deboned
1 tsp cummin
½ tsp powdered cinnamon
8 shallots
1 tsp coriander
2.5 cm piece fresh turmeric
1 tsp sugar
1 stalk lemon grass
2 tbsps roasted peanuts
Salt to taste
2 tbsps cooking oil

Serves 6 — 8

Method:

1. Cube the chicken meat, drain and put aside.
2. Grind coriander, cummin, turmeric, peanuts, salt and sugar. Mix this with the powdered cinnamon, diced shallots and 1 tbsp cooking oil. Marinate the chicken with this mixture.
3. Using special skewers, skewer 5 pieces of meat on one skewer, as in Kebabs.
4. Grill over burning coal, constantly sprinkling cooking oil over the meat using crushed lemon grass.
5. Turn over and continue grilling until the chicken is cooked.
7. Serve with peanut sauce.

Peanut Sauce

Ingredients:

300 gms peanuts — roasted
2.5 cm piece ginger
A piece of galangal
3 tbsps pounded chillies
2 stalks lemon grass
1 cup sugar
1 bombay onion
½ cup tamarind juice
Salt to taste

Method:

1. Grind the roasted peanuts. Put aside.
2. Grind lemon grass, ginger and galangal until fine.
3. Slice bombay onion and stir fry until soft.
4. Add in ground chillies and the other ground ingredients.
5. Add in tamarind juice and lastly peanuts, sugar and salt. Simmer until the gravy thickens.
6. To serve, arrange a few sticks of satay on a plate and serve with a bowl of peanut sauce, cucumber and sliced bombay onion. Satay also goes very well with compressed rice.

Ayam Percik *(Grilled Chicken with Gravy)*

Ingredients:

1 medium sized chicken
4 cloves garlic
6 shallots
5 cm piece ginger
1 tsp salt

Serves 6 — 8

Method:

1. Cut the chicken into two. Clean and drain it.
2. Pound the shallots, garlic, ginger and salt.
3. Marinate the chicken with the pounded ingredients for 20 minutes.

Gravy

Ingredients:

2 coconuts
2.5 cm piece ginger
15 shallots
1 tsp aniseed
1 slice lime

Method:

1. Squeeze coconut to get the milk. Do not use water for the first squeeze. Use some water for the second squeeze.
2. Pound shallots, ginger and aniseed until fine. Add into the coconut milk. Pour this mixture into a pan and heat over a medium fire. Put in salt and sugar.
3. Squeeze in lime juice. Stir until the mixture thickens.
4. Roast chicken over a low charcoal fire and sprinkle gravy over the chicken. Turn the chicken over and baste with gravy again.
5. Repeat until the chicken is cooked.

The Malays believe that before slaughtering an old chicken, give it a tablespoonful of vinegar. This helps to tenderise the meat.

Ayam Berempah *(Spicy Chicken)*

Ingredients:

1 medium sized chicken
2 tbsps aniseed
1 tsp cummin
6 cardamoms
1.5 cm piece ginger
2.5 cm piece dried turmeric (or 1 tsp turmeric)
1 clove garlic
5 red chillies
1 stalk lemon grass
3 tbsps coriander
1 tsp black pepper
7 cloves
5 cm piece cinnamon
A piece of galangal
20 shallots
2 bombay onions
2 slices dried sour fruit (optional)
4 cups coconut milk — from 1 coconut
Some shrimp paste (optional)

Serves 6 — 8

Method:

1. Toast all ingredients except red chillies, lemon grass and bombay onions. Pound finely.
2. Cut bombay onions into 4 and cut chillies lengthwise.
3. Clean the chicken and cut into 8 pieces.
4. Squeeze coconut to get 4 cups of milk.
5. Cook chicken with coconut milk over a medium fire.
6. Bring gravy to a boil and add in the pounded ingredients.
7. Put in crushed lemon grass together with bombay onions, red chillies and salt to taste.
8. Simmer till chicken is tender, and gravy thick.

Ayam Goreng Istimewa

(Special Fried Chicken)

Ingredients:

1 chicken
300 gms flour
4 tbsps margarine
2 tbsps salt
4 eggs
½ tbsp sugar
Oil for deep frying

Serves 6 — 8

Method:

1. Cut the chicken into small pieces. Wash and drain well.
2. Mix well together flour, margarine, eggs, sugar and salt.
3. Put in the chicken pieces, and coat well.
4. Heat oil in a deep pan and deep fry the chicken pieces a few at a time until brown and crisp.

Ayam Golek *(Spicy Grilled Chicken)*

Ingredients:

1 whole chicken
5 cloves garlic
4 cups coconut milk — extracted from 1 coconut
1 tsp coriander seeds
1 tbsp tamarind pulp
3 hard-boiled eggs
Salt to taste
Chicken liver and gizzard

Serves 6 — 8

Method:

1. Clean the chicken well and drain.
2. Pound or grind the garlic and coriander seeds finely.
3. Slice finely the chicken innards and mix with 1 tsp of the ground ingredients.
4. Chop the eggs roughly and add to the mixture. Stuff the chicken with the mixture and sew up the opening.
5. Squeeze out the milk from the coconut, mix with tamarind and salt. Add in the remaining ground ingredients.
6. Boil the chicken in this mixture until the oil surfaces.
7. Take the chicken out of the pot and grill it in the oven until tender.

Pecal Ayam Bersantan

(Chicken in Coconut Milk)

Ingredients:

1 chicken
10 fresh red chillies
Thumb-sized piece shrimp paste
2 eggs
3 candlenuts
2 lime leaves
2 shallots
2 cloves garlic
2 cups coconut milk — from ½ grated coconut
1 tsp salt
2 tsps sugar

Serves 6 — 8

Method:

1. Clean the chicken and cut into 2. Wash and drain well.
2. Rub salt all over the chicken. Roast the chicken and when it is half cooked take it and tap it gently a few times. Roast again till chicken is tender.
3. To make the gravy — grind all the ingredients except lime leaves. Mix the coconut milk and lime leaves in a saucepan. Heat and bring to boil. The gravy should be slightly thick.
4. Place the chicken on a platter and pour the gravy over.

Ayam Masak Tomato

(Chicken in Tomato Sauce)

Ingredients:

1 chicken
30 dried red chillies
5 cloves garlic
2 large onions
2 tomatoes
1 cup tomato sauce
1 tbsp sugar
5 cm piece ginger
1 star anise
2 cm piece cinnamon stick
½ cup oil
2 cups thick coconut milk — from 1 grated coconut
2 cups green peas
3 cloves
2 tsps turmeric powder
Salt to taste

Serves 6 — 8

Method:

1. Clean the chicken and cut into bite-sized pieces. Drain and mix well with salt and turmeric powder.
2. Heat oil in a deep pan and fry the chicken pieces until crispy.
3. Grind the dried chillies until fine. Pound coarsely the shallots and ginger.
4. Heat 3 tbsps oil and fry the ground chillies, pounded shallots and ginger, cloves and star anise.
5. Add coconut milk and bring to boil.
6. Add tomato sauce, sugar, salt and cinnamon. Stir constantly.
7. Add in the fried chicken pieces. Simmer for 5 minutes.
8. Add in the sliced onions and tomatoes and green peas.
9. Turn the chicken pieces to mix well with the gravy.
10. Serve hot with Nasi Minyak.

> *If the coconut palm is planted beside the house, it is believed that the head of the household will not have an easy life.*

Ayam Rendang Santan

(Chicken Rendang in Coconut Milk)

Ingredients:

1 chicken
5 cm piece ginger
3 red chillies — cut lengthwise
6 shallots
Thumb-sized piece shrimp paste
1 cup thick coconut milk ⎫ From 1 grated
2 cups thin coconut milk ⎭ coconut
3 stalks lemon grass — crushed
4 'belimbing' (Carambola — optional)
½ tbsp sugar
½ cup oil
6 cloves garlic
Salt to taste

Serves 6 — 8

Method:

1. Clean the chicken and remove the skin. Cut into medium-sized pieces.
2. Heat the oil and fry shallots and chillies until the shallots turn golden brown.
3. Crumble the shrimp paste and add in.
4. Add in the chicken pieces, lemon grass, 3 cups water and thick coconut milk. Bring to boil.
5. When the chicken is almost cooked, add the 'belimbing', sugar and thin coconut milk. Bring to boil.
6. Lower the heat and simmer until the chicken is really tender and the oil separates.

Ayam Goreng Asam

(Fried Chicken in Tamarind)

Ingredients:

5 chicken breasts
1½ tbsps sesame oil
2 tbsps vegetable oil
3 cloves garlic — crushed
½ cup tamarind juice
2 tbsps chilli paste
3 tsps salt

Serves 6 — 8.

Method:

1. Flatten the chicken breasts with the side of a cleaver. Marinate with all the ingredients. Leave aside for 30 minutes.
2. Put on a rack under a grill and cook until both sides are golden brown, basting with extra oil and juices if necessary.
3. Alternatively, deep-fry the chicken over moderate heat.

Bubur Kacang Merah
(Red Beans Porridge)

Ingredients:

300 gms red beans
2 cm piece ginger — sliced
1 screwpine leaf
1 block plam sugar
2 cups sugar
4 cups thin coconut milk ⎫ Extracted
1 cup thick coconut milk ⎭ from 1 coconut
½ tsp salt
1 tbsp sago

Serves 6 — 8

Method:

1. Boil the red beans in 4 cups water until the beans expand. Add in the ginger, screwpine leaf and salt.
2. Add in palm sugar and sugar. Stir until the sugar dissolves.
3. Put in the thin coconut milk and bring to boil.
4. Add the sago and thick coconut milk. Stir constantly.
5. When the sago becomes transparent and shiny, remove the screwpine leaf.
6. Serve either hot or cold in small serving bowls.

Kuih Tas *(Sugar-coated Glutinous Rice Cakes)*

Ingredients:

500 gms glutinous rice flour
½ grated coconut
3 cups water
Pinch of salt
Oil for deep frying

Coating:

2 cups sugar
1 cup water

Serves 6 — 8

Method:

1. Mix together the flour, salt and coconut.
2. Add in water and mix until of dough consistency. Form diamond shapes.
3. Heat oil and fry the cakes until golden. Lift and drain.
4. Put water and sugar for the coating in a pan and bring to boil until the mixture thickens.
5. Put in the cakes and stir until the sugar crystallizes and coats all the cakes evenly.
6. Lift and serve immediately.

Kuih Badak
(Sweet Potato Cakes with Savoury Filling)

Ingredients:

300 gms sweet potato
½ cup flour
Pinch of salt
Oil for deep frying

Filling:

½ grated coconut
20 gms dried shrimps ⎫
1 stalk lemon grass ⎪
2 fresh red chillies ⎬ Ground together
2 cloves garlic ⎪
2 shallots ⎭
½ tsp turmeric powder
Salt to taste

Serves 6 — 8

Method:

1. Scrape the skin off the sweet potatoes and cut into small cubes. Boil with salt until cooked.
2. Remove and mash.
3. Mix mashed sweet potato with flour and knead until soft.
4. Divide into equal portions.
5. Prepare the filling. Mix all the ingredients together and fry in 2 tbsps of oil until dry.
6. Take 1 portion of the sweet potato mixture and flatten slightly. Put in 1 tsp of the filling in the centre and seal.
7. Heat oil and fry the cakes until golden.

Pengat Pisang *(Banana Porridge)*

Ingredients:

6 ripe bananas — peeled and cut
5 cm piece ginger
3 cups thin coconut milk ⎫ Extracted
1 cup thick coconut milk ⎭ from 1 coconut
1 cup sugar
1 tbsp sago

Serves 4 — 6

Method:

1. Bring to boil the thin coconut milk together with ginger.
2. Add the sugar and banana. Stir constantly so that the coconut milk does not curdle. However, be careful so as not to break the banana.
3. When the bananas are cooked, add in the thick coconut milk and sago.
4. Bring to boil and when the sago becomes transparent, turn off the heat.
5. Serve either hot or cold.

Bubur Kacang Merah (Red Beans Porridge)

Cendol

Ingredients:

10 screwpine leaves
A few drops green food colouring
½ cup green pea flour
1 block palm sugar
1 tbsp sugar
1 coconut — grated
Pinch of salt

Serves 4 — 6

Method:

1. Pound the screwpine leaves and strain to extract juice.
2. Add enough water to make 2 cups pandan juice and also drop in the green colouring.
3. Mix the green pea flour with this mixture and cook over a medium flame, stirring continously until it bubbles.
4. Place a cendol frame or strainer over a basin of cold water containing ice cubes. Spoon the mixture into the strainer and press through with a spatula.
5. Drain off the water and chill the cendol.
6. Boil the palm sugar and white sugar with ½ cup water to get a syrup. Strain and cool.
7. Extract coconut milk using 2 cups water. Add in salt.
8. To serve, place 1 tbsp cendol in a small serving bowl or sundae glass, then add 1 tbsp syrup and ¼ cup coconut milk. Serve cold.

Banana Pancakes

Ingredients:

1 cup flour
1 tsp baking powder
2 eggs
½ cup milk
6 large ripe bananas
1½ tbsps castor sugar
Pinch of salt
1 tbsp oil
2 tbsps sugar

Serves 6 — 8

Method:

1. Sieve flour and baking powder into a bowl. Make a well in the centre, add the eggs and half of the milk.
2. Mix well and beat batter for 10 minutes until smooth and light. Add the remaining milk.
3. Mash bananas together with castor sugar and salt. Mix with the batter.
4. Grease a frying pan, heat it and fry the pancakes till brown on both sides. Repeat until all the mixture has been used up.

Kuih Rose *(Rose Cookies)*

Ingredients:

¼ coconut
¾ cup flour
4 tbsps rice flour
3 tbsps sugar
1 egg
Oil for deep frying

Serves 6 — 8

Method:

1. Extract 1 cup coconut milk.
2. Sieve both types of flour into a bowl, add sugar and mix well.
3. Make a well in the centre, drop in the egg and half the coconut milk. Mix to get a smooth batter.
4. Add the remaining coconut milk, beat the batter for 10 minutes and then let it rest for 30 minutes.
5. Heat the oil for deep-fat frying and heat the rose mould in oil.
6. When both the oil and mould are hot, lift the mould, shake away excess oil and dip into the batter so that the batter almost reaches the top of the mould. The mould should be evenly coated with a thin layer of batter.
7. Hold the mould in hot oil and shake gently when the batter browns and hardens so that it comes away from the mould.
8. Fry until golden brown. Drain well and cool before storing in an airtight tin.

Ubi Bersira

(Sugar-coated Tapioca Fritters)

Ingredients:

300 gms tapioca
½ grated coconut
Salt and sugar to taste
Oil for deep-frying

Serves 6 — 8

Method:

1. Grate the tapioca and keep aside the juice.
2. Mix in the grated coconut with a little bit of salt and also the tapioca juice.
3. Shape into balls and flatten slightly.
5. Deep-fry until golden. Keep aside.
5. Place the coating ingredients in a pan and bring to boil until the mixture thickens.
6. Put in the cakes and stir until the sugar crystallizes and coats all the cakes evenly.

Pulut Inti
(Gutinous Rice with Sweet Coconut Filling)

Ingredients:

50 gms margarine	
200 gms sugar	
3 coconuts — grated	
6 tbsps boiling water	
6 screwpine leaves	
600 gms glutinous rice	
250 gms brown sugar	
1 litre water	
Colouring	
Salt to taste	

Serves 6 — 8

Method:

1. Clean and soak the glutinous rice overnight and sieve it the next day.
2. Add ¾ litre water to the grated coconut and take the first squeeze of the coconut milk. Keep aside in a cool place.
3. Cook ¾ of the grated coconut on a low fire together with screwpine leaves, margarine, sugar, salt and water until it is thick and sticky. Take care not to let it burn. Put aside and cool.
4. Put the glutinous rice in a steamer that has been lined with banana leaves and four screwpine leaves.
5. Sprinkle salt over the rice.
6. Steam for about 10 minutes and pour some cool coconut milk on top.
7. Use a wooden spoon to knead it in evenly. Repeat until all the coconut milk has been used up.
8. Streak the glutinous rice with colouring, preferably blue. Put into small cups, turn over and top with 1 tsp of the filling.

Bingka Ubi *(Baked Tapioca Cake)*

Ingredients:

1 medium sized tapioca
2 cups sugar
2 blocks palm sugar
1 grated coconut

Serves 6 — 8

Method:

1. Grate the tapioca and grind together with the coconut.
2. Melt the sugar, palm sugar and screwpine leaves.
3. Mix thoroughly all the ingredients and put in a baking tin.
4. Bake in medium oven until done.
5. Cool the cake before cutting.

Kuih Ubi Berlapis
(Layered Tapioca Cake)

Ingredients:

600 gms tapioca — grated finely	
4 fresh red chillies	Pounded together
5 shallots	
2 cloves garlic	
2 tbsps dried shrimps — pounded	
3 cups thick coconut milk — extracted from 1 coconut	
½ cup tamarind juice	
Salt and sugar tc taste	
4 tbsps oil	

Serves 6 — 8

Method:

1. Mix together the coconut milk and the grated tapioca.
2. Heat oil and fry the pounded chillies, shallots and garlic until fragrant.
3. Add in the dried shrimps and fry for 10 minutes.
4. Add in the tamarind juice, salt and sugar and fry for 5 minutes. Remove from fire.
5. In an oven-proof dish, put in the tapioca mixture alternated with the fried ingredients in layers.
6. Bake in a moderate oven.

Kodok Nangka *(Jack-fruit Fritters)*

Ingredients:

6 pieces jack-fruit flesh — discard the seeds and mash
300 gms flour
2 cups water
Pinch of salt
Oil for deep-frying

Serves 6 — 8

Method:

1. Mix together flour, salt and water until smooth.
2. Add in the jack-fruit flesh and mix thoroughly.
3. Heat oil and deep fry the fritters using a teaspoon to drop the fritters into the oil. Fry until golden.
4. Serve hot with tea or for breakfast.

> *Banana leaves are said to impart a deliciously delicate flavour to the food cooked in them. They are used for both savoury and sweet dishes, usually when steaming, and grilling is involved.*

Simple Agar-Agar

Ingredients:

50 gms agar-agar strands — soaked for 5 minutes
300 gms sugar
2 litres water
4 screwpine leaves — washed and knotted
Few drops colouring

Serves 6 — 8

Method:
1. Boil agar-agar in water until it dissolves.
2. Add sugar and stir until dissolved. Strain.
3. Colour with a few drops of food colouring and pour into rinsed moulds. Chill to set.
4. Chopped fruits or fruit cocktail can also be added. First half-fill the mould, chill until almost set, add the fruits and pour in the remaining agar-agar mixture. Chill.

Agar-agar Keledek Bersantan

(Sweet Potato Jelly with Coconut Milk)

Ingredients:

175 gms sweet potatoes
20 gms agar-agar strands
4 cups cool water
2 screwpine leaves
1 cup sugar
1 cup thick coconut milk — from ½ grated coconut
2 tsps cocoa
Few drops yellow colouring

Method:
1. Scrub and boil the sweet potato until cooked. Skin and mash it, making sure that the fibres are strained out.
2. In a pan, boil the agar-agar strands with 4 cups water and screwpine leaves until the agar-agar dissolves.
3. Add sugar and stir until dissolved. Strain.
4. Mix half of the agar-agar mixture with the mashed potato, add a few drops yellow colouring and pour into a rinsed mould. Chill to set.
5. Stir the coconut milk into the remaining agar-agar. Keep warm so that the agar-agar does not set.
6. When the first agar-agar mixture has set, pour in 1 cm layer of the second mixture. Chill to set.
7. Meanwhile, blend cocoa with 1 tbsp water. Add to the rest of the agar-agar and bring to boil to cook the cocoa.
8. Pour over the set white layer. Chill to set.
9. Turn out of the mould to serve.

Bubur Kacang *(Green Beans Porridge)*

Ingredients:

500 gms green beans — boiled until soft
4 cups coconut milk — extracted from 1 coconut
2 pieces palm sugar
2 screwpine leaves — washed and knotted
Pinch of salt

Serves 6 — 8

Method:
1. Bring to boil the cooked grean beans with the coconut milk and screwpine leaves.
2. Add the palm sugar and a pinch of salt.
3. Continue boiling over a medium flame until the gravy thickens.
4. Serve hot, removing the knotted screwpine leaves.

Dodol Durian

Ingredients:

500 gms glutinous rice flour
1 tsp salt
850 gms brown sugar
850 gms sugar
9 cups coconut milk — extracted from 2½ grated coconuts
5 screwpine leaves
1 bowl durian flesh

Serves 6 — 8

Method:
1. Mix the glutinous rice flour with the coconut milk in a pan. Stir over a medium flame, making sure it does not burn.
2. When the mixture starts to thicken, add the sugar and durian flesh.
3. Stir slowly over a low flame until thick and glossy.
4. Cool and cut before serving.

Durian is a seasonal rather distinctive Malaysian fruit. Because of the powerful smell, foreigners take some time to get accustomed to it.

Jala Mas *(Golden Net)*

Ingredients:

15 duck eggs
600 gms sugar
2 tumblers water
1 screwpine leaf

Serves 6 — 8

Method:

1. Boil the sugar and water until the sugar dissolves. Add the screwpine leaves.
2. Stir in the egg yolks and pour into a mould. Slowly shake the mould so that the yolks sink in the sugar syrup.
3. The yolks will now appear like strands. Using a thin stick or skewer, join these strands so that they will form a net.
4. Sieve and cool.

This is a specialty of the East Coast states of Malaysia whose people are well known for their sweet tooth.

Dodol

Ingredients:

1.8 kg glutinous rice flour
300 gms rice flour
3.6 kg palm sugar
12 coconuts — extract as much milk as possible, separating the thin from the thick
10—15 screwpine leaves

Method:

1. Mix both types of flour with the thin coconut milk and strain into an iron pan.
2. Cook the palm sugar and screwpine leaves with a little bit of water and when it has dissolved pour into the pan.
3. Bring the mixture to boil over a very low flame, stirring continously.
4. When it is half-cooked add the thick coconut milk and continue stirring until cooked.
5. When mixture no longer sticks to the fingers, it is ready to be removed from the fire.

Old Malay folk believe that a pregnant woman should not pass a banana leaf over a fire to soften it. They believe that the child might be born with spots like the banana leaf.

Ondeh-Ondeh
(Sweet Potato Balls with Sweet Filling)

Ingredients:

600 gms sweet potato
1 tbsp tapioca flour
1 tbsp flour
1 tbsp sugar
½ grated coconut — white part only; add salt and mix well
5 screwpine leaves — shredded and pounded to extract the juice
1 block palm sugar — chopped
Salt to taste

Serves 6 — 8

Method:

1. Scrub the sweet potato and boil until soft. Mash and strain the fibres.
2. Prepare filling. Mix the chopped palm sugar with ordinary sugar.
3. Mix the mashed sweet potato with flour and knead well to get an elastic dough. Add screwpine juice to give the dough a green colour.
4. Shape the dough into marble-size balls and flatten them.
5. Put in 1 tsp of the filling in the centre and re-shape into balls.
6. Boil a pan of water and when it is boiling, drop in the cakes.
7. The cakes will float when cooked. Lift and strain.
8. Roll in the grated coconut and serve immediately.

Kuih Lupis
(Glutinous Rice Cakes with Sweet Syrup)

Ingredients:

600 gms glutinous rice — washed thoroughly
10 screwpine leaves — washed, shredded and pounded to obtain 1½ cups juice
1 block palm sugar
½ cup sugar
½ grated coconut — white part only
Banana leaves for wrapping

Serves 6 — 8

Method:

1. Cook the glutinous rice with the screwpine juice until the rice is cooked. Stir continously so that it does not burn. Set aside.
2. Soften the banana leaves over a flame and wrap the glutinous rice as you desire, tie with a piece of string on both ends.
3. Put in a steamer and steam over rapidly boiling water.
4. Prepare the sauce. Cook both types of sugar to make a syrup. Add screwpine leaf for its fragrance.
5. To serve: Cut the kuih lupis and serve with the syrup and grated coconut.

Kuih Keria *(Doughnuts)*

Ingredients:

600 gms sweet potatoes
60 gms flour
60 gms tapioca flour
120 gms granulated sugar
1 tbsp water
Oil for deep frying

Serves 6 — 8

Method:

1. Scrub the sweet potatoes well and boil them in their jackets.
2. When tender, peel and mash them. Force through a sieve to remove fibres.
3. Mix in the flours and knead together to get a firm dough. Add water if the sweet potatoes are too dry.
4. Turn dough onto a floured board and roll into a long roll about 5 cms in diameter.
5. Cut the roll into 12 equal slices and shape each slice into a round cake 1 cm thick. Make a hole in the centre of each cake.
6. Heat oil and fry the doughnuts until golden brown. Drain and keep aside.
7. Strain the oil and put in sugar and 3 tbsps water. Melt the sugar and boil until a very thick syrup is obtained.
8. Return the doughnuts to the pan and toss them in the syrup until well coated and the sugar crystallises.
9. Serve either for breakfast or tea.

Agar-agar Kentang *(Potato Jelly)*

Ingredients:

25 gms agar-agar
600 gms sugar
5 eggs
3 cups water
600 gms mashed potato
3 cups thick coconut milk — extracted from 1 coconut

Serves 6 — 8

Method:

1. Boil the agar-agar until it dissolves.
2. Beat the eggs until frothy, add in mashed potato and stir well. Strain.
3. Add sugar into the agar-agar, stir until the sugar dissolves and strain.
4. Mix together the potato mixture and the agar-agar mixture. Add the coconut milk and cook over low heat.
5. Keep on stirring until the mixture thickens. Pour into a mould and cool it.

Kuih Rengas *(Green Pea Fritters)*

Ingredients:

Filling:

500 gms green peas
6 cups water
½ grated coconut
1 cup sugar
¾ cups brown sugar
1 tsp salt
½ cup flour
Oil for deep frying

Batter:

300 gms rice flour
3 cups water
½ tsp turmeric powder
Pinch of salt

Serves 6 — 8

Method:

1. Boil the green peas until they expand. Add more water if necessary.
2. Add the coconut, brown sugar, sugar and salt. Stir until thick. Remove into a mixing bowl.
3. Mix thoroughly with flour. Using a tablespoon, spoon out the mixture and shape into balls. Flatten slightly and keep aside.
4. Prepare batter. Mix together all the ingredients until smooth.
5. Heat oil and fry the cakes, dipping each into the batter and frying until golden.

Serawa Durian *(Durian Sweet)*

Ingredients:

8 pieces durian flesh — discard the seeds
3 tbsps sugar
2 tbsps chopped palm sugar
2 screwpine leaves
1 tbsp corn flour — blended with some water
2½ cups thick coconut milk — extracted from ½ grated coconut

Serves 6 — 8

Method:

1. Mix together the durian flesh, coconut milk and screwpine leaves.
2. Bring to boil and stir constantly.
3. Add in sugar, palm sugar and a pinch of salt.
4. Leave on the fire until it thickens. Add the blended cornflour if necessary.
5. Serve with bread.

CHINESE

Cookery writers who specialise in Chinese food constantly equate the merits of a Chinese meal with the qualities of a good novel — it must start immediately with a situation and follow through with characterization and suspense.

The secret of Chinese cooking lies in its preparation. Food is sliced, shredded or cut according to certain predetermined rules. For very tender, almost velvety meat, the meat should be sliced along the grain; for a slightly crunchier texture, it should, ideally, be sliced against. Vegetables are often diagonally sliced both for aesthetic appeal and for a semblance of regularity.

There are no laws governing what is served with what but there are philosophical and practical requirements which are taken into consideration. Menus which start with soups and work their way through to desserts are unknown. Instead, depending on the grandness of the occasion, a selection of four, six, eight, ten or up to almost any number of dishes is served in a course - type procedure. Each dish is savoured separately in order to extract the full goodness.

The final choice, however, depends, as it always has done, on the capabilities of the cook, both in culinary skills and in terms of the availability of money and ingredients. But starting with absolutely fresh ingredients, relatively few seasonings are used in any given dish. It is more the balance of ingredients that provides variety.

Table-setting consists of chopsticks, a selection of bowls of different sizes (for rice, soup, meat dishes and so on) and a soup spoon, if soup is to be served. Napkins, as they are used in the West, are unknown. Instead, a hot, damp hand towel is handed to guests both before and during the meal. Also, in contrast to western custom, the pride of place traditionally reserved for the guest of honour is often as far away from the host as possible but always directly across from the doorway or opening through which the food will come.

SOUPS

Soft Bean Curd Soup

Ingredients:

1 piece soft bean curd

30 gms small fresh prawns — shelled

1 clove garlic — crushed

1 large onion — sliced

3 cups water

Salt and pepper to taste

Spring onions for garnishing

Serves 2 — 4

Method:

1. Carefully cut the beancurd into 4.
2. Heat 1 tbsp oil in a pan and fry the garlic until fragrant. Add in the sliced large onion and fry until limp.
3. Add water and salt and bring to the boil.
4. When the soup boils, add the beancurd and cook for 5 minutes more.
5. Serve hot, garnished with chopped spring onions and a shake of pepper.

Steamed Melon Soup

Ingredients:

1 Chinese winter melon

3 tbsps lotus seeds

1 cup chicken meat — diced

4 Chinese mushrooms — diced

½ cup button mushrooms

2 cm piece ginger — sliced

5 cups chicken stock

2 tsps salt

Serves 4 — 6

Method:

1. Slice off 2.5 cm from the top of the melon.
2. Using a tablespoon, scoop out the soft centre of the melon, so you get a bowl-shaped melon.
3. The top of the melon bowl could be decorated.
4. Place the melon bowl in a large pan of boiling water. The water should cover the melon completely. Cover and cook over low heat for 20 minutes.
5. Remove the melon and place it in a basin of cold water. Drain well and stand the melon in a heatproof bowl.
6. Soak the lotus seeds in cold water overnight to soften. Boil for 30 minutes until tender.
7. Leave in cold water to cool, then peel off the skin and push out the shoot from the top.
8. Place the chicken meat, Chinese mushrooms, button mushrooms, lotus seeds and ginger in the melon and add enough stock to fill slightly more than ¾ of the melon.
9. Add salt and steam the melon for 1½ hours.
10. Serve hot as it is.

Duck in Lemon Soup

Ingredients:

1 kg duck pieces

6 cups water

2 lemons

1 tsp salt

Pepper to taste

Fresh coriander leaves

Serves 6 — 8

Method:

1. Clean the duck and wipe dry.
2. Place the duck in a deep casserole and add in water, and halved lemons.
3. Add salt and pepper to taste.
4. Cover and cook over low heat for 4 hours until the duck is very tender.
5. Season to taste and garnish with coriander leaves before serving.

Chicken and Corn Soup

Ingredients:

150 gms chicken meat

1 egg white

3 cups chicken stock

1 tin creamed sweetcorn

2 tsps salt

1 tsp soy sauce

1 tsp sesame oil

Pepper to taste

3 tbsps oil

2 tbsps cornflour

Serves 4 — 6

Method:

1. Mince the chicken meat and mix well with egg white and 3 tbsps water.
2. Pour the stock into a large bowl and stir in the creamed corn.
3. Add salt, soy sauce, sesame oil and pepper.
4. Heat 3 tbsps oil in a pan and pour in the seasoned corn mixture.
5. Let the mixture boil for a couple of minutes.
6. Thicken the soup by adding the cornflour blended with 3 tbsps water, stirring all the time.
7. When the soup is thick and boiling, stir in the chicken meat.
8. Remove the soup from the heat as soon as it boils again.
9. Season and serve with pepper.

Soft Bean Curd Soup

66

Fish Ball Soup

Ingredients:

300 gms Spanish Mackerel
1 tsps tapioca flour
1½ tsps salt
150 gms choy sum (mustard greens)
10 strands so hoon
1 tsp preserved cabbage
4 tbsps oil
2 cloves garlic — chopped
5 cm ginger — sliced
1 tbsp soy sauce
Pepper to taste

Serves 4 — 6

Method:

1. Clean and fillet the fish. Scrape off the flesh with a tablespoon. Knead the fish flesh well on a chopping board using the flat side of a kitchen knife until smooth.
2. Add tapioca flour and 1 tsp salt and work it in with 4-5 tbsps water until you get a soft and sticky paste.
3. Wet your hands and shape the fish balls. Dip each ball in salt water before placing it on a plate.
4. Wash the mustard greens and cut into 5 cm lengths. Wash the preserved cabbage and soak the so hoon.
5. Heat oil and fry the garlic until golden brown. Remove and set aside.
6. Make fish stock. Lightly brown the ginger slices and fry the fish bones and skin for 2 minutes. Add in 4 cups water and ½ tsp salt. Simmer for 30 minutes.
7. Strain the fish stock, return to saucepan and bring to boil. Add the fish balls.
8. When the soup boils, add the mustard greens, so hoon and preserved cabbage. Bring to boil again.
9. Remove from heat, season well with soy sauce, salt and pepper.
10. Serve hot as a starter garnished with the browned garlic.

> *Radish is a very nutritious vegetable, especially in soups.*

Watercress and Pork Soup

Ingredients:

300 gms pork
600 gms watercress
1 tsp soy sauce
1 tsp salt

Serves 4 — 6

Method:

1. Clean the pork and cut away the excess fat.
2. Clean watercress and pluck off the green leaves and young shoots, leaving only the stems.
3. Place the pork in a saucepan with 6 cups water and bring to boil.
4. Add watercress stems and simmer the soup for 1½ hours.
5. Take out the pork and slice it into thin slices.
6. Remove the watercress stems and throw them away.
7. Bring soup to boil again and add salt, watercress leaves and shoots.
8. Bring to boil again and remove from heat. Season to taste.
9. Take out the watercress shoots and arrange on a serving dish. Arrange sliced pork on top and sprinkle soy sauce and pepper over it before serving.
10. Serve soup separately.

Beef and Radish Soup

Ingredients:

300 gms beef
1 Chinese radish
10 peppercorns
1 star anise
1 tsp salt
1 tbsp soy sauce
Pepper
2 tsps chopped spring onions

Serves 4 — 6

Method:

1. Clean and cut the beef into cubes. Halve the radish lengthwise and cut each half diagonally into 3 cm pieces.
2. Place the beef, radish, peppercorns and star anise with 6 cups water in saucepan and bring to boil.
3. Lower the heat and simmer for 1½ hours.
4. Season with salt, soy sauce and pepper and serve garnished with spring onions.

Mee Hoon Soup

Ingredients:

500 gms rice vermicelli — soaked to soften	
100 gms pigs liver } Sliced thinly	
100 gms lean pork }	
60 gms shrimps — peeled	
125 gms mustard greens	
2 cloves garlic	
6 cups chicken stock	
¼ cup thin soy sauce	
3 tbsps oil	
Salt to taste	

Serves 4 — 6

Method:

1. Heat oil and fry garlic until fragrant for 1 minute.
2. Add vermicelli and fry for 2 minutes. Transfer to a serving bowl.
3. Add liver and pork to pan and fry for 5 minutes, adding more oil if necessary.
4. Add shrimps and soy sauce. Season to taste.
5. Pour in the stock and bring to boil.
6. Add the mustard greens and simmer for 3 minutes.
7. To serve, pour boiling soup over the vermicelli.

Shark's Fin Soup

Ingredients:

120 gms dried shark's fin	
120 gms sliced chicken flesh — boiled	
1 tsp pepper	
4 shallots — sliced	
1 clove garlic — sliced	
120 gms crab meat	
4 cups chicken stock	
1 tsp salt	
3 cm piece ginger	
1 tbsp cornflour blended with water	

Serves 4 — 6

Method:

1. Clean the shark's fin. Soak overnight or for at least 8 hours. Place in a pan of water and boil for 2-3 hours.
2. Heat oil in a deep frying pan. Fry sliced ginger, sliced shallots, sliced garlic until fragrant.
3. Add chicken stock, salt and pepper. Bring to boil.
4. Stir constantly. Add in the blended cornflour to thicken the soup.
5. Serve hot.

Thick Corn Soup

Ingredients:

6 cups vegetable stock	
2½ cups tinned creamed corn	
½ tsp salt	
¼ tsp ground pepper	
1 tsp sesame oil	
4 tbsps cornstarch blended in 4 tbsps water	
1 dsp hot red pepper	

Serves 4 — 6

Method:

1. Heat the stock and creamed corn in a pot and bring to the boil.
2. Add the salt, pepper and sesame oil and allow to simmer for a couple of minutes.
3. Stir in the blended cornstarch and cook until soup thickens.
4. Remove from heat and pour into soup bowls.
5. Sprinkle with red pepper.
6. Serve in individual bowls as the first course in a Chinese meal.

Chinese Beef Soup

Ingredients:

300 gms beef steak	
1 tsp tapioca flour	
2 tsps soy sauce	
¾ tsp salt	
Pepper	
2 pieces soft bean curd	
2 tbsps oil	
2 shallots — sliced	
2 tbsps green peas	
1 stalk spring onions — chopped	

Serves 4 — 6

Method:

1. Clean and slice the steak thinly and season with tapioca flour, soy sauce, salt and pepper. Leave for 25 minutes.
2. Clean and cut each piece of bean curd into 8 pieces.
3. Heat 2 tbsps oil in saucepan and brown the shallots. Add in 3 cups water.
4. Bring to boil and add ½ tsp salt, bean curd and green peas.
5. When the peas are cooked, add the steak, stirring continuously.
6. When the soup boils, add the spring onions and remove from heat.
7. Season to taste and serve at once.
8. You can also serve this soup with mee hoon (rice vermicelli). Soak the mee hoon in cold water and scald.

Curry Laksa

Ingredients:

250 gms yellow noodles
4 tbsps oil
3 shallots — sliced
1 cm piece ginger ⎫ Sliced 1 fresh red chilli ⎭
1 fresh green chilli
150 gms prawns — shelled and deveined
100 gms fresh oysters
100 gms fish balls
4 cups thick coconut milk — from 1 coconut
100 gms beansprouts
2 tbsps curry powder
1 bunch kesum leaves
Salt to taste

Serves 4 — 6

Method:

1. Scald the noodles in hot water. Drain well and spread 1 tbsp oil evenly into the noodles.
2. Heat 3 tbsps oil and fry the shallots and ginger until fragrant. Add in curry powder and fry further until fragrant.
3. Add the ginger, prawns and chillies. Stir-fry for 3 minutes.
4. Add the coconut milk and bring to boil.
5. Add the oysters and fishballs and season to taste.
6. Lastly add the kesum leaves and beansprouts.
7. To serve, place the noodles in individual bowls and pour over the gravy making sure that each bowl will contain the oysters, prawns and fishballs.

Chee Cheong Fun

Ingredients:

1 packet/500 gms twin rice noodles (chee cheong fun)
1 tbsp Chinese barbecue sauce
1 tbsp light soy sauce
1 tsp sesame oil
1 tsp chilli sauce
1 tbsp toasted sesame seeds

Serves 4 — 6

Method:

1. Cut the rice noodles into thin strips.
2. Place them in a bowl of boiling water and set aside for 5 minutes.
3. Drain and transfer into a large bowl.
4. Add the rest of the ingredients and toss lightly until well mixed.
5. Serve immediately with fresh, cut chilli.

Loh Mai Kai *(Chicken in Glutinous Rice)*

Ingredients:

450 gms glutinous rice
5 Chinese mushrooms
½ chicken
2 tbsps soy sauce
½ tsp thick soy sauce
2 tbsps oyster sauce
2 tsps sesame oil
1 tbsp sugar
¼ tsp pepper
7 tbsps oil
100 gms roast pork
225 gms fresh pork
1 tbsp cornflour
Salt to taste
1 stalk coriander leaves — chopped

Serves 4 — 6

Method:

1. Soak the glutinous rice overnight. Rinse and drain well.
2. Soak the mushrooms and cut in half.
3. Cut the chicken into bite-sized pieces. Season with ½ tbsp thin soy sauce, 1 tbsp oyster sauce, 1 tsp sesame oil and 1 tsp sugar.
4. Slice the roast pork into 1 cm cubes and season with ½ tbsp soy sauce, ½ tsp thick soy sauce, 1 tbsp oyster sauce, 1 tsp sesame oil, the remaining sugar and pepper.
5. Heat 2 tbsps oil and fry chicken until cooked and all the gravy absorbed. Remove and set aside.
6. Heat another 2 tbsps oil, add in pork and toss for a minute.
7. Add mushrooms and ¼ cup water, cover and simmer for 10 minutes.
8. Blend cornflour with ¼ cup water and thicken gravy. Set aside.
9. Mix the glutinous rice with 3 tbsps oil, 1 tbsp soy sauce, ½ tbsp sugar and ½ tsp salt.
10. Divide chicken, roast pork, fried pork and mushrooms into 10 equal portions. Place each portion in a bowl.
11. Divide the rice into 10 portions also and cover the ingredients of each bowl with 1 portion of rice. The bowls should only be half full.
12. Steam the bowls of rice in a steamer for 30 minutes or until the rice is well-cooked.
13. Turn each bowl of rice onto a serving plate and serve garnished with chopped coriander leaves.

Curry Laksa

Fried Kway Teow

Ingredients:

1 kg kway teow — cut into 1 cm strips
450 gms fresh prawns — shelled
400 gms oysters — scalded and shells removed
500 gms bean sprouts — tails removed
2 fresh chillies ⎫ Pounded
6 cloves garlic ⎭
200 gms chicken flesh — cut into strips
250 gms squid — cleaned and cut into strips
1 tbsp thin soy sauce
1 tbsp thick soy sauce
Salt and pepper to taste
3 tbsps oil

Serves 4 — 6

Method:

1. Heat oil in a deep pan and fry pounded garlic and chillies until fragrant.
2. Increase heat and add in chicken. Fry for 2 minutes.
3. Add prawns and squid and stir fry for 2 more minutes. Add the oysters.
4. Pour in both types of soy sauce, salt and beansprouts.
5. Mix thoroughly and stir fry for 2 more minutes.
6. Serve immediately garnished with sliced chillies.

> *Luck is something you can never have too much of, and the reunion dinner table at Chinese New Year is loaded with food, the names of which pun on luck and goodwill, depending on the intonation. Oysters (ho see) symbolise good things, a type of seaweed (fatt choy) means prosperity, pig's trotters represent a windfall.*

Wonton Mee

Ingredients:

1 tbsp water chestnuts
2 cm piece ginger
150 gms mustard greens
300 gms roast pork
1 stalk spring onions — chopped
1 tsp tapioca flour
1 tsp salt
3 tsps thin soy sauce
3 tsps sesame oil
1 egg white
Pepper
25 wonton skins
5 tbsps oil
3 shallots — sliced
6 cups chicken stock
4 tsps oyster sauce
360 gms fine egg noodles

Serves 4 — 6

Method:

1. Dice the water chestnuts finely.
2. Cut off 2 thin slices of ginger and pound the rest to extract ginger juice.
3. Pluck off the young shoots of the mustard greens.
4. Slice the roast pork into 1 cm slices.
5. Mix the minced pork with water chestnuts, ginger juice, chopped spring onions, tapioca flour, ½ tsp salt, 1 tsp soy sauce, ½ tsp sesame oil, egg white and pepper. Mix thoroughly.
6. Spread out the wonton skins and put 1 tsp of the filling in the centre. Press opposite corners together.
7. Heat 2 tbsps oil and fry the sliced shallots and ginger until brown. Add the stock and ½ tsp salt, 2 tsps soy sauce and pepper.
8. In a separate pan, boil 12 cups water. Add the wontons, cover and cook for 4 minutes until the wontons float. Lift out and place in cold water. Drain well and keep aside.
9. Prepare 4 serving bowls. In each bowl, place ¼ tbsp vegetable oil, ¼ tsp sesame oil, ½ tsp oyster sauce, ¼ tsp soy sauce and pepper.
10. Bring to boil the water in a saucepan. Put in the noodles and stir to separate the strands. Cook for 2 minutes. Take the noodles out using a slotted spoon and put them in a basin of cold water. Remove, shake off the excess water and put them in the boiling water again.
11. Remove at once, drain well and place in one of the prepared 4 bowls. Mix thoroughly.
12. Boil the mustard greens lightly in boiling stock. Remove to a dish.
13. To serve, place a portion of mustard greens, wontons and sliced roast pork over the noodles in each bowl before pouring the boiling stock over. Serve with pickled green chillies.

Char Mee *(Fried Yellow Noodles)*

Ingredients:

250 gms yellow noodles

3 cm piece ginger — chopped finely

8 shallots — sliced

3 dried black mushrooms

65 gms beef — cut thinly

3 tbsps cooking oil

2 cloves garlic — sliced

65 gms fresh prawns — shelled and deveined

1 stalk mustard greens — cut into 3 cm lengths

1 tbsp thick soy sauce

Serves 4 — 6

Method:

1. Soak the mushrooms and remove the stems. Slice thinly.
2. Boil water and scald the noodles for 2-3 minutes.
3. Heat oil and fry sliced shallots, garlic and ginger until golden brown and fragrant.
4. Add the prawns and mushrooms and fry until prawns are cooked.
5. Add the mustard greens and fry for 3 minutes. Add the meat and fry until the meat is tender.
6. Add the noodles and mix well. Add the soy sauce, mix well and serve immediately.

Fish Porridge

Ingredients:

½ cup rice

2 tbsps oil

300 gms fish fillets

2 tsps soy sauce

1 tsp sesame oil

½ tsp salt

6 cm piece ginger — shredded finely

1 stalk spring onions — chopped finely

1 stalk coriander leaves — chopped finely

Pepper

¼ packet rice vermicelli

Serves 4 — 6

Method:

1. Wash rice well and boil in 6 cups water with 2 tbsps oil.
2. When it boils, turn down the heat and allow the broth to simmer for 1½ hours.
3. Wash and slice the fish thinly. Marinate in a mixture of soy sauce, sesame oil, salt and pepper.
4. In individual serving bowls, dish out broth and place the fish slices, ginger strips on top. Garnish with chopped spring onions, coriander leaves and pepper.
5. Fry the rice vermicelli in hot oil till golden and crispy, and sprinkle on top.

***Char Mee** (Fried Yellow Noodles)*

Chicken Rice

Ingredients:

1 chicken

2 tsps sesame oil

1 tsp thin soy sauce

1 cube chicken stock

450 gms rice

4 cloves garlic — chopped

2 tbsps oil

2 tbsps salt

For Sauce:

10 chillies

6 cm piece ginger — chopped

1 tbsp tomato sauce

1 tbsp vinegar

1 clove garlic

Serves 4 — 6

Method:

1. Boil enough water to cover the whole chicken in a large pan. Put in the chicken, lower the heat and cook the chicken covered for 10 minutes. Turn off the heat and leave the chicken in the water for 40 minutes.
2. Remove the chicken and put it in cold water for 15 minutes.
3. Hang the chicken to dry and brush it with 1 tsp sesame oil mixed with 1 tsp soy sauce.
4. Cut off the chicken legs, wing tips and neck and put them back in the water to boil. Add chicken cube.
5. Heat 1 tbsp oil and fry the chopped garlic until brown and fragrant.
6. Add the rice, stir-fry for one minute and add enough chicken stock to cook it. To the remaining stock add salt and pepper to taste, and a little ginger and garlic to make a tasty soup.
7. To the rice add salt and pepper to taste and 1 tsp sesame oil. Cook until the water is absorbed and the rice is cooked.
8. Make the chilli sauce. Pound together the chillies, garlic and ginger finely.
9. Heat 1 tbsp oil and fry the pounded ingredients until fragrant. Add in 1 tsp salt, 1 tsp sugar, tomato sauce, vinegar, 1 tsp sesame oil and 4 tbsps stock. Season well.
10. To serve, cut the chicken into bite-sized pieces and serve with the rice, chilli sauce and bowls of steaming soup.

The Chinese believe that it is bad luck to spill rice while eating. Rice is also considered good therapy for all illnesses. As long as the patient can continue eating rice, there is hope of a cure.

Fried Rice

Ingredients:

2 tbsps boiled shrimps
1 medium-sized onion — chopped
½ cup precooked green peas
2 red chillies — sliced
400 gms cold, cooked rice
2 eggs
Salt and pepper to taste
1 stalk fresh coriander leaves — shredded

Serves 4 — 6

Method:

1. Heat the oil and fry the onions until light brown.
2. Add the rice and fry for a couple of minutes, stirring continuously.
3. Push the rice aside and crack the eggs into the centre of the wok.
4. Stir well for 3 minutes.
5. Add the prawns, peas and salt and pepper, and remove from heat.
6. Serve garnished with coriander leaves and red chillies.

Lam Mee

Ingredients:

500 gms thick yellow noodles
300 gms streaky pork
½ chicken
300 gms fresh prawns — shelled
2 tsps cornflour
2 tsps water
5 shallots — sliced and fried
1 head lettuce — sliced
1 egg
1 tbsp oil

Serves 4 — 6

Method:

1. Boil pork and chicken until soft. Remove and shred. Return the chicken bones to the boiling stock.
2. Add the prawns and when they are cooked, remove and slice.
3. Season the stock well with salt. Add the cornflour blended with water to thicken the gravy.
4. Scald the noodles with boiling water.
5. Put the noodles in individual serving bowls. Put in the meats, prawns and sliced lettuce. Pour the gravy. Garnish with fried shallots and shredded omelette.
6. To make omelette. Beat the egg with a fork. Glaze a pan with 1 tbsp oil. Swirl the omelette and lift out as soon as it is cooked. Shred.
7. Serve with sambal belacan.

Fried Meehoon

Ingredients:

357 gms fine rice vermicelli
2 cloves garlic — crushed
2 tsps coriander — ground
½ tsp turmeric powder
Peanut oil
8 dried Chinese mushrooms — soaked
90 gms prawns — shelled
125 gms white fish
2 medium onions — sliced
125 gms beansprouts
2 eggs — lightly beaten
4 red chillies
3 stalks spring onions — chopped

Serves 4 — 6

Method:

1. Soak the vermicelli in cold water for 5 minutes, then scald them in boiling water. Drain well.
2. Mix the crushed garlic and pounded coriander with turmeric powder.
3. Heat 1 tbsp oil and fry the garlic mixture for 2 minutes.
4. Remove the stems from the mushrooms and slice thinly.
5. Dice into small cubes the fresh prawns and fish. Add to the garlic with mushrooms. Fry on medium heat for 5 minutes. Remove from pan.
6. Add 2 tbsps oil to the pan and fry the sliced onions and chillies.
7. Add the vermicelli, season with salt and stir thoroughly. Add the beansprouts and stir-fry for 1 minute. Remove from pan.
8. Pour in the beaten egg, swirl to make a thin omelette. Cook until set and remove from pan. Shred.
9. Add the fried seafood to the fried noodles, mix well and serve with shredded omelette, and chopped spring onions.

> *To the Chinese, eating noodles is a symbol of longevity because noodles never seem to end.*

Steamed King Prawns

Ingredients:

6 king prawns — heads removed

Salt and pepper to taste

Spring onions for garnishing

Serves 4 — 6

Method:

1. Marinate the prawns in salt and pepper and keep aside for 5 minutes.
2. Steam over rapidly boiling water until the prawns are cooked.
3. Serve with shredded spring onions and chilli sauce.

Steamed Fish With Ginger And Spring Onion

Ingredients:

500 gms whole garoupa or white pomfret

2 tsps Chinese rice wine

½ tsp salt

½ tsp white pepper

5 stalks spring onions — chopped

4 cm piece ginger — shredded

2 tsps oil

2 tsps thin soy sauce

2 stalks coriander leaves — chopped

Serves 4 — 6

Method:

1. Clean the fish, remove scales and intestines. Wash well with salt water to get rid of the fishy smell. Make several deep diagonal cuts across each side.
2. Season with rice wine and let stand for 10 minutes.
3. Rub the fish with salt and pepper and place on a lightly oiled plate.
4. Place half of the shredded spring onions and ginger inside the fish. The remaining spring onions and ginger should be scattered over the fish.
5. Sprinkle oil, soy sauce and 2 tsps water on the fish.
6. Cover and steam the fish in a steamer over rapidly boiling water until tender. Take care not to overcook the fish.
7. Serve immediately on a serving plate garnished with coriander leaves. Pour the cooking liquid over.

Prawns In Red Sauce

Ingredients:

500 gms large raw prawns

2 tbsps oil

4 stalks spring onions — shredded

3 cloves garlic — crushed

4 cm piece ginger — chopped

1 fresh red chilli — chopped

3 tsps Chinese rice wine

1 tbsp thin soy sauce

1 tsp sugar

Salt and pepper to taste

½ tbsp tomato puree

4 tbsps chicken stock

1 tsp cornflour

Serves 4 — 6

Method:

1. Snip off the legs of the prawns, leaving the shell intact. Wash well, drain and set aside.
2. Heat oil and fry the garlic, ginger and chilli for 1 minute.
3. Add the prawns and fry for 5 minutes, turning the prawns occasionally so that they cook evenly.
4. Pour in the rice wine and soy sauce. Add sugar, salt and pepper. Stir gently.
5. Add the tomato puree and stir again.
6. Thicken sauce with cornflour blended with a little water and stir on medium heat.
7. Dish out the prawns and pour the sauce over.
8. Serve garnished with shredded spring onions.

Stuffed Crab

Ingredients:

½ cup crab meat

½ cup water chestnuts

1 stalk spring onion — chopped

2 tbsps cornflour

1 tsp salt

½ cup prawns — shelled and minced

2 tbsps minced meat

½ tbsp sesame oil

1 egg — beaten

1 tsp white pepper

1 crab shell — cleaned

Serves 4 — 6

Method:

1. Mix all the ingredients thoroughly.
2. Stuff the mixture into the crab shell.
3. Fry the stuffed crab in heated oil over a medium flame.
4. Serve immediately.

Steamed King Prawn

Sweet and Sour Prawns

Ingredients:

500 gms medium-sized prawns

3 cups cold water

1 tsp fresh ginger — grated

2 egg whites

3 tbsps cornflour

5 stalks spring onion

1 small green cucumber — sliced

2 small onions — chopped

1 large tomato — sliced

Salt

Oil for deep frying

For the sauce:

¼ cup white vinegar

¾ cup orange juice

3 tbsps sugar

1 tbsp arrowroot

Pinch red colouring

1 tbsp cold water

Serves 4 — 6

Method:

1. Shell and devein the prawns, leaving only the last segment of the shell and tail intact.
2. Wash and soak them in cold water with half teaspoon salt for 20 minutes.
3. Drain and then blot them on kitchen paper.
4. Place them in a dry bowl and sprinkle with another half teaspoonful of salt.
5. Sprinkle the ginger over and mix well.
6. Add the egg whites and cornflour and stir thoroughly ensuring that the prawns are thoroughly coated with mixture.
7. Cover and refrigerate for 4 hours or longer, overnight would be ideal.

To prepare the sauce:

1. Combine the white vinegar, orange juice, salt and colouring.
2. Bring to the boil, remove from heat and stir in the arrowroot mixed with cold water.
3. Return to heat and stir continuously until the sauce boils and thickens.

To fry the prawns:

1. Heat enough oil for deep-frying.
2. When the oil is hot, put in half of the prawns and fry for just under a minute — be careful not to overcook them or they will lose their succulence and become leathery.
3. Lift out with a wire spoon and drain on grease-proof paper.
4. Heat the oil and fry the remaining prawns.
5. After draining, place the prawns in a serving dish and pour the sauce over.
6. Garnish with spring onion, cucumber, onions and tomato.

Steamed Fish

Ingredients:

1 medium-sized pomfret — slit on both sides of the body

2.5 cm pieces fresh ginger — cut into strips

3 black mushrooms (soaked in hot water for 20 minutes or longer) — shredded

2 tbsps light soy sauce

1 tsp sesame oil

1 tbsp vegetable oil

1 stalk spring onion — chopped

1 tsp oyster sauce

Salt and pepper to taste

Serves 4 — 6

Method:

1. Place the cleaned fish on an ovenproof glass platter and season with salt and pepper.
2. Mix the sesame oil, oyster sauce and light soy sauce together.
3. Heat a pan with 1 tbsp oil and stir-fry the mushrooms.
4. Pour in the mixed sauces and stir.
5. Remove from heat and pour over the fish.
6. Sprinkle the ginger over the fish.
7. Place the plate in a steamer, cover and steam for 8-10 minutes. Note that the water in the steamer should be boiling when the plate is placed in it.
8. When the fish is cooked, remove from the steamer and garnish with the spring onions.

Prawn Fritters

Ingredients:

600 gms prawns — shelled

2 tsps cornflour

Golden breadcrumbs

2 eggs — lightly beaten

2 tbsps sesame oil

1 tsp butter

Salt and pepper to taste

Oil for deep frying

Serves 4 — 6

Method:

1. Mince the prawns.
2. Season with salt and pepper.
3. Add the cornflour, butter, half the egg mixture and 1 tbsp sesame oil.
4. Shape the prawn mixture into bite-sized balls and dip in the rest of the egg mixture.
5. Heat the oil to a high temperature and then add the other tbsp of sesame oil.
6. Fry the fritters rolled in crumbs, for about three minutes until golden grown.
7. Serve with chilli sauce.

Mussels In Tow Cheong

Ingredients:

600 gms mussels
3 cloves garlic — chopped
3 shallots — chopped
3 cm piece ginger — sliced thinly
1 fresh red chilli — sliced
1 tbsp tow-cheong
3 tbsps oil
1 tsp sugar

Serves 4 — 6

Method:

1. Wash mussels under running water to get rid of all the sand and mud. Leave in a basin of water for 1 hour.
2. Pound the tow-cheong into a paste.
3. Heat the oil in a deep pan and fry the garlic and shallots until brown and fragrant.
4. Add the tow-cheong paste and stir gently for 4 minutes.
5. Add ginger, chillies and mussels. Stir-fry over a high heat for a minute before adding sugar.
6. Continue stir-frying until the mussels are cooked (the shells will open).
7. Season and serve immediately.

Fried Prawns

Ingredients:

600 gms fresh prawns
7 cups oil
3 shallots — sliced
6 cloves garlic — chopped
1 red chilli — sliced thinly
2 tbsps rice wine
Salt and pepper to taste

Serves 4 — 6

Method

1. Cut away the whiskers and legs of the prawns but leave the shells intact. Remove the sac from the head. Wash in salt water and drain well.
2. Heat oil and deep fry the prawns until cooked. Remove and keep aside.
3. Pour out all the oil from the pan. Using the same oil-coated pan, fry the sliced shallots and garlic until light brown.
4. Add the chilli, rice wine and salt.
5. Add the fried prawns and mix well together with the other ingredients in the pan.
6. Add pepper and serve at once.

Har Lok

(Fried King Prawns, Cantonese Style)

Ingredients:

1 kg king prawns
1 tbsp sliced garlic
1 tsp thin soy sauce
5 candlenuts — pounded
1 tsp sugar
2 tsps cornflour blended with water
1 tbsp sliced ginger
1 tbsp sliced shallots
1 tbsp rice wine
1 tsp salt

Serves 2 — 4

Method:

1. Clean the prawns and wash with salt water. Drain and remove tails.
2. Heat oil in a deep frying pan. Fry the prawns for 4 minutes. Remove and drain.
3. Remove oil and leave just enough to fry the garlic, shallots and ginger.
4. Add soy sauce, rice wine and pounded candlenuts. Mix well for ½ minute. Add the prawns.
5. Season well. Add the blended cornflour to thicken the gravy. Stir for another 2 minutes and turn off heat.

Spicy Prawns

Ingredients:

10 medium raw prawns
1 fresh red chilli
1 stalk spring onion
1 tsp spiced salt
3 cloves garlic
1 tsp cornflour
3 tbsps oil

Serves 4 — 6

Method:

1. Slice the chillies and spring onion and soak the prawns for 10 minutes in cold water.
2. Trim off the legs of the prawns and season with half of the spiced salt. Leave aside for 15 minutes.
3. Drain the prawns well and sprinkle on cornflour.
4. Heat oil and fry garlic for just 30 seconds.
5. Add the prawns and fry until cooked.
6. Add the rest of the spiced salt and stir-fry on a moderate flame for just 30 seconds.
7. Dish out and serve immediately.

Fried Prawns In Lime Juice

Ingredients:

600 gms medium sized prawns
2 eggs — beaten
2 tbsps cornflour
2 limes
1 tbsp chilli sauce
Salt to taste
Oil for deep-frying

Serves 4 — 6

Method:

1. Shell the prawns, slit down the back and remove the black vein. Wash well and drain.
2. Mix in cornflour and salt to the beaten eggs.
3. Heat oil in a wok. Dip the prawns into the batter and deep-fry until golden and crispy.
4. Lift immediately to a serving plate.
5. Slice the limes thinly and arrange around the prawns.
6. Serve immediately with chilli sauce.

Steamed Garoupa

Ingredients:

1 large garoupa
8 Chinese mushrooms — halved and steamed
3 cm piece ginger — pounded
1 lemon
4 tbsps fish sauce
½ tsp white pepper
1 tsp thin soy sauce
1 tsp thick soy sauce
Several kai lan leaves (broccoli)
Salt to taste

Serves 4 — 6

Method:

1. Clean the fish, wash and cut into 2.
2. Season the fish well with the pounded ginger, pepper, soy sauce and salt.
3. Steam the fish in a steamer over rapidly boiling water until cooked.
4. Place the fish on a plate and garnish with steamed mushrooms and kai lan leaves.
5. Squeeze lemon juice over the fish and sprinkle with salt.
6. Let stand for 10 minutes before serving.

The Chinese believe it is good to plant a lime or orange tree in the compound of their house. Limes and oranges signify prosperity and matrimonial harmony.

Steamboat

Ingredients:

500 gms medium-sized prawns
20 fishballs
30 hard-boiled quail's eggs
250 gms fillets of fish
500 gms oysters
500 gms rice vermicelli
250 gms black Chinese mushrooms — soaked in water till soft
250 gms canned button mushrooms
Lettuce leaves
Water convulvulus (kangkong)

Sauce:

15 fresh red chillies
1 tbsp vinegar
Lime juice
1 tsp salt
3 cm piece ginger
3 tbsps castor sugar
1 clove garlic

Soup:

12 cups chicken stock
2 tbsps oil
2 stalks spring onions
1½ tbsps sesame oil
1 tsp white pepper
2 cubes chicken soup
1 tsp thin soy sauce
1 tsp salt
5 slices ginger

Serves 6 — 8

Method:

1. Boil stock in a large pot.
2. Add chicken cubes, ginger, sesame oil, cooking oil and thin soy sauce.
3. When water boils, add pepper and salt. Pour into steamboat.
4. Make the sauce: Grind together the chillies, ginger and garlic. Mix well with vinegar, salt and castor sugar. Squeeze in lime juice.
5. To eat, each person dips the food of his/her choice into the boiling soup. When the food is cooked, it is then dipped into the chilli sauce.
6. If the steamboat equipment is not available, you can also use an electric rice cooker in which to boil the soup.

Steamed Pomfret

Ingredients:

1 medium sized white pomfret
2 tbsps thin soy sauce
1 tbsp corn oil
1 tsp white pepper
1 tsp salt

Serves 4 — 6

Method:

1. Clean the fish but do not remove tail and fins.
2. Steam the fish in a steamer over rapidly boiling water until the fish is cooked.
3. Heat the oil and stir in the thin soy sauce.
4. Pour the sauce over the steamed fish.
5. Place the fish on a flat plate and sprinkle with salt and pepper.
6. Serve hot garnished with shredded spring onions and sliced red chilli.

Crystal Prawns

Ingredients:

30 medium-sized raw prawns
1 tbsp ginger wine
1 tbsp water
4 stalks spring onions
3 cm piece ginger — sliced
1 carrot — sliced
Oil
Pepper and salt to taste

Serves 4 — 6

Method:

1. Shell the prawns leaving heads and tails intact. Devein the prawns using a very sharp knife and cutting almost through the prawns.
2. Marinate the prawns in ginger wine, water, pepper and salt for 5 minutes.
3. Cut spring onions into 9 cm lengths. Shred both ends of each piece and soak in iced water so that the ends curl.
4. Cut the carrot and ginger slices into nice decorative shapes with a vegetable cutter, if available.
5. Heat 3 tbsps oil in a pan and stir-fry the prawns until they turn pink and curl.
6. Lift immediately from the pan as the prawns should not be overcooked.
7. Serve immediately garnished with spring onions and cut vegetables.
8. Serve with chilli sauce or thick soy sauce.

Sweet Sour Fish

Ingredients:

1 black pomfret
1 egg white
6 tbsps cornflour
4 tbsps tomato sauce
½ tbsp vinegar
5 stalks spring onions
5 stalks coriander leaves
2 cloves garlic — chopped finely
Oil for deep frying
½ cucumber
1 red chilli
Salt and sugar to taste

Serves 4 — 6

Method:

1. Scale the pomfret and remove the entrails. Wash well with salt water.
2. Remove the head and slit in half, taking care not to break the skin.
3. Fillet the fish and score lengthwise and cross-wise, taking care not to cut through the skin.
4. In a plate, mix 1 tsp salt, ½ tsp sugar, 1 egg white, 3 tbsps cornflour and 3 tbsps water. Marinate the fillets and the fish head for 15-20 minutes.
5. Clean and shred the cucumber, chilli and spring onions. Cut the coriander leaves into 3 cm lengths.
6. Mix ½ cup water, tomato sauce, vinegar, 2 tsps sugar, ½ tsp salt and 2 tsps cornflour.
7. Coat seasoned fish with cornflour and deep fry until brown and crisp. Place on a warmed dish.
8. Heat 2 tsps oil in a separate clean pan and fry the garlic until fragrant.
9. Add tomato sauce mixture, stirring gently until the gravy boils and thickens. Season well and pour over the fish.
10. To serve, garnish with shredded cucumber, chillies, spring onions and coriander leaves.

> *Women in confinement are usually served steamed fish with plenty of ginger. They are not allowed to eat spicy food and the ginger helps in expelling wind from the body.*

Fried Oyster Omelette

Ingredients:

5 tbsps vegetable fat
4 tbsps cornflour
300 ml water
4 eggs
12 fresh oysters
2 tsps fish sauce
1 tsp chilli paste or 1 red chilli — sliced
1 spray fresh coriander leaves — shredded
3 stalks spring onions — chopped

Serves 4 — 6

Method:

1. In a flat frying pan, heat 2 tbsps vegetable fat to a fairly high temperature.
2. Mix the flour and water to a thin liquid and pour into the pan.
3. Allow to brown lightly.
4. Crack the eggs into the batter and spread them round, whipping them lightly.
5. Turn up the heat and fry till brown on one side.
6. Flip over and cook till brown on the other side.
7. Gradually add the rest of the vegetable fat as the omelette is frying.
8. When the omelette is golden, shred it into large pieces and add the oysters.
9. Add the sauce and chilli and stir well.
10. Serve garnished with coriander leaves and spring onions on its own as a snack or as an accompaniment to boiled rice.

Steamed Crabs

Ingredients:

1 kg crabs — remove the top shell and cut into 2

Sauce:

6 fresh red chillies	
2 cloves garlic	**Pounded together**
1 tsp vinegar	
Salt and sugar to taste	

Serves 4 — 6

Method:

1. Put the crabs on a steaming tray and steam over rapidly boiling water until cooked.
2. Prepare the sauce. Mix all the ingredients together. Add in ½ cup water or more if the sauce is too thick.
3. Serve the steamed crabs immediately with the sauce.

Fish With Hot Bean Paste

Ingredients:

500 gms red snapper	
1 cm piece ginger	**Chopped finely**
3 cloves garlic	
2 tbsps thin soy sauce	
2 tbsps hot bean paste	
1 tbsp Chinese rice wine	
2 tbsps sugar	
½ cup water	
2 tsps Chinese brown vinegar	
1 tsp sesame oil	
1 stalk spring onion — chopped	
2 tsps cornflour	
Oil for frying	

Serves 4 — 6

Method:

1. Clean and scale the fish. With a sharp knife, make deep diagonal cuts across each side.
2. Heat oil and fry the fish for 2 minutes on each side. Lift out and set aside.
3. Drain oil from the pan leaving just 1 tbsp. Fry the chopped garlic and ginger for 2 minutes. Add the soy sauce, bean paste, rice wine and sugar and stir.
4. After 1 minute, add water and bring to the boil.
5. Add the fish and simmer until the fish is cooked. Turn once.
6. If desired, thicken sauce with cornflour blended with a little water.
7. Remove fish to a serving plate and spoon sauce over. Sprinkle with brown vinegar and sesame oil before serving.
8. Serve immediately garnished with chopped spring onions.

The Chinese believe that chewing asam gelugor (tamarind) can help get rid of bad breath. They also believe that tamarind is an aphrodisiac.

Abalone In Oyster Sauce

Ingredients:

454 gms canned abalone

5 dried Chinese mushrooms

4 Chinese mustard cabbage leaves

4 spring onions

Hot water

For the sauce:

1 tbsp oyster sauce

1 tsp thin soy sauce

1 tbsp Chinese wine

¾ cup water

½ tbsp flour

Serves 4 — 6

Method:

1. Drain the liquid from the can of abalone.
2. Slice the abalone into very thin slices.
3. Soak the mushrooms in hot water for 30 minutes.
4. Slice each mushroom into 4.
5. Cut the cabbage into bite-sized pieces.
6. Cut the spring onions into similar lengths.
7. Combine the oyster sauce, soy sauce and wine.
8. Mix the cornflour with water until smooth and add to the above mixture.
9. Stirring constantly, bring to the boil in a small pan.
10. Add the mushrooms, cabbage and spring onions.
11. Cook, stirring constantly until the vegetables are tender but still crisp. This should take about a couple of minutes.
12. Put in the abalone and heat over a low temperature. Be careful not to cook the abalone on high heat or for longer than necessary or it will toughen.

> *Raw fish is traditionally eaten from the 7th until the 15th day of the Lunar Year. Eaten during this time, it is supposed to bring good luck and prosperity the whole of the following year.*

Sweet And Sour Crabs

Ingredients:

1 kg crabs — remove top shell and cut into 4

1 clove garlic — crushed

1 cm piece ginger — sliced

2 fresh red chillies — sliced

1 large onion — cut into wedges

2 stalks spring onions — shredded

¼ cup white vinegar

⅓ cup water

2 tbsps tomato sauce

2 tsps cornflour — blended with 2 tsps water

1 egg — beaten

1 tbsp oil

Serves 4 — 6

Method:

1. Heat oil in a pan and fry the garlic and ginger until fragrant.
2. Add the onion wedges and brown slightly.
3. Add the vinegar, tomato sauce and water. Bring to boil and season to taste with salt and sugar.
4. Stir in the beaten egg. If necessary thicken the gravy with cornflour.
5. Add the crabs and cook until done.
6. Serve hot garnished with sliced chillies and shredded spring onions.

Lucky Rawfish

Ingredients:

12 pieces of white fish fillet

1 carrot

1 white radish

1 cm piece ginger

1 cucumber

1 tsp lime juice or vinegar

1 bunch mint leaves

Serves 4 — 6

Method:

1. Clean the fish, wash and drain well. Slice thinly.
2. Scrape the radish and carrots and slice thinly lengthwise.
3. Peel the cucumber and slice thinly lengthwise.
4. Mix the mint and lime juice with the fish to get rid of the unpleasant fishy smell.
5. When the ingredients are ready, place on a flat dish.
6. Serve with plum sauce, light soy sauce, sliced chillies, pickled green chillies and mustard. Squeeze lime juice over the raw fish and sprinkle with pepper.

Egg Noodles and Minced Beef

Ingredients:

120 gms black mushrooms

1 tsp sesame oil

3 cloves garlic

2 cm piece ginger

600 gms egg noodles

1 capsicum

360 gms minced beef

3 shallots

2 tbsps white sauce

1 stalk spring onion

2 red chillies

Salt to taste

2 tbsps oil

Serves 4 — 6

Method:

1. Soak the mushrooms and slice thinly. Also slice the red chillies thinly.
2. Heat oil in a pan and fry the minced beef for 2 minutes. Remove and set aside.
3. Using the same oil, fry the pounded shallots, garlic, ginger and mushrooms.
4. Add the minced beef, spring onions and salt.
5. Add the white sauce and simmer for 5 minutes.
6. Scald the egg noodles and pour the fried ingredients over.
7. Serve hot.

Braised Pork Leg

Ingredients:

1 leg of pork

5 tbsps thin soy sauce

50 gms brown sugar

4 tbsps rice wine

1 tbsp brandy

2 stalks spring onion

5 cm piece ginger — crushed

Serves 4 — 6

Method:

1. Clean the pork leg well and score the skin. Place in a saucepan and cover with water. Bring to boil and skim off the scum.
2. Mix in all the remaining ingredients, cover saucepan and simmer for 30 minutes.
3. Turn the pork over, cover and simmer again for 2 hours or until pork is tender.
4. When gravy has reduced to half, cook for a while longer until thick.
5. Remove pork from saucepan and place on serving plate.
6. Slice thinly and then pour sauce over.

Sweet Sour Pork

Ingredients:

300 gms lean pork

1 tsp salt

2 tbsps sugar

Pepper

1 egg — beaten

1 cucumber

1 large onion

2 tomatoes

1 capsicum

1 stalk spring onion — cut into 2 cm lengths

½ tbsp vinegar

2 tbsps tomato sauce

1 tsp chilli sauce

½ tsp sesame oil

Oil for deep frying

Serves 4 — 6

Method:

1. Clean and cut the pork into 7 cm pieces.
2. Put the pork in a pan with enough water to cover and cook for 30 minutes.
3. Peel the cucumber, quarter it lengthwise and remove the core. Cut each quarter into 2 cm pieces.
4. Quarter the onion and tomatoes. Cut into 2 cm pieces. Remove seeds from capcisum and cut also into 2 cm pieces.
5. Prepare gravy: Mix together ½ tsp salt, sugar, vinegar, tomato sauce, chilli sauce and sesame oil with ½ cup water.
6. Heat oil for deep frying. Roll the seasoned pork in the remaining cornflour and fry over high heat until cooked and crispy.
7. Drain off the oil from the pan leaving just 1 tbsp.
8. Fry the onion quarters for 1 minute then add the gravy mixture. Bring to boil.
9. Add the capsicum, tomatoes and cucumber pieces.
10. Thicken gravy with ½ tsp cornflour blended with 2 tbsps water.
11. Season to taste, and add the fried pork pieces. Turn the heat off immediately.
12. Serve hot garnished with spring onions.

> *The Chinese traditionally serve roast suckling pig on many important occasions with the hope that "your halls will be full of jade and gold."*

Stir-fried Beef With Celery

Ingredients:

500 gms fillet beef — sliced
1 celery stick — sliced thickly
1 tbsp shredded ginger
1 tbsp Chinese rice wine
1 tbsp sesame oil
1 tsp salt
1 tsp pepper
4 tbsps water
2 tbsps oil

Serves 4 — 6

Method:

1. Using the back of a cleaver, pound the beef.
2. Heat oil and fry beef over high heat for 30 seconds.
3. Add celery and ginger and fry for another 30 seconds.
4. Add water, wine, sesame oil and seasoning. Bring to boil.
5. Mix well and cook until the liquid has dried up.
6. Serve hot as a course in a Chinese meal.

Braised Beef

Ingredients:

400 gms beef shank — cut into 3 cm cubes
1 turnip — cut into large cubes
1 stalk spring onions — cut into 3 cm lengths
3 cm piece ginger — sliced thinly
1 clove garlic — sliced
3 tbsps oil
6 tbsps thin soy sauce
½ tbsp sugar
1 star anise
2 cups water

Serves 4 — 6

Method:

1. Heat oil in a pan and fry the ginger, garlic, spring onions and beef for 5 minutes.
2. Remove to a saucepan and cover with water.
3. Add in soy sauce, sugar, star anise and cook covered until the beef is tender.
4. Add in the turnip and simmer until turnip is soft.
5. Dish out and serve hot.

Pork In Preserved Spinach

Ingredients:

500 gms belly pork
4 tbsps thin soy sauce
4 tbsps oil
100 gms preserved spinach
3 shallots — sliced
3 cm piece ginger — sliced
1 tbsp sugar
1 tbsp rice wine
1 tsp salt
Oil for deep frying

Serves 4 — 6

Method:

1. Clean the pork. Season with ½ tsp salt, ½ tsp sugar and pepper.
2. Mix the beaten egg well into the pork. Add 2 tbsps cornflour, mix well and let stand for 30 minutes.
3. Using a skewer, prick the skin all over, dab dry with a clean cloth. Rub 2 tbsps soy sauce all over the skin.
4. Heat oil and fry the pork, skin side down, for 5 minutes until the skin is golden brown.
   Cover the pan while frying so that the oil does not splash all over.
5. Remove pork from oil and cool it. Cut into 1 cm thick pieces.
6. Arrange the pork, skin downwards in a soup bowl.
7. Soak and wash the preserved spinach, rinse in hot water and squeeze out the water. Cut into 5 cm strips.
8. Heat a clean dry pan and fry preserved spinach over a medium flame for 7 minutes. This is to get rid of the strong flavour.
9. Heat 3 tbsps oil and fry the sliced shallots and ginger until light brown.
10. Add the preserved spinach and toss in the oil.
11. Add ½ cup water mixed with 2 tbsps soy sauce, sugar, rice wine and salt. Simmer for 5 minutes, covering the pan.
12. Spoon the mixture over the pork slices and steam over rapidly boiling water for 1 hour.
13. To serve, invert bowl on to a serving dish. Serve hot.

> *Pork is favourite meat of the Chinese. Traditionally they do not eat beef as the cow is considered an indispensable beast of burden.*

Sweet Sour Spareribs

Ingredients:

550 gms spareribs
4 cloves garlic — chopped finely
1 tsp salt
½ tbsp thin soy sauce
½ tbsp rice wine
Pepper
1 tbsp tomato sauce
1 tbsp Worcestershire sauce
½ tsp sesame oil
½ tbsp sugar
3 tbsps tapioca flour
Oil for deep frying
1 tomato — sliced

Serves 6 — 8

Method:

1. Clean and cut the spareribs into 7 cm lengths. Season with garlic, salt, soy sauce, rice wine and pepper. Let stand for 1 hour.
2. Prepare gravy. Mix together tomato sauce, Worcestershire sauce, sesame oil, sugar and 3 tbsps water.
3. Coat the spareribs in tapioca flour and fry in hot oil over medium heat for 5 minutes. Remove the spareribs.
4. Reheat oil and fry the spareribs again for 1 minute. Remove and drain on absorbent paper.
5. Drain off all the oil from the pan. Pour in the gravy mixture and boil until thick.
6. Add the fried ribs. Mix thoroughly.
7. Serve garnished with tomato slices.

Barbecued Spareribs

Ingredients:

550 gms spareribs
3 tbsps fish sauce
2 tbsps Hoi Sin sauce
½ tbsp thick soy sauce
1 tbsp rice wine
1 tbsp sugar
5 cucumber slices

Serves 6 — 8

Method:

1. Season spareribs in mixture of sauces, rice wine and sugar. Let stand for 2 hours, turning them over every 30 minutes.
2. Bake the spare ribs in an oven at 230°C until the meat is brown and cooked.
3. Alternatively, cook the spare ribs over a charcoal fire for 15 minutes on each side until cooked.
4. Cut the ribs and serve garnished with cucumber slices.

Honey Baked Ham

Ingredients:

800 gms uncooked ham
3 tbsps honey
50 gms sugar
3 tbsps oil
1 large sheet greaseproof paper
2 lotus leaves

Serves 6 — 8

Method:

1. Steam the ham for 30 minutes. Remove skin, fat and bone and cut into thin slices.
2. Mix together the honey, sugar and oil.
3. Arrange the ham slices on the greaseproof paper and pour over the honey mixture.
4. Wrap the ham with greaseproof paper and then wrap in lotus leaves.
5. Bake the wrapped ham in a moderate oven for 2 hours.
6. Cool for 15 minutes before removing the wrappers.
7. Serve at once.

Braised Beef With Radish

Ingredients:

350 gms shin beef
1 radish
3 tbsps oil
1 clove garlic — sliced
3 cm piece ginger — sliced
1 star anise
1 large onion — quartered
7 pepper corns
4 tbsps thin soy sauce
½ tbsp sugar
1 tsp salt
1 stalk coriander leaves — chopped

Serves 4 — 6

Method:

1. Clean and cut the beef into 4 cm cubes.
2. Cut radish into 4 cm pieces also.
3. Heat 3 tbsps oil and fry the garlic, ginger and onion until light brown.
4. Add beef and stir well for a few minutes. Add 2 cups water, star anise, peppercorns, soy sauce, sugar and salt. Simmer in a covered pan for 2 hours.
5. When the beef is tender, add radish and cook for 30 minutes until radish is tender.
6. Season to taste and serve immediately garnished with coriander leaves.

Beef In Oyster Sauce

Ingredients:

500 gms topside beef

2 tsps sugar

2 tbsps cornflour

2 tbsps thick soy sauce

2 tsps sesame oil

2 tsps rice wine

1 tbsp beef stock

12 dried mushrooms — soaked

1 green pepper ⎫
1 red pepper   ⎭ Cut into 2 cm squares

5 stalks spring onions — cut into 3 cm lengths

3 tbsps oil

4 tbsps oyster sauce

Pepper

2 tsps sesame oil

Serves 4 — 6

Method:

1. Slice meat into very thin strips. Marinate in a mixture of sugar, cornflour, soy sauce, sesame oil, rice wine and beef stock. Leave for 15 minutes.
2. Drain the mushrooms and keep 3 tbsps of the liquid. Remove stem of the mushrooms.
3. Heat oil in a wok and fry meat for 2 minutes. Lift out and keep warm.
4. Reheat oil and fry the peppers, spring onions and mushrooms for 2 minutes.
5. Add oyster sauce and mushroom liquid mixed with cornflour and white pepper. Bring to boil. Simmer until the sauce thickens.
6. Return the meat to the wok and bring to boil once.
7. To serve, sprinkle sesame oil.

Char Siew *(Chinese Roast Pork)*

Ingredients:

550 gms pork

3 tbsps fish sauce

3 tbsps sugar

1 tbsp Chinese rice wine

Serves 4 — 6

Method:

1. Cut the pork into 3 cm strips. Marinate for 2 hours in a mixture of fish sauce, sugar and rice wine. Turn over every 30 minutes.
2. Grill the seasoned pork for 15 minutes on each side under a very slow grill.
3. Brush the pork with the seasoning every 5 minutes so that the meat will not be too dry.
4. Cook the remaining seasoning in a pan until thick and pour over the pork.

Stewed Pork Shoulder

Ingredients:

500 gms pork shoulder

3 tbsps oil

1 tsp Chinese spice (five-spice powder) — tied in a muslin bag

2 tsps fish sauce

1 tbsp oyster sauce

1 tbsp thick soy sauce

1 thumb sized piece rock sugar

2 tsps Chinese rice wine

Salt to taste

Serves 4 — 6

Method:

1. Clean the meat and tie into a neat roll with thread.
2. Bring to boil 2 cups of water in a pan and put in the meat roll, turning constantly. Do this for 10 minutes.
3. Remove the meat and keep the stock for later use.
4. Heat 3 tbsps oil in a pan and put in the meat, turning frequently until the meat is well browned.
5. Add the stock and spice and boil for 10 minutes.
6. Add the fish sauce and allow the meat to simmer slowly for 1½ hours.
7. Add the oyster sauce when the meat is tender, together with thick soy sauce, rock sugar and rice wine.
8. Season well with salt and serve immediately garnished with mustard greens.

Minced Pork Steamed With Mushrooms

Ingredients:

8 Chinese mushrooms

1 tbsp thin soy sauce

2 tbsps tapioca flour

500 gms minced pork

Salt and pepper to taste

Serves 4 — 6

Method:

1. Soak the mushrooms until soft, remove stems and chop finely. Season with soy sauce and 1 tbsp tapioca flour.
2. Mix the minced pork with 1 tbsp tapioca flour, salt and pepper. Gradually add 2 tbsps water and mix well.
3. Mix the mushrooms in and place pork mixture in a dish and steam over rapidly boiling water for 30 minutes.

Fried Beef With Spring Onion

Ingredients:

325 gms fillet steak
1 tsp salt
2 tsps thin soy sauce
Pepper
1 tbsp tapioca flour
¼ tsp bicarbonate of soda
8 cm piece young ginger — sliced thinly
5 stalks spring onions — cut into 4 cm lengths
1 egg
4 tbsps oil

Serves 4 — 6

Method:

1. Clean and slice beef thinly across the grain.
2. Season with salt, soy sauce, pepper, tapioca flour and bicarbonate of soda. Mix thoroughly.
3. Rub a pinch of salt into the sliced ginger and wash away the salt.
4. Beat the egg with pepper and ½ tbsp oil.
5. Heat oil and lightly fry the ginger for a minute.
6. Add the sliced beef, spring onions and 1 cup water. Cover the pan and let cook for 3 minutes.
7. Mix the ingredients well for a few minutes.. When the beef has changed colour and the ingredients are well mixed, turn off the heat.
8. Make a well in the centre of the ingredients and pour in the beaten egg. Mix well.
9. Serve immediately.

> *A porcelain spoon can help tenderise meat. This is because it retains heat longer. Put spoon into pot as meat is simmering.*

> *At a traditional Chinese wedding, you'll usually find a tray of roast pig (size varies according to financial status). It can even be scaled down to just a pig's stomach and a large piece of roast pork. This symbolises gratitude, the stomach symbolising the mother's womb that nourished the bride before she was born.*

Fried Beef With Spring Onion

Shredded Pork With Tow Cheong

Ingredients:

350 gms pork
1 tsp soy sauce
2 tsps tapioca flour
2 tsps rice wine
1 stalk spring onion — cut into 4 cm lengths
1 tbsp tow cheong
2 tsps sugar
Oil for deep frying

Serves 4 — 6

Method:

1. Clean and shred the pork thinly. Season with mixture of soy sauce, tapioca flour and 1 tsp rice wine. Let stand for 30 minutes.
2. Heat oil and fry pork for 3 minutes. Remove from oil and drain.
3. Leave just 2 tbsps oil in pan. Heat and fry tow cheong for 3 minutes.
4. Add sugar and 2 tbsps water. Bring to boil.
5. Add in ½ tsp rice wine and fried pork. Mix thoroughly.
6. Add in the spring onion, season to taste and serve.

Beef Stew

Ingredients:

1 kg stewing beef
3 star anise
1 large onion — sliced
3 cm piece ginger — sliced
1 lemon rind
2 tbsps oil
5 cloves garlic
2 tsps black peppercorns — crushed
1 cup thick soy sauce
¼ cup rice wine
4 tbsps sweet bean paste

Serves 4 — 6

Method:

1. Cut meat into 5 cm cubes. Put in a saucepan with enough water to cover the meat.
2. Add star anise, sliced onion, ginger and lemon rind.
3. Bring to the boil, reduce heat and simmer for 2 hours.
4. Heat oil in a pan and fry the chopped garlic and peppercorns.
5. After 1 minute, add in soy sauce, rice wine and bean paste. Bring to the boil and remove from heat.
6. Cover and cook for another hour.
7. To serve, remove the star anise and lemon rind.

Fried Chicken Wings

Ingredients:

5 pairs chicken wings — tips cut off and washed and drained well
1 tbsp thin soy sauce
½ tbsp thick soy sauce
Lettuce leaves and cucumber slices for garnishing
Oil for deep-frying

Serves 6 — 8

Method:

1. Marinate the chicken wings in the thin and thick soy sauce for 10 minutes.
2. Heat oil and deep fry until brown and crispy. Remove and drain.
3. Serve with lettuce leaves and cucumber slices.

Chicken Fu-Yung With Prawns

Ingredients:

350 gms chicken breast meat — cut into cubes
1 medium onion — chopped
3 cm piece ginger — chopped finely
225 gms prawns — shelled and cleaned
2½ tbsps flour
2½ tbsps butter
1½ dl stock
1½ dl top of milk
1 tbsp cornflour — blended with 4 tbsps water
Salt and pepper to taste
1½ tbsps oil

Serves 4 — 6

Method:

1. Heat oil in a pan and fry the onion and ginger over high heat for 1 minute.
2. Add in the chicken and stir-fry for 1 minute then add the prawns and cook for another minute. Dish out and keep in a warm bowl.
3. In the same pan, add in the flour and butter and stir over low heat until well mixed. Slowly pour in the stock and stir until a fine sauce is produced.
4. Add salt and pepper and top of milk. Stir over low heat to blend thoroughly.
5. Add in the chicken and prawns and cook over medium heat.
6. Gradually pour in the cornflour and stir until the sauce thickens.
7. Dish out and serve immediately.

Fried Chicken in Black Sauce

Ingredients:

1 chicken — cleaned and cut into 8 pieces
1 tsp mixed spice
1 large onion — sliced
3 red chillies — halved lengthwise
2 tbsps soy sauce
1 tbsp vinegar
2 tbsps granulated sugar
2 tsps powdered turmeric
Oil for deep frying

Serves 6 — 8

Method:

1. Blend the turmeric powder with 1 tsp water to form a paste.
2. Rub the chicken pieces with this paste.
3. Fry the chicken until almost crispy and remove from fire. Set aside.
4. Fry the sliced large onions in the same oil until limp.
5. Add the mixed spice, soy sauce, vinegar and sugar.
6. Add some water if the gravy is too thick.
7. Add the chillies and chicken and stir until well mixed.
8. Serve with plain boiled rice.

Chicken in Oyster Sauce

Ingredients:

1 chicken
1 tbsp sesame oil
4 tbsps oyster sauce
3 stalks kai lan (Chinese broccoli)
1 tbsp rice wine
1 tsp sliced garlic

Serves 4 — 6

Method:

1. Clean the chicken well.
2. Boil some water in a pot and put in the chicken. Lower the heat and boil for 15 minutes.
3. Lift out the chicken and pour cold water over it.
4. Dip again into the boiling water and boil for another 10 minutes.
5. Drain the chicken and let it cool for 1 or 2 hours before cutting it into small cubes. Remove all the bones.
6. Arrange the chicken pieces on a platter. Garnish with scalded kai lan.
7. To serve, pour over oyster sauce.
8. To make sauce. Fry garlic in 1 tbsp oil until fragrant. Mix well with sesame oil, rice wine and oyster sauce.

Stewed Mushroom and Chicken Feet

Ingredients:

12 black mushrooms
2 tsps salt
½ tbsp vinegar
6 cups chicken stock
24 chicken feet
2 stalks spring onions
2 tbsps sliced ginger

Serves 6 — 8

Method:

1. Soak mushrooms in warm water. Drain and remove the stalks.
2. Clean the chicken feet and boil.
3. Mix well the chicken feet with chicken stock, vinegar, salt, spring onions and ginger.
4. Place in a steamer and steam for 30 minutes.
5. Add in the mushrooms and steam for another 20 minutes.
6. Serve hot with plain boiled rice.

Braised Chicken In Ginger Wine

Ingredients:

6 chicken drumsticks or breast pieces
4 tbsps oil
2 tbsps black soy sauce
4 tbsps ginger wine
2 tbsps oyster sauce
1 tsp sugar
1 knob vegetable fat
750 ml water

Serves 4 — 6

Method:

1. Cut the chicken pieces into reasonably-sized serving portions.
2. Heat the oil to a moderately high temperature and fry the chicken until the skins are golden-brown.
3. Drain and set aside.
4. Place all the other ingredients in a heavy-bottomed pot and add the chicken.
5. Cover and allow to simmer for half an hour until the gravy thickens.

Peking Duck

Ingredients:

1 duck
3 tbsps honey
2 cloves
2 stalks spring onions — chopped
2½ cups water
5 cm piece ginger
1 cucumber

For dough:

3 cups flour
2 tbsps sesame seed oil
3 tbsps Worcestershire sauce
1 tsp sesame oil
1 cup hot water
2 tbsps cold water
1 tsp sugar

Serves 4 — 6

Method:

1. Clean the duck and hang in a cool and dry place for a few hours.
2. Put water in a pan with honey, ginger, cloves and chopped spring onions. Bring to boil for 5 minutes.
3. Hold the duck by the neck and soak it in the mixture. Slowly pour the sauce into the duck. Lift and hang for 2 more hours.
4. Strain the mixture and keep aside the ginger, onions, cloves and spring onions.
5. Prepare the batter. Sieve the flour in a large bowl and add in water. Knead for 5 minutes until smooth. Cover with a moist cloth and leave for 15 minutes.
6. Roll out the dough to 1 cm thickness and cut into lengths of 6 cm.
7. Spread each piece with sesame oil and put another piece on top. Roll it flat.
8. Fry the pieces in a non-stick pan without oil until both sides are evenly browned. When all the pieces are cooked bake in the oven for about 10 minutes.
9. Roast the duck and put the ginger, cloves and spring onions inside it. Roast for 1 hour.
10. Make the dip. Mix sesame oil, Worcestershire sauce, 2 tbsps water and 1 tsp sugar together. Bring to boil.
11. Cut into small pieces and serve with the dip together with slices of cucumber and the pancakes.

Steamed Chicken

Ingredients:

1 whole chicken	
½ cup water	
2 tbsps thick soy sauce	
1 tsp sugar	
4 black mushrooms — soaked in hot water	
1 cube chicken stock	
1.5 cm pieces ginger	
2 tbsps vinegar	
½ tsp sesame oil	
Salt to taste	

Serves 4 — 6

Method:

1. Cut the chicken into 6 pieces and wash well. Place on a steaming tray.
2. Melt the chicken cube in hot water. Add ginger, soy sauce, vinegar, sugar, sesame oil and salt and mix well.
3. Pour over the chicken pieces and steam for 45 minutes.
4. When the chicken is tender, add in the sliced mushrooms.
5. Steam for another 10 minutes and serve hot.

Steamed Chicken with Sausage

Ingredients:

2 cups chicken meat	
4 cm piece ginger	
2 tbsps tapioca flour	
2 tbsps soy sauce	
Pepper	
2 Chinese sausages	
4 dried black mushrooms — soak in a little water	
2 tbsps oil	
½ tsp salt	
1 tbsp rice wine	

Serves 4 — 6

Method:

1. Cut the chicken meat into bite-sized pieces.
2. Pound the ginger and extract its juice.
3. Season the chicken with 1 tbsp tapioca flour, 1 tbsp soy sauce, ginger juice and pepper.
4. Slice sausage, wash and quarter mushrooms.
5. Season mushrooms with 1 tbsp tapioca flour, 1 tbsp soy sauce, 2 tbsps oil and ½ tsp salt.
6. Mix chicken meat with sausages and mushrooms and add rice wine and pepper.
7. Put ingredients in a heat-proof dish and steam over boiling water for 20 minutes.
8. Serve garnished with chopped coriander leaves.

Crisp Peking Duck

Ingredients:

1 whole duck	
2 stalks coriander leaves	
2 tsps cinnamon powder	
2 tsps cummin seeds	
5 stalks spring onions — chopped	
5 cm piece ginger sliced thinly	
2 tsps cloves	
1 cucumber — sliced	
1 tomato — sliced	
Oil for cooking	
1 tsp sugar	
2 tsps soy sauce	
1 tbsp Chinese rice wine	

Serves 4 — 6

Method:

1. Clean the duck and marinate with 1½ tsps salt, white pepper, 1 tsp sugar, 2 tbsps soy sauce and 1 tbsp Chinese rice wine. Leave aside for 20 minutes.
2. Place the duck in a greased pan and cover with muslin cloth.
3. Put the ginger slices, spring onions, coriander leaves and spices on the muslin cloth.
4. Steam for 1 to 1½ hours. Remove from fire.
5. Deep fry the duck until golden brown.
6. Serve garnished with slices of cucumber and tomato.

Chickens served up at special occasions must be plump and succulent, as the Chinese believe you risk shrinking your luck with one that's scrawny.

Spicy Chicken

Ingredients:

1.5 kg chicken
3 cm piece ginger
4 shallots
½ tsp mixed spice
1 tsp salt
½ tsp sugar
1 tbsp thin soy sauce
½ tsp sesame oil
1 tbsp rice wine
½ tsp pepper
1 egg yolk
5 tbsps cornflour
Oil for deep frying

Serves 6 — 8

Method:

1. Clean the chicken and cut into small pieces.
2. Pound ginger and shallots.
3. Season the chicken with pounded ginger and shallots, mixed spice, salt, sugar, soy sauce, sesame oil, rice wine and pepper. Let stand for 2 hours.
4. Beat the egg yolk and mix in with the seasoned chicken pieces.
5. Coat each chicken piece with cornflour.
6. Heat the oil and deep fry the chicken pieces for 5 minutes or until golden brown.
7. Serve hot.

Steamed Duck in Lotus Leaf

Ingredients:

1 piece duck breast
Abalone
6 thin slices of beef
1 cucumber — sliced
1 piece large lotus leaf
5 button mushrooms
1 carrot — sliced
1 tsp soy sauce
1 cm piece ginger — pounded
Salt and pepper to taste

Serves 4 — 6

Method:

1. Marinate duck meat with soy sauce, pounded ginger and pepper.
2. Clean the lotus leaf and place the meat on it.
3. Arrange abalone, sliced carrot, button mushrooms, slices of beef and sprinkle with salt.
4. Wrap the lotus leaf and steam until well cooked.
5. To serve, garnish with slices of cucumber.

Duck Stewed with Ginger

Ingredients:

1 duck
2 tbsps thin soy sauce
2 tsps thick soy sauce
5 dried Chinese mushrooms
70 gms young ginger
2 cloves garlic
2 stalks spring onions
300 gms lettuce
½ tbsp tow cheong
½ tsp salt
1 tsp sugar
2 tsps sesame oil
Pepper
Oil for deep frying
1 tbsp tapioca flour
1 tbsp Chinese rice wine

Serves 4 — 6

Method:

1. Clean the duck and cut into small pieces. Season with 1 tsp each of both the soy sauce.
2. Soak the mushrooms, remove the stems and halve them.
3. Slice the ginger thinly. Chop the garlic.
4. Cut spring onions into 4 cm lengths and clean the lettuce leaves.
5. Pound the tow cheong.
6. Prepare the gravy. Mix 4 cups water with salt, sugar, sesame oil, pepper, 1 tbsp thick soy sauce and 1 tsp thin soy sauce.
7. Heat oil for deep frying and fry the duck pieces until well browned. Remove the duck pieces and drain out all the oil, leaving just 2 tbsps in the pan.
8. In the oil, fry the garlic and ginger until brown.
9. Add in the preserved bean paste and stir fry for 1 minute.
10. Add the fried duck pieces, mushrooms and gravy.
11. When the meat is tender, bring to the boil rapidly to reduce the gravy. Thicken with tapioca flour blended with 2 tbsps water.
12. Season to taste and add in the rice wine and spring onions.
13. Serve on a bed of boil lettuce.

VEGETABLES

Stir Fried Mixed Vegetables

Ingredients:

8 dried Chinese mushrooms
250 gms snow peas
250 gms canned bamboo shoots
1 small carrot
80 gms frozen peas
2 tbsps oil
½ tsp salt
½ tsp sugar
1½ tsps dark soy sauce
2 tsps Chinese rice wine
½ cup chicken stock
½ tsp sesame oil

Serves 4 — 6

Method:

1. Soak mushrooms in cold water.
2. Wash snow peas and remove strings.
3. Drain bamboo shoots and slice thinly.
4. Scrape carrot and slice thinly.
5. Thaw the peas.
6. Simmer carrots in boiling water for 2 minutes. Drain well.
7. Drain mushrooms and slice thinly.
8. Heat oil in a wok and fry the bamboo shoots with carrots for 2 minutes. Season with salt, sugar, soy sauce and Chinese wine and add in the mushrooms followed by snow peas.
9. Stir fry for 2 minutes and add in chicken stock. Bring to boil.
10. Thicken gravy with corn flour blended with cold water.
11. Sprinkle sesame oil before serving.

Chinese Pickle

Ingredients:

1 cucumber
1 small Chinese radish
1 carrot
1 slice unripe papaya
2 red chillies
1 cup vinegar
3 tbsps sugar
1 tbsp salt

Serves 4 — 6

Method:

1. Clean and cut all the vegetables into thin slices. Sprinkle salt over them, toss to mix and let stand for 30 minutes.
2. Wash the vegetables to remove the salt and squeeze out all the water with a clean, dry kitchen towel. Allow to dry in a cool place.
3. Put all the vegetables in a bowl and add vinegar and sugar. The vinegar should be enough to cover all the vegetables.
4. Season to taste, adding more sugar if necessary. Leave for at least 6 hours.

Eggplant With Crab Sauce

Ingredients:

5 eggplants
1 tbsp fish sauce
1 tbsp vinegar
1 tsp sugar
4 tbsps oil
2 cloves garlic — chopped
½ cup crabmeat
½ tsp tapioca flour
Pepper
1 red chilli — shredded

Serves 4 — 6

Method:

1. Grill the eggplants until soft and cooked. Skin and halve them lengthwise and quarter each length.
2. Place on a platter.
3. Make the gravy. Mix fish sauce, vinegar and sugar in 1 cup water.
4. Heat the oil and fry the garlic until brown. Add in the gravy mixture and then the crabmeat.
5. Bring to boil and thicken with tapioca flour blended with 1 tbsp water.
6. Season gravy to taste and pour over the eggplant.
7. Sprinkle pepper and garnish with shredded chilli before serving.

Seasoned Bamboo Shoots

Ingredients:

500 gms canned young bamboo shoots
2 tbsps sweet bean paste
2 tbsps dark soy sauce
1 tbsp sugar
3 tsps Chinese rice wine
2 tbsps water
250 gms spinach
2 tsps sesame oil
Oil for deep frying

Serves 4 — 6

Method:

1. Drain bamboo shoots and cut into 2 cm cubes. Place in a large strainer and fry in hot oil. Remove and drain.
2. Place bamboo shoots in a dry pan with bean paste, soy sauce, sugar and rice wine.
3. Add 2 tbsps oil and bring sauce to the boil. Add water and simmer until the bamboo shoots are tender. Season with pepper.
4. Soften spinach in hot water. Drain.
5. Stir-fry the spinach in 1 tbsp oil for 2 minutes, then arrange on a platter.
6. Place seasoned bamboo shoots on top and sprinkle with sesame oil.

Stir Fried Mixed Vegetables

Beansprouts With Mushrooms

Ingredients:

300 gms beansprouts

200 gms prawns — shelled and drained dry

3 stalks spring onions

2 cloves garlic — crushed

1 red chilli — sliced

3 tbsps oil

1 tsp salt

6 dried Chinese mushrooms — soaked and sliced

Serves 4 — 6

Method:

1. Heat the oil to a high temperature and fry the crushed garlic until golden brown.
2. Add the prawns and carry on frying until they turn pink.
3. Add the beansprouts, mushrooms and spring onion and stir well.
4. Fry for half a minute or less.
5. Add salt to taste and serve garnished with sliced chillies.

Vegetable Omelette

Ingredients:

4 eggs

60 gms Chinese roast pork

60 gms canned bamboo shoots

3 dried Chinese mushrooms — sliced

1 small carrot

1 cm piece ginger

8 stalks spring onions

Salt and pepper to taste

1 tsp sesame oil

1 tsp cornflour

2 tbsps water

3 tbsps oil

1 fresh red chilli

Serves 4 — 6

Method:

1. Beat the eggs lightly and set aside.
2. Shred thinly the roast pork and bamboo shoots.
3. Drain the mushrooms and shred thinly.
4. Scrape the carrot and cut into matchstick pieces.
5. Shred the ginger and cut the spring onions into 2 cm lengths.
6. Season the eggs with salt and pepper. Add in sesame oil, cornflour blended with water and set aside.
7. Heat oil in a frying pan and fry the meat and vegetables until slightly softened.
8. Pour in the egg and stir evenly.
9. Cut in halves and turn. Cook the other side and put on a plate.
10. Serve garnished with shredded red chilli.

Mixed Vegetables and Beancurd in Claypot

Ingredients:

8 beancurd squares

1 medium carrot

12 dried Chinese mushrooms — soaked

4 stalks spring onions

60 gms canned bamboo shoots

30 gms cloud ear fungus — soaked

100 gms chicken liver

8 cups water

Soy sauce to taste

Chinese brown vinegar to taste

Serves 4 — 6

Method:

1. Slice or dice the beancurd and set aside.
2. Scrape carrot and slice thinly.
3. Drain mushrooms and cut each in half.
4. Thinly slice bamboo shoots.
5. Drain cloud ear fungus.
6. Clean and slice chicken liver.
7. Bring water to boil in a claypot and put in the carrot, mushrooms, spring onions, bamboo shoots, fungus and liver. Boil for 10 minutes.
8. Season to taste with soy sauce and Chinese brown vinegar.

Loh Hon Chye *(Mixed Vegetables)*

Ingredients:

1 head kai choy (mustard greens)

1 carrot

6 dried Chinese mushrooms

6 tbsps oil

2 shallots — sliced

1 tsp salt

½ cup button mushrooms

½ cup straw mushrooms

12 fried min kun (gluten balls)

½ tsp tapioca flour

Serves 4 — 6

Method:

1. Clean and cut the mustard greens into 2 cm lengths. Slice the carrot. Soak the mushrooms to soften, then halve them.
2. Heat 5 tbsps oil and fry the shallots until golden brown. Add in the greens and fry for 1 minute.
3. Add the carrot and Chinese mushrooms and toss all together until well mixed. Add salt.
4. Add ½ cup water and allow vegetables to simmer for 10 minutes.
5. When vegetables are tender, add the button mushrooms, straw mushrooms and fried gluten balls and cook for 5 minutes.
6. Thicken gravy with tapioca flour blended in 1 tbsp water.
7. Season to taste and serve immediately.

Kai Lan With Oyster Sauce

Ingredients:

30 gms young fresh kai lan (Chinese broccoli)
Oyster sauce according to taste
½ tsp rice wine
½ tsp salt
¼ tsp sugar

Serves 4 — 6

Method:

1. Boil water in a pot and add in rice wine, salt and sugar.
2. Dip the kai lan into the boiling water for a few seconds. When the kai lan has softened remove and rinse under running water. This is to ensure that the kai lan remains crispy. Dip into boiling water again. Drain and cool.
3. Arrange the kai lan on a serving plate.
4. Prepare oyster sauce. Mix oyster sauce with some hot water to dilute it.
5. To serve, pour the oyster sauce over the kai lan.

Stuffed Marrow

Ingredients:

1 vegetable marrow
¼ cup shrimps
½ large onion
¼ cup minced pork
1 tbsp diced yambean
1½ tsps tapioca flour
½ tsp salt
1½ tsps sesame oil
Pepper
6 tbsps oil
2 tbsps chopped spring onions

Serves 4 — 6

Method:

1. Scrape off the skin of the marrow, clean it and scoop out the central pith with a teaspoon.
2. Shell, clean and chop the shrimps.
3. Dice the onion to get 1 tbsp diced onion.
4. Mix the chopped shrimps, minced pork, yam bean, onion, 1 tsp tapioca flour, ½ tsp salt, 1 tsp sesame oil and pepper. Knead the ingredients well.
5. Stuff the marrow with this mixture.
6. Heat oil in a saucepan and fry the marrow, turning it frequently until evenly browned.
7. Add 1 cup water with ¼ tsp salt to the pan.
8. Cover the pan and allow the marrow to simmer for 30 minutes until tender.
9. Blend ½ tsp tapioca flour with 1 tbsp water and thicken the gravy with it.
10. Add in the spring onions, season to taste and serve whole or sliced.

Chinese White Cabbage with Crab and Egg Sauce

Ingredients:

600 gms Chinese white cabbage
1 cup stock
1 tsp salt
½ tsp sugar
½ tsp sesame oil
Pepper
5 tbsps oil
2 tsps fish sauce
2 shallots — sliced
½ cup crabmeat
1 egg — beaten

Serves 4 — 6

Method:

1. Discard the old leaves and use just the tender young leaves at the centre of the cabbage. Wash and cut into 5 cm lengths.
2. Mix 1 cup stock with ½ tsp salt, ½ tsp sugar, sesame oil and pepper for gravy.
3. Boil 2 cups water with ¼ teaspoon salt in a pan and when it boils put in the white cabbage. Cover and cook for 5 minutes.
4. Rinse vegetables in cold water and drain well.
5. Heat 2 tbsps oil in a pan and toss cabbage. Add in fish sauce. Arrange cabbage leaves on a platter.
6. Heat another 2 tbsps oil and fry the shallots until golden brown. Add the gravy mixture and crabmeat.
7. When the gravy boils, thicken with tapioca flour blended with 1 tbsp water.
8. Season to taste and turn off the heat.
9. Add in a beaten egg and 1 tbsp oil. Stir once and pour over the cabbage
10. To serve, sprinkle pepper and serve immediately.

> *Traditionally, the claypot was the only cooking utensil available in China and thus evolved the art of claypot cooking which has been perfected over the years.*

SWEETS

Almond Jelly

Ingredients:

| 300 gms gelatine powder |
| 4 tbsps sugar |
| ¼ tin evaporated milk |
| 1 tsp almond essence |
| 2½ cups water |
| 1 standard-sized can lychees |

Serves 4 — 6

Method:

1. Pour the milk and water into a saucepan.
2. Add the gelatine and sugar and dissolve over low heat.
3. Put in the almond essence and mix well.
4. Pour the contents into a glass bowl and set aside to cool before placing it in the refrigerator to chill.
5. When the jelly has set, cut into cubes and serve together with lychees and syrup.
6. Serve in small porcelain bowls as a dessert.

Steamed Honey Sponge

Ingredients:

| 30 gms honey |
| 185 gms butter |
| 100 gms sugar |
| 5 eggs |
| 1 cup fresh milk |
| 375 gms plain flour |
| 2 tbsps baking powder |

Serves 4 — 6

Method:

1. Mix honey with butter, then blend in a quarter of the sugar.
2. Beat until light and smooth.
3. Separate eggs. Beat the yolks into the butter mixture gradually with remaining sugar. Beat until smooth.
4. Add in milk and sift on flour with baking powder. Fold in. Leave to stand for 15 minutes.
5. Whip egg whites until fairly stiff and fold into the mixture.
6. Line the bottom of a baking tin with grease-proof paper and grease lightly. Line the sides with thin cardboard to aid steam to reach all around the cake evenly.
7. Pour in the batter and steam over boiling water for 40 minutes.

Candied Banana Fritters

Ingredients:

| 4 big bananas — peeled and cut into pieces |
| 1 egg |
| 5 tbsps flour |
| 5 tbsps water |
| 1 tbsp oil |
| 6 tbsps sugar |
| 6 cups oil |
| 1 tsp sesame seeds — toasted |

Serves 4 — 6

Method:

1. Beat egg in a small bowl, add cornstarch, flour and water to make batter.
2. Sprinkle flour on the pieces of banana and coat each piece with batter. Deep-fry in hot oil until golden. Remove and drain.
3. Heat 1 tbsp oil in a frying pan, add sugar and water, stir-fry for a while over low heat to make syrup.
4. Turn off heat, add in fried bananas to mix carefully.
5. Serve immediately on a plate brushed with sesame oil. Sprinkle toasted sesame seeds on the bananas.

Mandarin oranges, bananas and pineapples signify good luck to the Chinese. You'll usually find these fruits on the family altar in a Chinese home, particularly at Chinese New Year. The Mandarin oranges (kum) signify gold or wealth; pineapple (wong lai) means prosperity is in store; bananas (koong chew) signify luck first thing in the morning.

Almond Jelly

Toffee Apples

Ingredients:

2 medium-sized eating apples
100 gms plain flour
1 egg
1½ cups water
1 tbsp oil
2 tbsps white sesame seeds
Vegetable oil for deep frying
Iced water
Ice cubes

Serves 4 — 6

Method:

1. Oil a serving plate lightly.
2. Peel apples, remove cores and cut each into 8 pieces.
3. Lightly beat the egg and combine with ½ cup water and flour to make a smooth, thick batter.
4. Heat the oil for deep-frying.
5. Mix sugar with 1 cup water and 1 tbsp oil and bring to boil.
6. Simmer until it forms a thick, light-coloured toffee. Test if toffee is ready by dropping a spoonful into iced water. If it hardens immediately the toffee is ready.
7. Add sesame seeds to the toffee and set near the cooker.
8. When the oil is almost at smoking point coat several pieces of apple with the batter. Put into the oil and fry until golden brown.
9. Lift out using a pair of chop sticks and put into the toffee mixture.
10. When coated transfer to the iced water to harden. Place on the oiled plate.
11. Cook all the apple pieces and serve immediately with the iced water. Dip into the iced water if the toffee begins to soften.

> *Fruits and vegetables have considerable significance for the Chinese. Sugar cane, for instance, (kum chair) means 'I have gold to lend'; persimmons, star fruits, melon and pomegranate represent happiness and fertility because they are either sweet or contain a lot of seeds.*

Pumpkin Cake

Ingredients:

1 small pumpkin
300 gms rice flour
25 shallots — sliced thinly
10 tbsps dried shrimps — soaked and pounded slightly
4 tbsps oil
2 tsps salt

Serves 4 — 6

Method:

1. Skin the pumpkin and cut into wedges.
2. Boil the wedges until well cooked through. Mash
3. Set aside to cool.
4. Sieve the rice flour into the pumpkin mash.
5. Mix well to a consistency like that of mashed potatoes.
6. In a frying pan, heat the oil and fry the shallots lightly.
7. Add in the shrimps and continue to fry for a couple more minutes and then put in the salt.
8. Drain away half the oil and stir the mixture into the pumpkin mash.
9. Grease a medium-sized baking tin and pour in the pumpkin mixture.
10. Steam for about 45 minutes to an hour depending on the size and content of the baking tin.
11. Allow to cool before cutting into squares.
12. Serve hot or cold with golden syrup.

Steamed Cake

Ingredients:

2 eggs
50 gms brown sugar
75 ml fresh milk
100 gms self-raising flour
1 tbsp vegetable fat
Golden syrup for topping

Serves 4 — 6

Method:

1. Beat the eggs in a bowl until light.
2. Stir in the sugar and milk.
3. Fold in the sifted flour and mix well.
4. Melt the fat and leave to cool before pouring into the batter.
5. Pour the batter into a greased 20 cm tin and steam vigorously for 20-30 minutes.
6. Remove the cake from the tin and cut into squares or triangles.

Lotus Seed Paste Dumplings

Ingredients:

400 gms lotus seed paste	
500 gms wheat flour	
200 gms fat	
1 tsp bicarbonate of soda	
5 tbsps sugar	
150 ml water	
Oil for deep frying	

Serves 4 — 6

Method:

1. In a mixing bowl, sieve the flour and bicarbonate of soda.
2. Rub in the fat, add in the water gradually.
3. Knead the mixture into a soft dough and divide it equally into 2 portions.
4. Knead each portion separately and divide into approximately 20 portions.
5. Form each portion into rounds and flatten with a rolling pin.
6. Place one round on another and roll once more. This should result in rounds each formed by two pieces of dough.
7. Fill each round with about 2 tbsps of lotus seed paste and roll into a ball.
8. Using the sharp tip of a knife, cut a criss-cross pattern at the top of each ball to form an open-petal shape but be careful not to cut into the filling.
9. Deep fry the dumplings until brown, drain and sprinkle each dumpling with sugar while hot.
10. Serve as a dessert or a tea-time snack.

In the wedding gift tray you'll find scattered around, some pine leaves and lotus seeds to wish the young couple 100 years of togetherness and a son every year, as well as a pair of pomegranates to wish them 100 children and 1,000 grandchildren. Pieces of rock sugar promise a sweet married life.

Shanghai Pancakes

Ingredients:

300 gms red beans	
180 gms sugar	
4 tbsps oil	
Batter:	
1 cup flour	
1 egg	
1 cup water	
Pinch of salt	
3 tbsps oil	

Serves 4 — 6

Method:

1. To make the paste. Soak the red beans overnight. Cook in a pressure cooker for 30 minutes. Wash them and pass through a sieve to remove the tough skin.
2. Pour into a calico bag and hang it up so that the water drips off.
3. Turn out the paste into a frying pan and cook over low heat with sugar and oil. The paste should be smooth and glossy.
4. To make batter. Sieve flour and salt into a bowl. Make a well in the centre, put the egg and ½ cup water in the well and mix to get a smooth batter.
5. Beat the batter for 10 minutes and then add the rest of the water. Let stand for 30 minutes.
6. Fry the pancakes in a hot, greased pan till they are lightly browned on both sides.
7. Turn pancakes onto a plate, spread the bean paste on it and fold the top and bottom over to get a long, rectangular-shaped cake.
8. When all the pancakes have been filled and folded over, heat 2 tbsps oil in a frying pan and fry each pancake again until well browned.
9. Cut each pancake into 3 cm pieces and serve sprinkled with sesame seeds.

INDIAN

Almost everybody, when asked what food they would associate with the Indian sub-continent would be bound to reply, "curry", little realising that not every spiced dish is a curry and curry is not just one dish. It includes a whole range of dishes, each distinctly different according to the spices and herbs used in varying combinations. Spices, imaginatively used, are the most important features of Indian cooking: hot or mild, pungent or bland, there is something to suit every palate.

And unlike many Western cooks who indiscriminately use the same curry powder for every dish, the Indian cook carefully chooses her spices to enhance the flavour of the main ingredient. Thus while cardamom and cloves will do wonders for mutton, fenugreek will be all-important when it comes to fish curry.

The recipes included in this section have been selected from all the different regions of the Indian subcontinent.

The recipes included in this section, like the diversity of the Indian people in Malaysia — the Tamils, the Malayalees, the Sikhs, the Punjabis, the Sinhalese — have been selected to represent the different regional culinary styles of India.

ACCOMPANIMENTS

Spiced Tea

Ingredients:

4 cups boiling water
1 tsp fresh tea
4 cardamom pods — bruised
1 small piece cinnamon stick
Pinch of saffron strands
2 tbsps finely flaked almonds
Sugar to taste

Serves 4 — 6

Method:

1. Brew the tea and allow to steep for 5 minutes.
2. Add the spices.
3. In each individual bowl or cup, put a teaspoonful of flaked almonds.
4. Pour the tea over the almonds, sweeten to taste and drink hot.

Dhall *(Lentils)*

Ingredients:

1 cup dhall
1 large onion — sliced
2 cloves garlic — chopped
1.5 cm piece ginger — shredded
2 cups water
2 large tomatoes — quartered
A pinch turmeric powder
Salt to taste
1 tsp cummin
3 — 4 dried chillies — roughly broken into a few pieces
4 tbsps ghee or butter

Serves 4 — 6

Method:

1. Clean, wash and drain the dhall. Put into a deep pan with two cups water, garlic and ginger, salt and turmeric, and simmer till dhall is soft and mashable.
2. In a small wok or frying pan, heat ghee or butter.
3. When hot, add dried chillies, cummin, and when crackling, add sliced onions. Fry till onions are golden.
4. When onions are golden, add the tomatoes, fry for a few minutes, then add the cooked dhall, and let it simmer for about 5 minutes.
5. Serve hot with rice and vegetables and fried fish, or with vegetables and chapatis.

Mee Rebus *(Curried Noodles — Indian Style)*

Ingredients:

600 gms thick yellow noodles
300 gms bean sprouts — scalded
4 eggs — hard-boiled and sliced
200 gms cooked prawns
2 potatoes — boiled and sliced
2 bean cakes (tow foo) — fried and sliced
200 gms cooked beef — sliced thinly
5 red chillies — sliced
2 stalks spring onions — chopped
1 cup thick coconut milk — from ½ grated coconut
20 shallots — sliced
4 cloves garlic — chopped
1 cup prawns — shelled and chopped
2 onions — chopped fine
2 tomatoes — sliced
4 tbsps oil
1 — 2 tsps sugar
Salt to taste
½ cup sliced shallots — fried crisp and brown for garnishing
A few lemons — halved

Serves 4 — 6

Method:

1. Heat oil in a wok and fry the garlic and shallots till golden.
2. Stir in curry powder paste and curry leaves, stirring well until fragrant and oil separates.
3. Stir in tamarind juice, sugar and salt, and bring to boil.
4. Add prawns, onions, tomatoes and coconut milk and cook for 5 minutes before removing from heat.
5. Arrange cooked ingredients — meat, prawns, bean curd, potatoes, eggs, bean sprouts individually on a large platter. Dish gravy out into a bowl. Set aside fried shallots, chillies and spring onions for garnishing.
6. Serve in individual bowls, putting in noodles, topping with cooked ingredients. Pour over the gravy and garnish. Squeeze some lemon juice on for a deliciously piquant flavour.

Cardamoms are believed to be a slimming agent and can also aid in relieving urinary complications.

Fresh Mint Chutney

Ingredients:

1 cup firmly packed mint leaves
6 spring onions
2 fresh green chillies — roughly chopped
Salt to taste
2 tsps sugar
1 tsp garam masala
⅓ cup lemon juice
2 tsps water

Serves 4 — 6

Method:

1. Blend the mint leaves with spring onions and all other ingredients to a smooth puree.
2. Pack the chutney into a small dish, smooth the surface, cover and chill.
3. Serve as an accompaniment with meals or as a dip for pakoras..

> *Traditionally, grinding stones were used to blend the chutney. A pestle and mortar can also be used but the leaves must be finely chopped first.*

Pakoras *(Savoury biscuits)*

Ingredients:

3 cups plain flour
½ cup semolina
4 tbsps ghee
½ tsp dill seeds
1 tsp black peppercorns — crushed fine
Salt to taste
Oil for deep frying

Serves 4 — 6

Method:

1. Mix all the ingredients except the oil together and rub in well. Knead into a hard dough with a little water.
2. Roll out dough about 1.5 cm thick and using a cutter, cut out into rounds about 5 cms in diameter. Or cut into rectangles, about 2 cm x 5 cms in size.
3. Prick all over with a fork and deep-fry in hot oil over low heat till golden.

> *Fenugreek was used to reduce fevers and soothe intestinal inflammation.*

Avial

Ingredients:

1 carrot
1 potato
1 cucumber
1 brinjal
8 — 10 French beans
1 cooking banana
1 yam (Keladi)
2 large onions ⎫
4 green chillies ⎬ Ground
1 tsp cummin ⎪
1 cup water ⎭
½ grated coconut — ground
½ cup yoghurt
½ tsp turmeric powder
1 tbsp oil
3 — 4 sprigs curry leaves
Salt to taste

Serves 4 — 6

Method:

1. Wash and cut the vegetables lengthwise into 5 cm strips.
2. Put vegetables into a pan with water, turmeric and salt. Cover and cook for 20 minutes.
3. When the vegetables are cooked, add all the ground ingredients and cook on low heat. Stir well.
4. Add the curd and mix well. Cook for 5 minutes then remove from heat.
5. Add 1 tbsp oil to curry leaves, and sprinkle on the avial.

Tandoori Fish

Ingredients:

1 large pomfret (about 1 kg) — remove head and tail
6 cloves garlic
1 tsp cummin
½ tsp turmeric powder
Juice of one lime
4 tbsps unflavoured yoghurt
2 drops red colouring
Salt to taste

Serves 4 — 6

Method:

1. Grind cummin and garlic.
2. Cut deep slits on both sides of the fish, rub lime juice over, and keep aside for 10 minutes.
3. Combine ground cummin and garlic with yoghurt, turmeric, salt and colouring, and rub into the fish. Leave to marinate for 30 minutes.
4. Grill the fish or barbecue over a charcoal stove, basting with ghee, seasoned with crushed cardamom seeds and a little chilli powder. Serve piping hot.

Fresh Mint Chutney

Rasam *(Pepper Water)*

Ingredients:

1 tbsp tamarind pulp
1 clove garlic
½ tsp ground black pepper
1 tsp ground cummin
4 cups cold water
2 tsps salt
2 tbsps chopped fresh coriander
1 tomato — quartered
2 tsps oil
1 tsp black mustard seeds
8 sprigs curry leaves

Serves 4 — 6

Method:

1. Squeeze out tamarind juice and strain.
2. Put tamarind juice, garlic, pepper, cummin, tomato, cold water, salt and coriander into a saucepan and bring to the boil.
3. Turn down heat and simmer for 10 minutes.
4. In a separate saucepan heat the oil and fry mustard seeds and curry leaves until the leaves turn brown.
5. Add to the simmering soup and serve hot.

Sweet Tomato Chutney

Ingredients:

1 kg ripe tomatoes — chopped
½ cup raisins
1 tsp mustard seeds
1 tsp cummin
1 tsp fenugreek seeds
2 sprigs curry leaves
1 cup vinegar
1 tsp chilli powder
½ tsp turmeric powder
½ tsp salt
1½ cups brown sugar
½ cup oil

Serves 6 — 8

Method:

1. Heat oil in a deep pan and fry mustard, cummin and fenugreek seeds till fragrant and crackling.
2. Add chopped tomatoes, curry leaves, raisins, brown sugar, chilli powder, turmeric and salt. Cook, stirring occasionally, till ingredients are well blended and liquid dries.
3. Add vinegar and simmer over low heat till oil separates. Cool and bottle.
4. This chutney must be kept in the refrigerator.

Uppuma *(Savoury Semolina)*

Ingredients:

2 cups semolina
4½ tbsps vegetable oil
1 tsp black mustard seeds
8 — 10 curry leaves
1 tbsp urad dhall (black lentils)
1 tbsp channa dhall (yellow split peas)
4 dried red chillies
1½ cups finely chopped onion
1 tbsp sliced fresh red or green chillies
1 tbsp grated fresh ginger
1½ cups diced vegetables (peas, carrots, cauliflower)
2 cups hot water
1½ tsps salt
2 tsps ghee
Squeeze of lemon juice

Serves 4 — 6

Method:

1. In a saucepan heat 1½ tablespoons oil and fry semolina until golden.
2. Remove the semolina from the pan, wipe pan and heat remaining 3 tablespoons oil.
3. Fry mustard seeds, curry leaves and both types of lentils, and the dried chillies, broken into pieces.
4. When the lentils are golden add onions and fry stirring, until soft.
5. Add fresh chillies, ginger and vegetables, stir and cook for about 8 minutes.
6. Add water and salt, and bring to the boil, add semolina and stir till mixture boils. Keep stirring till quite dry. Cover pan and cook on low heat till semolina is cooked through.
7. Add ghee and stir. Squeeze lemon juice and serve warm or cold.

> *Cummin was prescribed by early Hindu medicine for jaundice, piles and other organic complaints. The seeds were also bruised, mixed to a paste and applied to relieve pain in the sides. Together with other drugs, cummin formed a stimulating linament.*

Roti Canai

Ingredients:

600 gms flour	
1 cup warm water	} Mixed together
1 tsp salt	
3 tbsps ghee	
1 egg	
Sugar to taste	

Serves 6 — 8

Method:

1. Mix together flour, water, sugar and egg. Knead until a soft dough is formed.
2. Form into small balls and keep overnight.
3. When you are ready to make the roti canai, spread the ghee on the balls and flatten.
4. Heat an iron griddle and fry the rotis individually until cooked.
5. Serve hot with a curry or dhall.

Pea Pulau

Ingredients:

1½ cups long grain Indian basmati rice
1½ cups peas
1½ tbsps ghee
6 cloves
2.5 cm stick cinnamon
½ tsp turmeric powder
2 cups hot water
Salt to taste
1 large onion — sliced fine

Serves 4 — 6

Method:

1. Fry sliced onion till brown and keep aside for garnishing.
2. Wash and soak the rice for about 30 minutes. Drain.
3. Heat ghee in a heavy-bottomed pan, add cloves, cinnamon and turmeric for a minute.
4. Add rice and salt to taste and fry gently for a few minutes, stirring constantly.
5. Add peas and hot water and mix thoroughly.
6. Turn rice into rice cooker and cook until rice is done and liquid absorbed.
7. Serve garnished with fried onion.

Chapatis

These are light flat discs of unleavened wholemeal bread served with a curry or dhall. Traditionally, they are cooked on a large spherical plate placed over a heat source. This is, of course, not always available in the average kitchen and a compromise may be made by using a heavyweight frying pan or an iron griddle.

Ingredients:

225 gms "atta" (Indian wholemeal) flour
A knob of ghee
Some lukewarm water
Salt to taste

Serves 4 — 6

Method:

1. Put the flour, ghee and salt in a mixing bowl.
2. Add the water gradually and mix to form a firm dough.
3. Knead the dough for ten minutes or longer bearing in mind that the longer the dough is kneaded, the lighter the resulting chapati will be.
4. Put the dough back in the mixing bowl, cover with a damp tea towel and leave to stand for at least an hour; overnight would be ideal.
5. Divide the dough into small balls and roll out thinly on a lightly floured board.
6. Heat the frying pan or griddle until very hot and cook the chapatis one at a time for about one minute, turning them over occasionally.
7. As each one is cooked, wrap in a clean dry tea towel to keep them warm.
8. Serve immediately with curry or dhall. Chapatis should be served fresh as when reheated, they can become rather hard and leathery.

> *Aniseeds can help cure nervous headaches. They are crushed, mixed with oil of cloves and rubbed into the back of the neck, forehead and temples.*

Roti Canai

Idli *(Steamed Rice Cakes)*

Ingredients:

300 gms uncooked rice
250 gms black lentils
2 tbsps cooked rice
Pinch of salt

Serves 4 — 6

Method:

1. Soak the rice and lentils separately in water for 4-5 hours.
2. Grind finely the uncooked rice and cooked rice, then grind the lentils separately.
3. Mix the rice and lentils together, add salt.
4. Pour this thick paste into small moulds and steam till cooked about 20 minutes. Serve with curries or chutneys.

Hoppers *(Appam)*

Ingredients:

225 gms long grain or Basmati rice
1 tsp salt
7 cups coconut milk — from ½ grated coconut
Pinch baking soda
A little butter

Serves 4 — 6

Method:

1. Grind the rice and mix together with the salt and coconut milk and a pinch of bicarbonate of soda. Leave overnight.
2. Before cooking whip the batter to make it light.
3. Heat a small omelette pan with a little butter and pour in a little of the batter. Turn the pan so that the batter runs up the sides to give a lacy effect.
4. When the batter becomes firm in the centre remove with a fish slice and keep warm in a tea cloth.

> *Hoppers are quite similar to thosais and originated from South India. Traditionally hoppers are cooked in earthenware pots with rounded bottoms which are placed in the ashes of a slow charcoal fire.*
>
> *The batter is poured in and the pot spun quickly to make the batter swirl round into the hotter parts of the pot. This gives a lacy crisp border to the hopper. This method of cooking needs skill and therefore it is easier to use a small omelette pan to make the hoppers. Just swirl the batter so that it runs up the sides.*

Idli

Puri

This is essentially a deep-fried chapati traditionally served at breakfast with coffee.

Ingredients:

225 gms "atta" (Indian wholemeal) flour
100 gms ghee
Lukewarm water
Vegetable oil for deep frying
Pinch of salt

Serves 4 — 6

Method:

1. Rub the ghee and salt into the flour.
2. Gradually add some water to the mixture to form a firm dough.
3. Divide into 2.5 cm pieces and roll out thinly.
4. Heat the vegetable oil in a wok to a high temperature.
5. If the oil is of the right temperature, the puri, when dropped in the pan, will immediately puff up and float to the surface.
6. Fry until pale golden brown and drain on greaseproof paper.
7. Serve immediately with a dry curry and vegetables.

Vegetable Biryani

Ingredients:

3 cups rice — half-cooked
1 cup carrots — chopped
1 cup peas
½ cup corn
½ cup french beans — sliced thinly
1 cup onions — chopped
1 cup chopped tomatoes
½ cup ghee
1 tbsp chopped coriander leaves
3 sticks cinnamon, cardamoms and star anise

Serves 4 — 6

Method:

1. In a heavy pan, heat the ghee and fry the onions, cinnamon, cardamoms, star anise and carrots, french beans and tomatoes.
2. Fry until the mixture turns a light brown.
3. Add the rice, corn, peas, coriander leaves and salt and turn down the heat.
4. Cover the pan and remove from heat.
5. Place in a steamer and steam until the rice is cooked.
6. Garnish with red chillies if so desired.
7. Serve as with chicken biryani or pilau.

Murtaba

Anyone who has seen murtaba being made will find it almost impossible to believe that it can be made at home as the "mamak roti" men who have spent a lifetime making these parchment thin rotis achieve this by flinging a handful of dough in ever-widening curves.

An egg-sized lump becomes a large, smooth sheet in about the space of a minute. It is then cooked on a griddle and filled with savoury meat and seasoned beaten egg.

At home, you may not be able to put on such a spectacular display but it is possible to get the required thinness by soaking the balls of well-kneaded dough in oil for an hour or more and then spreading them with the hands much as though you were smoothing down a bed sheet.

Work on a smooth surface, then carry the thin pastry to the hot griddle over a rolling pin as fingers may easily make holes. The edges will be somewhat thicker than the centre but this does not matter.

The problem encountered in a domestic kitchen is getting a griddle large enough to cook murtaba on but there's no law that murtaba must be of a specific size and smaller ones taste just as well.

Ingredients:

| 3 cups plain white flour |
| 1 tsp salt |
| 1 tbsp ghee |
| 1 cup lukewarm water |
| ½ cup oil |

Serves 4 — 6

For the filling:

| 500 gms minced meat |
| 2 tbsps ghee |
| 1 large red onion — sliced fine |
| 2 cloves garlic — crushed |
| ½ tsp fresh ginger — grated |
| 1 tsp turmeric powder |
| 1 tsp garam masala |
| 1½ tsps salt |
| 2 tbsps fresh coriander leaves — finely chopped |
| 1 fresh red chilli — finely sliced |
| 2 eggs — beaten |
| Salt and pepper |
| 1 onion — finely sliced |

Method:

For the roti:

1. Place the flour and salt in a large bowl and rub in the ghee.
2. Add the water and mix to a fairly soft dough.
3. Knead the dough for ten minutes or longer.
4. Divide the dough into equal-sized balls and place them in a small bowl containing the oil.
5. Leave for at least an hour.

To make the filling:

1. Heat the ghee and fry the onion until it is soft.
2. Add the garlic and fresh ginger and continue to fry until the onion is golden brown.
3. Add the turmeric and chilli powder and stir for a few seconds.
4. Put in the meat and carry on frying, stirring constantly, until it is well-cooked.

To cook the murtaba:

1. Season the beaten eggs with salt and pepper and set aside in a small bowl.
2. On a smooth surface, spread a little oil from the bowl and flatten one of the dough balls with a rolling pin.
4. Gently press with the fingers, spreading the dough until it is almost as thin as strudel pastry.
4. Heat the griddle and grease it lightly with ghee.
5. Drape the roti over a rolling pin and transfer it on to the griddle.
6. It will cook very quickly so spoon on some beaten egg and spread it over the middle portion of the roti with the underside of the spoon.
7. Sprinkle some meat over and just before folding, add a few slices of onion.
8. Fold over the sides of the roti, in an envelope-like fashion to enclose the filling completely.
9. Turn it over and cook the other side, spreading a little more ghee or oil on the griddle before putting it down.
10. Cook until crisp and golden on both sides.
11. Serve hot either on its own or with a bowl of curry gravy or dhall.

Biryani

Biryani is a rich pilau often layered with meat of some kind and steamed very gently so that the flavours blend. It is the masterpiece of many Eastern cooks and the main feature at festive dinners.

Chicken Biryani

Ingredients:

A

2.5 cm piece stick cinnamon	Ground to a fine paste
4 cardamoms	
1 nutmeg	

B

1 medium-sized onion	Ground
½ cup ginger	
¼ cup garlic	

C

¼ cup cashewnuts	Ground and mixed with ½ cup water to form a paste
½ tsp chilli powder	
1 tbsp aniseed	
½ tsp turmeric	

1 medium sized chicken — cut into 6 pieces

1 bunch coriander leaves

1 spray mint leaves

3 medium-sized onions — thinly sliced

3 screwpine leaves

5 cups rice — half-cooked

250 gms ghee

1 cup tomato puree

Serves 6 — 8

Method:

1. In a large pan, put in the ghee and fry the onions lightly.
2. Add the ground spices, A.
3. Fry for a couple of minutes and then add the tomatoes, chillies, pandan, mint and coriander leaves.
4. Fry for a few minutes and then put in the ground spices, B.
5. Fry for five minutes or until well-browned and then add the chicken and lower the heat.
6. Add the spices, C and the tomato puree and mix slowly.
7. When the chicken is cooked, add the half-cooked rice and lower the heat to a minimum.
8. Cover with a couple of clean dish cloths and cook until the rice is well-done.
9. Serve immediately with curries or dhall and vegetables.

Paratha

This is probably the most popular of Indian breads — rich, layered, flaky and deliciously flavoured with ghee, it makes up a complete meal when served with a curry or dhall but may also be eaten as an in-between snack with butter and sugar.

The secret behind the perfect paratha lies in the rolling and folding technique in order to achieve the light, layered effect.

Ingredients:

225 gms wholemeal flour

225 gms plain flour

200 gms ghee

1½ tsps salt

220 ml lukewarm water

Ghee for cooking

Serves 4 — 6

Method:

1. In a large mixing bowl, put in the wholemeal flour, plain flour, salt and a knob of the ghee.
2. Add a little water at a time and knead to form a soft dough which is wet to the touch.
3. Turn out onto a lightly floured board and knead for ten minutes or longer.
4. Put the dough back into the mixing bowl, cover with a tea towel and set aside for at least an hour.
5. Turn the dough out again on the board and divide into 12 portions.
6. Roll each portion into a ball.
7. Melt the ghee over a low heat and put it in a bowl.
8. Knead lightly and then roll each ball of dough as thinly as possible into a circular shape.
9. Dip a small brush in the melted ghee and brush each round lightly.
10. With a knife, make a cut from the centre of each circle to the outer edge.
11. Starting at the cut edge, roll the dough tightly into a conical shape.
12. Press the apex of the cone and the base towards each other and flatten slightly. The roll will now be a small, approximately round lump of dough again.
13. Lightly flour the board once more and roll out the dough as gently as possible, taking care not to press too hard and let the air out at the edges.
14. Grease liberally an iron griddle or heavyweight frying pan and heat over moderate heat.
15. Cook each paratha individually, turning it over occasionally and spreading more ghee until both sides are a golden brown.
16. Serve hot with a curry or dhall or butter and sugar.

Meatball Curry

Ingredients:

750 gms fine minced meat
1 medium onion — finely chopped
1 clove garlic — crushed
3 cm piece fresh ginger — finely grated
1 fresh red or green chilli — seeded and finely chopped
3 tbsps chopped fresh coriander or mint
1½ tsps salt
1 tsp garam masala

Gravy:

3 tbsps ghee
2 medium onions — finely chopped
1 clove garlic — finely chopped
3 cm piece fresh ginger — finely chopped
1 tsp turmeric powder
1 tsp garam masala
1 tsp chilli powder
2 ripe tomatoes — quartered
1 tsp salt
2 tbsps chopped coriander or mint
Lemon juice to taste

Serves 6 — 8

Method:

Meatballs:

1. Mix the minced meat thoroughly with all the other ingredients.
2. Shape into balls.

Gravy:

1. Heat ghee in a large heavy saucepan, brown the meatballs and set aside.
2. Using the same oil, fry the onions, garlic and ginger until soft and golden.
3. Add turmeric, garam masala and chilli powder. Fry for 1 minute.
4. Add tomatoes, salt and meatballs. Cover the pan and simmer for 25 minutes or until the gravy is thick and the meatballs soft.
5. Stir in the chopped herbs and lemon juice.
6. Serve with rice or chapattis.

The meatballs can also be fried and served with a sauce instead of cooking them in the gravy.

Spiced Mutton

Ingredients:

1 kg boneless mutton — cubed
1 cup yoghurt
¼ tsp asafoetida (Optional)
2.5 cm piece ginger — shredded
4 cloves garlic
1 tsp cummin
1 tsp khus khus
1 tsp coriander
4 cloves
½ tsp black peppercorns
2 tbsps unblanched almonds
1 medium onion — chopped
1 tsp turmeric powder
1 cup water
4 tbsps oil
Salt to taste
Coriander leaves for garnishing

Serves 6 — 8

Method:

1. Mix the yoghurt with the asafoetida and add mutton. Leave to marinate for 30 minutes.
2. Grind together the ginger, garlic, khus khus, cummin, coriander, cloves, cardamom, peppercorns and almonds, and add a few drops of water to form a smooth paste.
3. Heat oil in a pan and fry onions till golden. Stir in the turmeric and ground spices and fry for a few minutes, stirring all the time. Add a little water if mixture dries.
4. Bring to the boil and add meat mixture. Fry for 10 minutes.
5. Reduce heat, cover pan and simmer for 40 minutes or until meat is tender.
6. Remove cover, add water and cook until liquid dries.
7. Add mixed spices and coriander leaves. Dish out into an ovenproof dish and bake in low oven for 25 minutes.

It was said that the Brahmins of Kashmir chewed on garlic to inflame their baser passions.

Minced Meat And Potato Curry

Ingredients:

600 gms minced meat
3 large onions — finely chopped
2 cloves garlic — chopped
3 cm piece ginger — grated
1 tsp ground turmeric
3 tsps ground coriander
2 tsps ground cummin
3 tbsps lemon juice
600 gms potatoes — peeled and quartered
2 cups hot water
2 tsps garam masala
Salt to taste
4 tbsps ghee

Serves 6 — 8

Method:

1. Heat ghee and fry onions, garlic and ginger until limp and golden.
2. Add turmeric, coriander, cummin and stir for 1 minute.
3. Add salt and lemon juice.
4. Add meat and stir constantly until the meat is browned.
5. Add potatoes and hot water and bring to simmering point.
6. Lower heat and cook until potatoes are done and meat is tender. Stir occasionally so that the curry does not stick to the base of the pan.
7. Sprinkle garam masala and stir gently.
8. Serve garnished with chopped coriander leaves.

After a banana leaf meal, folding the leaf away from you means that you do not like the food. If you want to compliment the hostess, fold the leaf towards you.

Mutton With Drumstick Curry

Ingredients:

500 gms mutton — cleaned and cubed
6 drumsticks — skinned and cut into 2.5 cm lengths
2.5 cm piece stick cinnamon
4 cloves
½ tsp mustard seeds
½ tsp garam masala
½ cup thick coconut milk ⎱ From ½ grated
2 cups thin coconut milk ⎰ coconut
2 green chillies — slit lengthwise and seeded
1 tsp black peppercorns — ground
3 tbsps meat curry powder
1 tomato — quartered
2 large onions — sliced
4 tbsps oil
Salt to taste
1 sprig curry leaves
2.5 cm piece ginger — sliced fine
1 tsp turmeric powder
4 cloves garlic — chopped

Serves 6 — 8

Method:

1. Put mutton in a saucepan, cover with water, add half the ginger and garlic and bring to boil. Cook until mutton is tender and liquid absorbed.
2. Heat the oil in a pan and fry mustard seeds, onions, curry leaves and remaining ginger and garlic till brown.
3. Add curry powder, black pepper and turmeric and 2 tablespoons thin coconut milk and stir well.
4. Fry till oil separates, then add mutton and drumsticks and remaining thin coconut milk.
5. Bring to the boil, then reduce heat and cook till gravy is almost dry.
6. Add thick coconut milk and simmer till drumsticks are soft.
7. Add salt, tomatoes and chillies, and simmer for 10 minutes before dishing out.

Fried Meatballs

Minced Lamb

Ingredients:

500 gms lamb or mutton
2 dsps coriander
1 dsp cummin
1 tsp aniseed
10 dried chillies
2.5 cm piece fresh turmeric
2.5 cm piece stick cinnamon
4 cloves
4 cardamoms
10 small onions — sliced
2 cm piece ginger — shredded
1 cup coconut milk from ½ grated coconut
2 tomatoes — chopped
3 dsps oil

Serves 6 — 8

Method:

1. Heat frying pan (no oil), and brown the chillies, coriander, cummin, turmeric and aniseed. Remove from pan and grind fine.
2. Heat oil in a pan and brown the onions and ginger, cloves, cardamoms, cinnamon.
3. Add ground spices and fry till oil separates.
4. Add minced lamb and salt. Stir well and cover, simmering for 15 minutes.
5. Add coconut milk and tomatoes, and cook over medium heat till dry.

Madras Stick Curry

Ingredients:

500 gms lean mutton — cut into 2.5 cm cubes
½ cup ginger — thickly sliced
½ cup small onions — peeled and left whole
2 tbsps chopped onion
2 cloves garlic — chopped
2 fresh red chillies — cut lengthwise
1 tbsp curry powder
60 gms ghee

Serves 6 — 8

Method:

1. Pack cubed mutton, ginger slices and onions alternately on skewers. Keep aside.
2. Heat ghee in a pan and fry the chopped onion, garlic and chillies till golden.
3. Add curry powder and a little water and mix well then continue cooking for a few more minutes.
4. Pack the skewered meat in the gravy, cover and simmer over low heat till meat is tender. Add salt to taste.

Meat And Tomato Curry

(North Indian style)

Ingredients:

1 kg lamb or mutton
½ kg ripe tomatoes — blended or ground
2 large onions — sliced fine
8 tbsps oil
4 bay leaves
(A)
10 shallots
4 cm piece ginger
6 cloves garlic
6 fresh red chillies

} Grind together

(B)
4 cardamoms
2.5 cm stick cinnamon
10 black peppercorns

} Grind together

Serves 6 — 8

Method:

1. Heat oil in a deep pan and fry onion till golden. Add (A) and meat and brown well, sprinkling a little water if necessary to prevent the spices from burning.
2. Add tomato and stir well.
3. Add 4 cups water, bay leaves and salt to taste, and simmer over low heat until meat is tender.
4. Sprinkle (B) on, and serve hot, garnished with chopped coriander leaves.

Shami Kebabs

Ingredients:

500 gms minced beef
1 cup split peas
2 onions — chopped
1 tsp chilli powder
½ tsp turmeric powder
2 eggs
A few mint leaves
A small bunch coriander leaves
Salt to taste
Oil for frying

Serves 6 — 8

Method:

1. Soak split peas in water for several hours, then boil with mince till soft. Drain thoroughly.
2. Put through a mincer with chopped onion, mint, coriander leaves, salt, chilli powder and turmeric.
3. Mix with beaten egg and make into round cutlets.
4. Deep fry in hot oil and serve with chutney.

Mirch Ka Salan
(Mutton and Green Peppers — North Indian Style)

Ingredients:

500 gms mutton or lamb
6 green peppers (capsicums)
5 tbsps oil
½ tsp cummin
1 tsp chilli powder
½ tsp turmeric powder
1 tsp garam masala
500 gms potatoes
½ cup yoghurt
1 tsp sugar
1 bunch coriander leaves
6 cloves garlic
2.5 cm piece ginger } **Grind to a paste**
12 shallots
1 large tomato
Salt to taste

Serves 6 — 8

Method:

1. Heat oil in a deep pan or pressure cooker. Add cummin seeds.
2. When crackling, add mutton and brown well.
3. Add the ground spices and chilli powder, turmeric, garam masala, salt and sugar. Fry for 3 minutes.
4. Add capsicums and potatoes and fry for about 5 minutes.
5. Add the yoghurt and cook for a few more minutes, mixing the gravy thoroughly.
6. Add 2 cups water and simmer over low heat, or cook under pressure till meat is tender. Serve garnished with coriander leaves.
7. This recipe usually includes ¼ tsp onion seeds (Kalonji) if available. The seeds are added with the cummin.

Masala Fry

Ingredients:

500 gms beef steak — sliced into steak-size pieces
6 cloves garlic
3—4 dried chillies
1 tsp cummin } **Grind to a paste**
¼ tsp mustard seeds
1 dsp vinegar

Serves 6 — 8

Method:

1. Rub paste into meat with vinegar and a little salt, and leave to marinate for 30 minutes to an hour.
2. Heat oil in a heavy bottomed pan, put in meat slices, and fry slowly till quite brown and meat is tender.

Hot Beef Curry

Ingredients:

1 kg beef — cubed
1 tbsp ground aniseed
1 tbsp ground cummin
1 tbsp ground coriander
5 dried chillies — ground
1 stalk lemon grass
3 large onions — sliced fine
4 cloves garlic — crushed
½ tsp turmeric powder
2.5 cm piece stick cinnamon
1 tbsp ground black pepper
½ cup tamarind juice
4 cups coconut milk from ½ grated coconut
Salt to taste
4 tbsps oil

Serves 6 — 8

Method:

1. Mix the ground curry spices with a little water to form a paste and add to meat. Add ground chillies and mix well. Leave to marinate for 30 minutes.
2. Heat oil in a deep pan and fry the onions, garlic and lemon grass until fragrant.
3. Add the meat mixture and stir well.
4. Pour in tamarind juice, and simmer gently for 5 minutes.
5. Add coconut milk, salt and black pepper. Cover and simmer till meat is cooked.

Jhal Farazi

Ingredients:

500 gms cooked meat
4 potatoes — boil and dice
6 cloves garlic — chopped
3 cm piece ginger sliced fine
3 tsps chilli powder
2 onions — chopped
1 tsp garam masala
5 tbsps ghee
Salt to taste
½ tsp turmeric powder

Serves 6 — 8

Method:

1. Heat the ghee and fry onions till golden.
2. Add garlic, fry for 2 minutes.
3. Add cooked meat and potatoes with remaining spices and salt to taste. Stir well and fry over medium heat till dry.

Seek Kebabs

Ingredients:

500 gms minced beef
2 tbsps gram flour (split pea flour)
4 tbsps yoghurt
2 tsps garam masala
3 tsps salt
2 medium-sized onions — chopped
A small bunch coriander leaves
2 dsps lemon juice
1 tsp chilli powder
2 cm piece ginger

Serves 6 — 8

Method:

1. Put beef through a mincer with onion, ginger and coriander leaves.
2. Add salt, garam masala, chilli powder, lemon juice and gram flour, and mix and knead for several minutes till it becomes like a smooth dough.
3. Divide the 'dough' into 12 portions, and wrap each portion round a metal skewer in a sausage shape. Baste generously with yoghurt.
4. Place under a hot grill and brown well on all sides.
5. Serve hot with mint chutney or chilli sauce.

Spicy Meat Curry

Ingredients:

500 gms beef, mutton or pork
6 large onions — sliced
1 sprig curry leaves
1 tsp mustard seeds
1 tsp cummin
1 small piece turmeric
1 pod garlic
6 fresh red chillies
3 tbsps ghee
Vinegar and salt to taste

Serves 6 — 8

Method:

1. Cut meat into bite-sized pieces.
2. Grind garlic, chillies, mustard seeds, cummin, turmeric to a fine paste.
3. Heat ghee in a pan, add curry leaves.
4. Add the onions and fry till golden.
5. Add the ground spices and fry for 5 minutes.
6. Add meat. Stir well and brown for about 5 minutes.
7. Add ½ cup water. Stir well then cover and simmer for 30-40 minutes, or until meat is tender.
8. Remove cover, add salt and brown a little over high heat, adding vinegar to taste a few minutes before serving.

Pork Curry

Ingredients:

750 gms pork — cleaned and cubed
½ tsp chilli powder
1½ cups coconut milk
5 cm piece ginger — shredded
2 large onions — chopped
4 cloves garlic — chopped
1 tsp coriander — ground
1 tsp cummin — ground
Salt to taste
Brown sugar to taste

Serves 6 — 8

Method:

1. Put pork in a deep saucepan and pour in the coconut milk, ground spices, onion, ginger, garlic.
2. Bring to the boil slowly, add salt and brown sugar to taste.
3. Reduce heat and simmer, covered for an hour or until pork is tender. Serve hot.
   Note: You can add more chilli powder if you like your curry more pungent.

Pork Vindaloo

Ingredients:

750 gms pork — cubed
5 cm piece ginger ⎫
4 cloves garlic
20 dried chillies
2 tsp turmeric powder ⎬ Grind to a paste
10 shallots
1 tbsp cummin ⎭
½ cup water
Vinegar to taste
Salt to taste
2 sprigs curry leaves
1 tsp mustard seeds — ground coarsely
3 tbsps oil

Serves 6 — 8

Method:

1. Marinate the pork in the ground spices, salt and vinegar for about 30 minutes.
2. Heat oil in a pan or wok and add the mustard seeds. Fry until the seeds crackle.
3. Add curry leaves and pork and stir well; fry for a few minutes.
4. Add water and bring to the boil. Cover and reduce heat and simmer till the meat is tender and most of the liquid has been absorbed.

Mirch Ka Salan *(Mutton And Green Peppers)*

Mutton And Potato Curry

Ingredients:

1 kg mutton chops — each chop cut into half	
5 potatoes — halved	
6 fresh red chillies	
½ bunch coriander leaves	Grind and mix
4 cloves garlic	into paste with 2
2.5 cm piece ginger	tbsps coconut milk
2 cups thick coconut milk from 1 grated coconut	
1 tbsps cummin	
1 tbsp khus khus	
1 tsp black peppercorns	
1 tsp turmeric powder	
½ tsp ground nutmeg	
2 large onions — sliced	
Salt to taste	
4 tbsps oil	

Serves 6 — 8

Method:

1. Marinate mutton with ground spices for a few hours (overnight if possible).
2. Heat half the oil in a pan and fry the grated coconut, cummin and khus khus for a few minutes.
3. Add the peppercorns, turmeric and nutmeg and fry till fragrant. Remove from heat and cool.
4. When cool, put in a blender with remaining coconut milk and blend to a smooth paste.
5. Heat the remaining oil in a pan and fry the onions till golden.
6. Stir in the coconut and spice paste and fry for a while.
7. Add the meat mixture. Stir well and bring to the boil slowly.
8. Reduce heat, cover and simmer for 40 minutes or until meat is tender.
9. Add potatoes and salt to taste and cook till potatoes are soft.

Nutmegs are believed to be a cure for heart ailments. The nutmeg should be grated and placed in a glass. Mix with boiling water and some sugar. Drink while it is warm.

Easy Mutton Curry

Ingredients:

750 gms mutton or lamb — diced
4 large onions — ground
1 tbsp coriander seeds — ground
4 cloves garlic — chopped
5 cardamoms — seeds ground
2.5 cm piece stick cinnamon
1 tbsp chilli powder (more if you like your curry really hot)
1 tsp turmeric powder
1 tsp ground black pepper
1 cup oil
Salt to taste
Juice of 2 limes

Serves 6 — 8

Method:

1. Heat oil in a deep pan, and fry onions till brown, then add garlic, cardamom, chilli powder, cinnamon, turmeric and coriander.
2. Fry till fragrant, then add mutton and powdered black pepper.
3. Stir well and add salt to taste.
4. Add enough water to cover meat, and simmer till mutton is tender.
5. Before serving, pour in lime juice.
   Note: You can substitute 1½ cup coconut milk for the water for a richer and slightly different taste.

The Indians believe that drinking too much lime juice is not good for the stomach lining. However, if drunk with rock sugar in the evening, it is supposed to increase sperm production.

Mutton Korma

Ingredients:

600 gms boneless mutton
2 medium-sized red onions — chopped
2.5 cm piece ginger — sliced
4 cloves garlic — crushed
3 green chillies
1 tbsp black peppercorns
½ tsp turmeric powder
2 tbsps ground cummin
3 cardamoms — ground
1 stick cinnamon
2 tomatoes
Milk from half a coconut
1 tbsp fresh grated coconut
2 tbsps oil
Salt to taste
A few stalks coriander leaves

Serves 6 — 8

Method:

1. Grind together the chillies, black peppercorns and fresh grated coconut.
2. Mix together the turmeric, coriander, cummin and cardamoms with a little water to form a paste.
3. Boil the mutton pieces with a little of the sliced ginger, and crushed garlic in water until tender.
4. Heat a saucepan with oil and fry the onions, cinnamon and remaining ginger and garlic.
5. Add in the paste.
6. Fry until the oil begins to surface and then add the mutton, coating it well with the spices.
7. Pour in the coconut milk and bring slowly to the boil.
8. Cover and cook on low heat until the gravy thickens.
9. Add the salt, lime juice and coriander leaves.
10. Stir well and remove from heat.

Indians believe that a drink of ginger water every morning and night will help keep illness at bay.

Lamb Curry

Ingredients:

1.5 kg boneless shoulder of lamb
2 tbsps ghee
2 large red onions — chopped
4 cloves garlic — chopped
1 tbsp finely chopped fresh ginger
2 tbsps curry powder
2 tbsps vinegar
3 ripe tomatoes
2 fresh chillies
2 tbsps fresh mint leaves — chopped
1 tsp garam masala
1 tbsp fresh coriander leaves — chopped
Salt to taste

Serves 6 — 8

Method:

1. Cut the lamb into bite-sized cubes.
2. Heat the ghee in a saucepan and fry the onions, garlic and ginger until fragrant.
3. Add the curry powder and the vinegar, stirring thoroughly.
4. Add the lamb to the mixture and cook, stirring constantly.
5. Put in the tomatoes, chillies and mint.
6. Cover and cook over a low heat for about an hour or until the lamb is tender, stirring occasionally and adding a little hot water if necessary to prevent the meat from sticking to the pan.
7. Add the garam masala and coriander leaves for the last five minutes of the cooking time.

Mutton And Dhall Curry

Ingredients:

500 gms mutton — cubed
1 cup dhall — soaked
1 tsp garam masala
A small bunch coriander leaves
1 cup yoghurt
1 large onion — chopped
6 shallots 4 cloves garlic } Grind to a paste 1 tsp cummin
2 tsps chilli powder
½ tsp turmeric powder
4 tbsps oil
2 cups water

Serves 6 — 8

Method:

1. Marinate meat in yoghurt, ground spices, and salt for an hour.
2. Heat oil in a deep pan and fry onions till golden.
3. Add meat and fry briskly, browning meat well.
4. Add remaining marinade, garam masala, dhall and water.
5. Stir well, reduce heat and simmer till meat is tender and dhall is cooked.
6. Serve hot garnished with chopped coriander.

Liver Curry

Ingredients:

500 gms liver
2 onions — sliced
2 cloves garlic
4 cm piece ginger — sliced fine
2.5 cm piece stick cinnamon
½ tsp turmeric powder
½ tsp fenugreek
1 sprig curry leaves
10 dried chillies 1 dsp coriander seeds } Broil (no oil) in frying pan, then grind ½ tsp cummin
2 cups coconut milk — from 1 grated coconut
1 tbsp oil
Salt to taste

Serves 6 — 8

Method:

1. Wash and cut liver into thick slices. Put into a pan with coconut milk and all the ingredients except ghee.
2. Boil till liquid is almost absorbed.
3. Remove liver and fry in hot ghee till brown.
4. Add gravy and cook a little longer. Serve hot.

Spiced Mutton Chops

Ingredients:

500 gms mutton chops
3 onions — finely minced
3 tomatoes — chopped
200 gms peas
1 tsp garam masala
A small bunch coriander leaves — chopped
2 green chillies — chopped
½ tsp turmeric powder 1 tsp coriander powder 1 tsp cummin powder 3 cloves garlic — ground } Blend for marinade 2 cm piece ginger — ground 1 tsp chilli powder ½ cup yoghurt Salt to taste
4 tbsps oil

Serves 6 — 8

Method:

1. Marinate chops for 2 hours.
2. Heat oil in a pan and fry minced onions till golden.
3. Add tomatoes, chopped chillies, coriander, peas and garam masala, and fry for 2 minutes.
4. Add chops and fry briskly till brown, and oil separates.
5. Add water to cover chops and reduce heat. Simmer till meat is tender.
   Note: Chops can be pressure cooked for 20-25 minutes.

Shish Kebabs

Ingredients:

1 kg boneless lamb — cut into cubes
1 large capsicum — diced into 2.5 cm squares
4 cloves garlic — crushed
Juice of 1½ lemons
1 tsp ground black pepper
3 onions — halved
2 tsps salt
2 tbsps oil

Serves 6 — 8

Method:

1. Mix garlic, oil, lemon juice, salt and black pepper with meat, and leave to marinate in the refrigerator overnight.
2. Drain meat and mount on skewers, alternating meat, capsicum and onions.
3. Roast over a charcoal stove or grill in hot oven, brushing with marinade from time to time while cooking.

POULTRY

Chicken Tikka

Ingredients:

1 large chicken — deboned and cut into large pieces

For marinade:

4 cloves garlic — ground

2 cm piece ginger — ground

2.5 cm piece unripe peeled papaya — ground

1 red chilli — ground

1 tsp salt

½ cup curd

2 tbsps tomato sauce

Juice of ½ lime

1 tbsp oil

A pinch of nutmeg

For basting sauce:

4 cardamoms — seeds removed and ground

1 tsp ground black pepper

2 tbsps oil

Juice of ½ lime

Serves 6 — 8

Method:

1. Mix all the marinade ingredients and marinate chicken in it for 5 hours.
2. Skewer a few pieces of chicken on each skewer, and brown over a charcoal stove.
3. Keep basting the chicken with the marinade till all the mixture has been used up.
4. Finally, brush over with basting sauce. Serve piping hot.

Chicken Goulash

Ingredients:

1 medium-sized chicken — skinned and cut into large pieces

100 gms butter

125 gms cream

3 medium onions — finely sliced

4 cloves

½ bottle tomato sauce (more if required)

1 tsp chilli powder

Salt to taste

Serves 6 — 8

Method:

1. Heat butter in a large pan over low heat. Add cloves and onions and fry till transparent.
2. Add chicken and salt, and fry till golden and liquid has dried up.
3. Add tomato sauce and chilli powder — there should be enough sauce to coat chicken as well as for a thick gravy. Cook for five minutes.
4. Add cream and stir well. Cover the pan and simmer chicken over low heat till tender. Serve hot.

Chicken Pasandh

Ingredients:

3 chicken breasts — cut into 2 or 3 pieces each

½ cup ground coriander

4 tbsps ground cashewnuts

1 onion ⎱ Grind fine
6 cloves garlic ⎰

½ tbsp lime juice

5 tbsps yoghurt

2.5 cm piece ginger — crushed

2 sticks cinnamon ⎫
4 cloves ⎪
3 cardamoms ⎬ Grind fine
1 nutmeg ⎪
1 tbsp aniseed ⎭

½ tbsp chilli powder

1 cup oil

Salt to taste

Serves 6 — 8

Method:

1. Heat oil in a wok and fry onions, ginger, garlic, coriander and cashewnuts till fragrant.
2. Add all the remaining ground spices and chilli powder and lime juice and stir well for a few minutes.
3. Add chicken, mix well.
4. Add yoghurt and salt. Mix well.
5. Pour out chicken curry into a baking dish, and bake in a moderate oven for 1-1½ hours or until chicken is tender.

Chicken Masala

Ingredients:

1 medium-sized chicken — washed and cut into large pieces

5 large tomatoes — blanched and chopped roughly

10 shallots ⎫
2.5 cm piece ginger ⎪
1 pod garlic ⎪
1 cm piece turmeric ⎬ Grind to a paste and
1 tsp cummin ⎪ rub into chicken
4 cm piece cinnamon ⎪
4 cloves ⎪
3 cardamoms ⎭

Salt to taste

3 tbsps ghee

Serves 6 — 8

Method:

1. Heat a deep, heavy-bottomed pan, add the chicken and tomatoes, dot with the ghee.
2. Cover tightly and let it simmer till chicken is tender.
3. Fry for a few minutes till chicken is brown.
4. Serve garnished with chopped coriander leaves.

Chicken Tikka

Dry Chicken Curry

Ingredients:

1 large chicken
3 — 4 large onions — sliced fine
2.5 cm piece young ginger — sliced very fine
2 — 3 tbsps chilli powder
2 cm piece cinnamon stick
2 stalks spring onions — chopped
5 tbsps oil
Salt to taste
Juice of one lime

Serves 6 — 8

Method:

1. Heat the oil in a wok over high heat.
2. When oil is smoking, add the cinnamon stick, sliced ginger and half the onions, and fry till golden.
3. Add chicken pieces and salt and brown.
4. Add the chilli powder and fry over high heat, stirring gently. Cover and simmer over medium heat, until the liquid dries and the chicken is tender.
5. Add lime juice or one tablespoon vinegar, and the spring onions, and stir quickly before dishing out.

Pahari Chicken

Ingredients:

1 medium-sized chicken — skinned and cut into pieces
4 tbsps yoghurt — beaten with a fork till smooth and creamy
4 cardamoms
3 green chillies — finely chopped
3 green chillies
2.5 cm piece ginger } Grind to a paste
6 cloves garlic
1 tbsp coriander leaves — finely chopped
2 tbsps ghee
Salt to taste

Serves 6 — 8

Method:

1. Heat ghee, add chopped chillies and cardamoms and fry for 2 minutes.
2. Add ground paste and fry for another 2 minutes.
3. Add chicken and fry till golden.
4. Reduce heat. Add yoghurt, stir well and simmer on low heat till yoghurt is completely absorbed.
5. Add coriander leaves; remove from heat and serve hot.

Chicken Curry *(South Indian Style)*

Ingredients:

1 medium chicken — cleaned and cut into pieces
3 tomatoes — chopped
3 potatoes — quartered
2 large onions — chopped
2 cups thick coconut milk ⎞ From one
2 cups thin coconut milk ⎠ grated coconut
½ cups ground cashewnuts
(A)
2.5 cm piece stick cinnamon
2 cloves } Grind to a paste
3 cardamoms
6 black peppercorns
(B)
5 cm piece ginger } Grind
1 pod garlic
(C)
6 dried chillies
Small piece turmeric } Grind
2 tsps aniseed
1 cup oil
Salt to taste

Serves 6 — 8

Method:

1. Heat the oil in a heavy-bottomed pan and fry onions till golden.
2. Add tomatoes and fry for a few more minutes.
3. Add ground spices (A), and fry for a few minutes.
4. Add (B) and fry for 2 minutes.
5. Add (C) and fry well.
6. Add the chicken and fry, stirring well, till oil separates.
7. Pour in the thin coconut milk, and add the potatoes. Leave to simmer till chicken is tender.
8. Add thick coconut milk and ground cashewnuts. Season to taste and serve hot.

> *Chicken pieces for an Indian curry are cut smaller to allow for maximum penetration of the spices.*

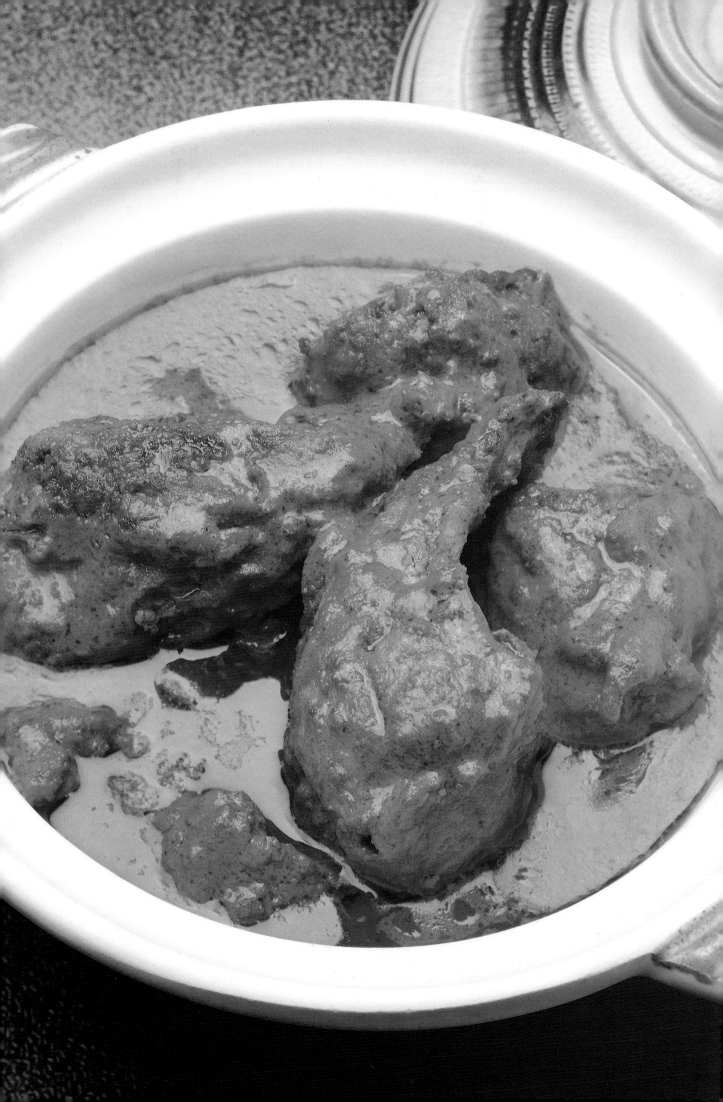

Chicken With Cummin

Ingredients:

1 medium chicken — cleaned and cut into pieces
1½ cups yoghurt
1 tsp ground black pepper
2 tsps whole cummin
2 large onions — sliced fine
2 cloves garlic — crushed
2.5 cm piece ginger — shredded
4 tbsps oil
Juice of 2 lemons
Rind of 1 lemon
½ cup flour

Serves 6 — 8

Method:

1. Rub lemon juice into chicken and leave aside for 30 minutes.
2. Drain chicken and rub with salt, pepper and flour.
3. Heat oil in a pan and fry the chicken pieces till golden. Remove from pan and keep aside.
4. Add onions, garlic, ginger and cummin to hot oil in pan and fry till brown.
5. Add the chicken pieces and lemon rind and stir well.
6. Add yoghurt and a little water, and stir well so that chicken is well coated with the gravy.
7. Reduce heat and simmer for an hour or until chicken is tender and gravy thick. Discard rind before serving.

Spiced Chicken

Ingredients:

1 medium chicken — cut into pieces
4 onions — sliced
2 cloves garlic — crushed
2 cm piece ginger — sliced
½ tsp black peppercorns — ground
½ tsp turmeric powder
3 green chillies — slit lengthwise and seeded
1 dsp vinegar
¼ cup tamarind juice
2 tbsps oil
Salt to taste

Serves 6 — 8

Method:

1. Heat oil in a deep pan and fry the onions till golden.
2. Add garlic and ginger and fry for 2 minutes.
3. Add chicken and stir well. Then cover pan and cook on low heat, stirring occasionally, for 30 minutes.
4. Add pepper, turmeric, chillies and tamarind juice. There should be enough liquid to just cover chicken.
5. Simmer until gravy is thick. Add vinegar, stir well, and serve hot.

Spicy Fried Chicken

Ingredients:

1.3 kg chicken — washed and jointed
2 cloves garlic — finely chopped
1 tsp salt
3 cm piece ginger — finely grated
1 tsp ground cinnamon
½ tsp ground nutmeg
½ tsp ground black pepper
1 tbsp ghee
2 tbsps oil
1 fresh green chilli — chopped
¾ cup cashew nuts — ground
2 hard-boiled eggs
2 tomatoes
½ cup green peas ⎫ Boiled Cauliflower sprigs ⎭

Serves 6 — 8

Method:

1. Mix garlic, salt, ginger and ground spices and rub all over the chicken joints. Set aside for 30 minutes.
2. Heat ghee and oil in a heavy pan and brown the chicken pieces.
3. Add ground cashew nuts and cook for 2 minutes.
4. Add ¼ cup water, cover and simmer over a low flame until chicken is cooked.
5. Lift out chicken pieces and put on a serving platter.
6. Put green peas and cauliflower sprigs in the pan and toss in the gravy.
7. Lift out and arrange with chicken pieces.
8. Garnish with hard-boiled eggs and serve with rice or parathas.

Dry Chicken Curry
(North Indian style)

Ingredients:

| 1 medium sized chicken — cut into large pieces |
| 2 large onions — sliced fine |

A:

1 tbsp coriander	
1 dsp cummin	
4 cloves	
2.5 cm piece cinnamon	**Grind to a paste**
4 cardamoms	
1 dsp khus khus	
1 tbsp black peppercorns	
3 red chillies	

B:

| 4 cloves garlic | Pound together and |
| 2.5 cm piece ginger | rub into chicken |

| Salt |
| ½ cup yoghurt |
| ½ cup coconut milk |
| 3 green chillies |
| 1 sprig curry leaves |
| 1 sprig coriander leaves — for garnishing |

Serves 6 — 8

Method:

1. Heat oil in a deep pan and fry onions until golden brown. Remove from pan.
2. Fry ground spices (A) over low heat, gradually adding yoghurt a little at a time until used up.
3. Add chicken, stir well till pieces are well coated with the spices.
4. Add coconut milk and curry leaves, and cook on high heat till the gravy dries.
5. Lower heat, add chillies and continue frying till oil separates and chicken is tender.
6. Serve garnished with coriander leaves.

Ginger juice helps boost a man's virility according to an old Indian belief.

Dry Fried Chicken

Ingredients:

| 1.5 kg chicken — jointed |
| 4 tbsps ghee |
| 3 large onions — sliced thinly |
| 2 tsps chilli powder |
| ¾ cup water |
| ¾ cup yoghurt |

Marinade:

| 2 cloves garlic — crushed |
| 3 cm piece ginger — grated |
| 1½ tsps garam masala |
| 2 tsps salt |
| 1½ tsps ground coriander |
| 1½ tsps ground cummin |
| 1 tsp ground turmeric |
| 2½ tbsps yoghurt |

Serves 6 — 8

Method:

1. Mix thoroughly together the marinade ingredients and rub well over the chicken pieces. Leave aside for 1 hour.
2. Heat ghee and fry the onions until golden. Remove from pan.
3. Using the same oil, fry the chicken pieces until golden brown on both sides.
4. Add the chilli powder, any remaining marinade and ¾ cup water.
5. Cover and simmer until tender.
6. Stir in the yoghurt, add fried onions and simmer for another 5 minutes.

Egg Curry

Ingredients:

6 eggs — hard-boiled and sliced in half	
2 onions — finely chopped	
3 cloves garlic — finely chopped	
2.5 cm piece ginger — shredded fine	
3 tsps ground coriander	
2 tsps ground turmeric	
1 tsp chilli powder	
4 tomatoes — diced	
½ cup hot water	
4 tbsps oil or ghee	
½ tsp garam masala	
Salt to taste	

Serves 6 — 8

Method:

1. Heat oil in a pan and fry the onions, garlic and ginger till soft and golden.
2. Add coriander, turmeric and chilli and fry for a minute.
3. Add tomatoes and season to taste. Stir over medium heat for 5 minutes.
4. Add hot water, cover and simmer till gravy thickens.
5. Stir in garam masala and the eggs.
7. Bring to the boil, then remove from heat.

Chicken With Yoghurt Curry

Ingredients:

1 medium chicken — cleaned and cut into pieces	
1 onion — chopped	
2 cloves garlic	
2 tsps chopped fresh ginger	
1 tsp garam masala	
¼ tsp chilli powder (more if required)	
A small bunch mint leaves	
1 tbsp ground turmeric	
¼ cup yoghurt	
1 cup chopped tomatoes	
2 tbsps oil	
Salt to taste	

Serves 6 — 8

Method:

1. Grind together the onions, garlic, ginger and mint leaves.
2. Heat oil in a deep pan and fry the pureed mixture, stirring all the time.
3. Add the turmeric, garam masala, salt and chilli powder, and cook for a few minutes.
4. Add yoghurt and tomatoes and cook until gravy thickens.
5. Add chicken and stir well till pieces are well coated with the gravy. Add a little water if gravy is too thick.
6. Cover pan and simmer until chicken is tender.

Duck Masala

Ingredients:

1½ kg duck — cleaned and cut into pieces	
1 large onion — sliced	
4 cardamoms	
1 small stick cinnamon	
2.5 cm piece ginger — shredded fine	
1 tsp turmeric powder	
½ tsp ground black pepper	
2 tsps ground coriander	
2 fresh red chillies — slit lengthwise	
2 tsps salt	
2 cups hot water	
2 tbsps vinegar	
5 potatoes — peeled and halved	
Half a cabbage — cut into wedges	
2 cups peas	
2 tbsps oil	

Serves 6 — 8

Method:

1. Heat oil in a large, heavy-bottomed pan, and fry cardamoms, cinnamon and onions till golden.
2. Add ginger, turmeric, pepper and coriander and fry for 2 minutes.
3. Add duck and cook till light brown.
4. Add chillies, salt, water and vinegar and stir well. Cover and simmer on low heat for 45 minutes or until duck is tender.
5. Skim off any excess fat, then add potatoes and cook until soft.
6. Add peas and adjust seasoning if necessary. Cook for a few more minutes then dish out.

> *Indian women grind dried turmeric into a paste with a little water, and rub it onto their face to keep their complexions clear and free of blemishes.*

VEGETABLES

Stuffed Brinjals

Ingredients:

4 round brinjals
1 large onion — chopped
100 gms ghee
100 gms green peas
100 gms carrots — diced
225 gms tomatoes
1 tsp finely chopped ginger
Salt and pepper to taste

Serves 4 — 6

Method:

1. Wash the brinjals and boil in salted water for 10 minutes until half-cooked.
2. Halve each brinjal and scoop out the pulp leaving 1 cm all the way around.
3. Season the brinjal cases with salt and pepper.
4. Heat ghee and fry the chopped onions lightly. Add the peas and diced carrots.
5. Chop the brinjal pulp and add to the frying pan. Add also tomatoes. Cook over low flame until vegetables are cooked.
6. Add salt and ginger. Fry for 2 minutes.
7. Fill brinjal cases with the cooked vegetables. Bake for 20 minutes until golden brown.

Prawn And Brinjal Curry

Ingredients:

500 gms brinjals
250 gms shrimps
1 cup thick coconut milk — from ½ grated coconut
2 tbsps curry powder (for fish)
3 onions — sliced
2 cloves garlic — chopped
Chilli powder to taste
Salt to taste
1 sprig curry leaves
½ tsp turmeric powder

Serves 6 — 8

Method:

1. Dice brinjals. Add salt and turmeric.
2. Heat oil in a wok and fry the brinjals till brown. Remove from wok.
3. Clean the shrimps. Add salt and a pinch of turmeric. Put into wok in which the brinjals are fried, and fry till brown and quite crisp. Remove from wok.
4. Add salt, curry powder, chilli powder and tamarind juice to coconut milk and mix well.
5. Heat a little oil in the wok, and fry onions, garlic and curry leaves till golden and fragrant.
6. Add fried brinjals and prawns.
7. Add the coconut milk mixture and allow to simmer till gravy thickens and oil comes to the top. Serve hot with rice.

Saag

Ingredients:

200 gms spinach or other greens
2 medium-sized turnips
1 tbsp ghee
½ tsp black mustard seeds
1 medium-sized red onion — finely chopped
1 tsp fresh ginger — grated
½ tsp chilli powder
½ tsp ground turmeric
½ tsp garam masala
Salt to taste

Serves 4 — 6

Method:

1. Wash the greens, removing any tough stalks.
2. Break the leaves into small pieces and put in a large pan with a sprinkling of water.
3. Scrape and dice the turnips and add to the pan.
4. Cover and cook over a low heat until the vegetables are soft.
5. Mash the vegetables gently.
6. In a frying pan, heat the ghee and fry the mustard seeds for a minute, then add the onion and ginger and fry until the onion is soft and golden brown.
7. Add the chilli, turmeric, salt and mashed vegetables.
8. Stir and cook for five minutes, then sprinkle with garam masala.
9. Cover and leave on the lowest possible heat until the liquid evaporates.
10. Add salt to taste and dash of lemon juice if desired.

A puree of leafy greens, it is served as an accompaniment to chapatis or rice and curry. A meal of chapatis and saag provides the mainstay of many a hefty, turbaned and bearded Sikh "jaga" or night-watchman, whose job it is to keep an eye on the building from his spartan-like bed of macrameed jute.

Stuffed Brinjals

Pakoras *(Vegetable Fritters)*

Ingredients:

¾ cup chick pea flour
¼ cup self-raising flour
1½ tsps crushed garlic
1 tsp garam masala
1 cup water
2 potatoes
1 brinjal
2 onions
1 head cauliflower
½ tsp chilli powder (optional)
Salt to taste
Oil for deep frying

Serves 4 — 6

Method:

1. Mix the flours with garlic, garam masala, salt, chilli powder and water.
2. Beat until smooth and light. Cover the bowl and set aside for 1 hour or longer.
3. Peel the potatoes and cut into very thin round slices. Soak in cool water.
4. Slice the brinjal thinly.
5. Peel the onions and cut in halves lengthways, then into thin slices.
6. Separate the cauliflower segments.
7. Heat oil in a frying pan. Dip individual pieces of vegetable in the batter, allow any excess to drip off, and fry, a few at a time.
8. Serve warm with a chutney.

Snake Gourd Kootu

Ingredients:

1 medium-sized snake gourd — remove skin and cut into pieces
½ cup dhall
3 green chillies — sliced
2 large onions — sliced
½ cup thick coconut milk
½ tsp mustard seeds
1 sprig curry leaves
2 cups water
2 tsps ghee

Serves 4 — 6

Method:

1. Boil dhall in 2 cups water till cooked.
2. Add the gourd and cook till almost tender. Remove from fire.
3. Heat 2 tsps ghee in a pan, add sliced onions, chillies and mustard seeds. Fry for 2 minutes.
4. Add boiled vegetable, coconut milk and salt to taste, stir well, simmer gently over low heat.
5. When the vegetable is cooked, remove from heat and add curry leaves.

Pakoras

Bhendi Bhaji

Ingredients:

250 gms ladies fingers
1 tbsp vegetable oil
½ tsp panch phora
½ tsp turmeric powder
½ tsp chilli powder
½ tsp garam masala
1 medium-sized red onion — chopped
Salt to taste

Serves 4 — 6

Method:

1. Wash the ladies' fingers, remove the stalks and slice into bite-sized pieces.
2. Heat the vegetable oil to a moderate temperature and fry the panch phora for a minute.
3. Add the onion and continue to fry until the onion turns golden.
4. Put in the turmeric powder, chilli powder, garam masala and salt.
5. Add the ladies' fingers, stir well, cover and cook until it is soft but not mushy.
6. Serve as a vegetable accompaniment to rice or chapati.

Samosas

Ingredients:

10 spring roll skins
3 tbsps oil
1 clove garlic — crushed
1 large onion — sliced finely
2 red chillies — sliced
3 potatoes — boiled and diced finely
150 gms green peas
1 tsp beef curry powder
1 spray fresh coriander leaves — chopped
1 tbsp lemon juice
½ tsp salt
Oil for deep frying

Serves 6 — 8

Method:

1. In a frying pan, heat the 3 tbsps of oil and fry the onion until soft but not brown.
2. Add the crushed garlic and fry further for about a minute.
3. Turn down the heat, add the curry powder and fry gently for another couple of minutes.
4. Add the potatoes and peas and stir for a few seconds before adding all the other ingredients.
5. Stir well and set aside in a dish to cool.
6. Cut each spring roll skin into approximately 8 cm squares.
7. Place a tbsp of filling in each square and fold into a triangle.
8. Seal with a little water and deep fry until golden and crisp.

Sagoo *(Spiced Yellow Pumpkin)*

Ingredients:

250 gms yellow pumpkin
1 tbsp oil
2 tbsps lentils
1 tsp black mustard seeds
5 curry leaves
1 tsp finely chopped garlic
2 tsps ground coriander
1 tsp ground cummin
½ tsp ground turmeric
3 tbsps freshly grated coconut
Salt to taste

Serves 4 — 6

Method:

1. Peel and seed the pumpkin and cut into pieces.
2. Heat the oil in a saucepan and gently fry the lentils, mustard seeds and curry leaves until the lentils are golden and the mustard seeds pop.
3. Add garlic and fry for another minute. Add the ground spices and stir well.
4. Put in the pumpkin and enough water to just cover the vegetable.
5. Add salt, cover the pan and simmer until the pumpkin is half-cooked.
6. Sprinkle in the coconut and cook until pumpkin is tender.
   Note: Desiccated coconut can be used if fresh coconut is not available.

Palak Ka Saag *(Spinach)*

Ingredients:

500 gms spinach — washed and chopped
2 large onions — sliced thinly
2 green chillies — seeded and chopped
4 cloves garlic — chopped
Salt to taste
2 tbsps oil

Serves 6 — 8

Method:

1. Heat all in a pan, and when hot add garlic and brown.
2. Add onions and fry till golden.
3. Add chopped chillies and fry for a minute.
4. Add spinach, mix well, then cover and cook over a low fire till dry.
5. Add salt, stir well and serve hot.

Potatoes And Spinach

Ingredients:

750 gms potatoes — scraped and quartered
250 gms spinach — chopped
1 tsp turmeric powder
1 tsp garam masala
2 cm piece ginger — shredded fine
½ tsp chilli powder
1 tbsp ghee
Salt to taste

Serves 6 — 8

Method:

1. Heat ghee in a pan and fry the ginger for a few minutes.
2. Add turmeric, chilli powder and salt and stir for a minute.
3. Add potatoes and fry briskly for a few minutes. Reduce heat, cover and simmer till potatoes are almost done (about 10-15 minutes).
4. Add the spinach and cook uncovered for 15 minutes.
5. Add the garam masala and stir well. Serve hot.

Vegetable And Prawn Curry

Ingredients:

500 gms small prawns — shelled
2 brinjals — cut into 6 pieces each
4 ladies fingers — cut into 4 cm lengths
2 onions — chopped
2 cloves garlic — crushed
2.5 cm piece ginger — chopped
1 tsp turmeric powder
1 tsp ground fennel
3 tbsps oil
Salt to taste
1 tsp chilli powder
1½ cups coconut milk — from ½ grated coconut

Serves 6 — 8 -

Method:

1. Heat oil in a saucepan and fry the onions till golden.
2. Add garlic, ginger and chillies and fry for a few minutes.
3. Stir in the coriander, chilli powder, fennel and turmeric and fry, stirring constantly, till oil separates.
4. Add brinjals and ladies' fingers, salt and coconut milk. Bring to the boil and reduce heat.
5. Add prawns and simmer till gravy thickens (about 15 minutes).

Chick Pea Curry

Ingredients:

2 cups dried chick peas
3 tbsps ghee
1 tsp cummin
1 large onion — chopped
2.5 cm piece ginger — chopped
1 tsp turmeric powder
½ tsp ground cummin
1 tsp ground coriander } Combine to a fine paste with 2 tbsps water
1 tsp garam masala
¼ tsp chilli powder
1 tbsp chopped coriander leaves

Serves 4 — 6

Method:

1. Boil chick peas in 6 cups water and salt. Reduce heat and simmer for 1 hour.
2. Heat ghee in a saucepan and fry cummin for 1 minute.
3. Add onion and ginger and fry until the onion is golden.
4. Add paste to the pan and stir-fry for 3 minutes.
5. Add chick peas and liquid and bring to boil.
6. Reduce heat, cover and simmer for 30 minutes or until chick peas are tender.
7. Sprinkle coriander leaves and serve.

Pumpkin Kootu

Ingredients:

300 gms pumpkin — skinned, washed and cubed
3 dried chillies — sliced
3 shallots — sliced
½ tsp mustard seeds
½ cup thick coconut milk) from ½ grated
1 cup thin coconut milk) coconut
1 tsp sugar
1 tsp ghee
Salt to taste

Serves 4 — 6

Method:

1. Heat ghee in a frying pan, add mustard seeds and shallots and fry for 2 minutes.
2. Add pumpkin, thin coconut milk and salt to taste. Simmer.
3. When pumpkin is cooked, add thick coconut milk. Stir well and simmer a little longer on low heat.
4. Add sugar and cook till gravy thickens.

Vegetable Stew

Ingredients:

4 large potatoes or 500 gms new potatoes (whole or halve the large potatoes)
3 carrots — scraped, washed and cut into 2 cm rounds
250 gms cabbage or cauliflower — use cabbage leaves whole
2 large onions — sliced into thick rings
2 stalks spring onions — chopped into 2 cm pieces
2 fresh red chillies — sliced into half and seeded
2 green chillies — left whole
2.5 cm piece fresh ginger — sliced finely
4 cloves garlic — chopped
2.5 cm piece cinnamon
4 cloves
1 tsp peppercorns
4 cardamoms
Bay leaves
Salt to taste

Serves 6 — 8

Method:

1. Heat oil in a deep, large pan. Toss in cinnamon, cloves, cardamom, peppercorns, and when crackling, put in the chopped garlic.
2. When garlic is brown, add carrots, potatoes and onions and fry for two minutes.
3. Add stock and water to cover vegetables, and simmer till vegetables are almost done.
4. Add beans, cabbage, spring onions and chillies, and pepper and salt to taste. Simmer till the vegetables are cooked but not too soft.
   Note: For brown stew, brown 1 heaping tablespoon flour, mix to a paste with water and add to stew. Simmer till gravy thickens. For white stew, mix flour to paste with milk. Add to stew when gravy thickens, add a lot of butter.

Carrot Halva

Ingredients:

600 gms carrots — peeled and grated finely
70 gms ghee
½ tsp ground cardamom
1½ cups sugar
1 cup hot water
1½ cups cream
6 tbsps dried milk powder
25 gms almond — blanched and slivered
Silver paper for garnishing

Serves 6 — 8

Method:

1. Heat ghee in a heavy saucepan and add grated carrots. Cook uncovered over a medium heat, stirring constantly.
2. Turn heat down to the minimum and allow the carrots to cook until soft and there is almost no more liquid.
3. Make syrup. Boil sugar and water until sugar dissolves.
4. Add syrup to carrots and stir in the cream and milk powder.
5. Cook, stirring constantly, until the mixture is thick enough to come away from the sides, in one lump.
6. Turn onto a greased dish and smooth the top.
7. Decorate with slivered almonds and silver paper.
8. Serve cut into small squares or diamond shapes.

Vermicelli Pudding

Ingredients:

10 cups milk
1 cup broken vermicelli
10 tbsps sugar
4 tbsps sultanas
½ cup almonds — blanched and slivered
4 drops rose essence
2 tbsps chopped pistachios

Serves 6 — 8

Method:

1. Bring milk to the boil, stirring constantly.
2. Add vermicelli and continue cooking until the vermicelli is soft.
3. Add sugar, sultanas and almonds.
4. Remove from fire, drop in the essence and spoon into individual dessert bowls.
5. Serve warm or chilled, decorated with chopped pistachios.

Khir *(Rice Pudding)*

Ingredients:

2½ pints milk
½ cup rice
1 cup sugar
20 almonds — blanched, skinned and thinly sliced
1 tsp rose essence
½ cup raisins — washed
6—7 cardamoms — skins removed and seeds crushed

Serves 4 — 6

Method:

1. Pour the milk into a large, heavy-bottomed aluminium pan and bring to the boil.
2. Add the well-washed rice, and cook over medium heat for an hour, stirring constantly to prevent the mixture from sticking to the bottom and sides of pan.
3. Add sugar, raisins, almonds and crushed cardamom, and continue cooking over slow heat for another 15 minutes. By this time the rice should be well-cooked and blended into the milk.
4. Add rose essence and serve hot or cold.

Suji Halva *(Semolina Pudding)*

Ingredients:

115 gms semolina
175 gms sugar
1½ — 2 tbsps milk
2½ tbsps ghee
2 tbsps raisins
2 tbsps thinly sliced almonds
7 cardamoms — skinned and seeds crushed
240 mls water

Serves 6 — 8

Method:

1. Mix the sugar, milk and water and boil for a few minutes; remove from heat.
2. Melt the ghee in a large saucepan, add the semolina and fry gently over low heat for about 10 minutes, stirring constantly.
3. When ghee begins to separate from the semolina, and the mixture turns a deep golden, pour in the syrup.
4. Add raisins and cook over medium heat stiring constantly till all the liquid is absorbed (about 10 — 15 minutes).
5. Pour mixture into a greased shallow pyrex dish and sprinkle with almonds and crushed cardamom.
6. Serve hot or cold.

Poppadums

The poppadum is a crisp form of bread made from chick-pea flour. The recipe has not been included for although they seem a simple dish they are very difficult to make. Very few people would venture to make them because temperature and humidity must be taken into consideration when rolling the dough and there is a technique even in frying them.

Poppadums are easily available in any grocery store or delicatessen and are imported from India. They are about eight centimetres in diameter. After frying they should double in size. When frying poppadums, it is essential that the oil is kept clean. Poppadums gather dust, so before frying tap each raw one to clean, then drop into the pan of hot oil. The poppadums should sizzle immediately if oil is at the correct temperature. Fry 2-3 poppadums at a time turning once so that each side is browned well. Do not let the oil get overheated as poppadums will begin to burn. After frying each poppadum, drain on kitchen paper and serve immediately. If not using immediately, store in air-tight containers. In humid weather, poppadums tend to become soggy. To get them crisp again just place under a grill for a few seconds, but make sure they do not get toasted.

Firni *(Rice Pudding)*

Ingredients:

6 cups milk

6 tbsps ground rice

6 tbsps sugar

1 tsp ground cinnamon

Few drops rose essence

4 tbsps blanched almonds — finely chopped

Serves 6 — 8

Method:

1. Mix a little milk with the ground rice into a smooth cream.
2. Bring the rest of the milk to boil with sugar. Stir constantly with a wooden spoon.
3. Remove from heat and add the ground rice mixture. Return to heat, stirring constantly until the mixture boils and thickens.
4. Boil, stirring, for another 3-5 minutes.
5. Remove from heat. Sprinkle in cardamom, rose essence and half the almonds.
6. Pour into individual dessert bowls and garnish with the remaining almonds and silver paper.
7. Chill before serving.

Rasgula

One of the best-known of Indian desserts, it may be made in batches and stored in the refrigerator for a fairly long time. However, be sure that the container is well-sealed as it tends to absorb the other smells in the fridge.

Ingredients:

1 litre milk

4 tbsps lemon juice — warmed

900 gms sugar

2 tsps rose water

½ a lemon — chopped

6 cloves

6 cardamoms

1 litre water

Serves 6 — 8

Method:

1. Pour the milk into a large-sized pan and bring almost to the boil.
2. Remove from heat and add the lemon juice.
3. Stir lightly and leave to stand for a few minutes until solid lumps have formed.
4. Strain the curds through a piece of muslin and squeeze until dry.
5. Knead the curds into walnut-sized balls and set aside on a sheet of greaseproof paper.
6. In a large saucepan, heat the sugar and water until the sugar dissolves.
7. Add the lemon, cloves, cardamom and rose water.
8. Bring the mixture to the boil and then simmer until a heavy syrup is obtained.
9. Allow to cool and add the balls to the syrup. Serve warm or at room temperature, 1-2 rasgulas to a serving.

Murukku

Ingredients:

1½ cups rice flour
4 tbsps chick pea flour
2½ tsps salt
2 tsps cummin seeds
1 tsp chilli powder
2 tbsps ghee
½ cup thick coconut milk — from ½ grated coconut
Oil for deep frying

Serves 6 — 8

Method:

1. Mix the rice and chick pea flour with all the other dry ingredients.
2. Rub the ghee evenly into the flour and then add in enough coconut milk to form a soft dough.
3. Heat oil and force the dough into the oil in circles using the special Murukku presser.
4. Fry a few at a time on medium heat until golden brown and crisp, lift out and drain on absorbent paper.
5. Serve warm or cool completely and store in an airtight container.
   Note: If Murukku presser is not available, use an icing bag with a star nozzle.

Shakapare

Ingredients:

2 cups wholemeal flour (or plain flour if preferred)
2 tbsps ghee
1½ cups water
1½ cups sugar
½ cup water
Oil for deep-frying

Serves 6 — 8

Method:

1. Rub ghee into flour, and knead into a stiff dough with a little water or milk.
2. Roll out the dough about 1.5 cm thick, and cut into 2 cm squares.
3. Deep-fry over low heat until light brown. Dish out and keep aside.
4. In a saucepan, boil the sugar with ½ cup water until it is thick and coats the sides of the pan.
5. Add the fried 'biscuits' and stir quickly till coated with sugar. Remove and cool.

Gulab Jamun

Ingredients:

1 litre fresh milk
300 gms sugar
15 gms flour
Pinch of soda bicarbonate
Ghee for frying
30 gms cottage cheese
1 tsp rose essence

Serves 6 — 8

Method:

1. Boil the milk over a slow fire, stirring constantly to prevent burning, until it thickens to a very heavy consistency.
2. Melt sugar in a pan and add enough water to make a thick syrup. Add essence.
3. Mix the other ingredients with the cooked milk to form a fine dough, adding a few drops of milk or water if necessary.
4. Make small round balls from the dough (marble size), and deep-fry in ghee.
5. Remove and soak in syrup. Serve hot or cold.

Rasmalai

Ingredients:

3 cups powdered milk
¾ cup vinegar mixed with ½ cup water
3 tbsps ground semolina
8 cups water
3 cups sugar
2 cardamoms — skinned and seeds ground
600 mls water
1 glass milk thickened with a little cornflour

Serves 6 — 8

Method:

1. Put milk into a bowl, add 600 mls water and blend well. Pour into pan and bring to the boil.
2. Add vinegar and stir till milk curdles.
3. Drain the mixture through a muslin bag and leave to drip for an hour or so to make sure the 'cheese' is fairly dry.
4. Add cardamom and rub to a smooth paste. Knead in ground semolina.
5. Make flat oval pieces about 5 cms long from the dough.
6. Mix sugar and water in a pan and bring to the boil. Add the 'cheese' pieces and cook for 30 minutes.
7. Add thickened milk and cook for a few minutes over low heat.
8. Remove to dish and sprinkled with chopped almonds and glace cherries.

Lassi *(Yoghurt Drink)*

Ingredients:

1 cup yoghurt
3 cups iced water
Salt and pepper to taste
Pinch of cummin — toasted and ground

Serves 4 — 6

Method:

1. Beat yoghurt until smooth and gradually stir in iced water.
2. Season with salt, pepper and a pinch of toasted ground cummin.

Sweet Lassi

Ingredients:

1 cup yoghurt
3 cups iced water
Sugar to taste

Serves 4 — 6

Method:

1. Beat yoghurt till smooth and gradually stir in iced water.
2. Sweeten to taste.

Jalebi

These deep-fried Indian sweetmeats of batter filled with syrup are a favourite at Deepavali the Hindu Festival of Lights which is the most celebrated and most well-known of Indian festivals in Malaysia.

Ingredients:

Batter:
2 cups plain flour
½ cup rice flour
7 gms fresh yeast ½ tsp dried yeast and ½ cup lukewarm water
½ tsp saffron strands
2 tbsps boiling water
1½ tbsps yoghurt
Vegetable oil for deep frying

Serves 6 — 8

Syrup:
3 cups tepid water
3 cups sugar
1 tbsp corn syrup
½ tsp rose essence
1½ tsps orange food colouring

Method:

1. Sift both flours into a large mixing bowl.
2. Add the fresh yeast. If using dry yeast, stir it in half a cup of lukewarm water and set aside for five to ten minutes to activate it.
3. Put the saffron strands in a cup and leave to soak for 10 minutes in boiling water.
4. Add the saffron strands in water to the flour.
5. Put in the dry yeast mixture. If using fresh yeast, add half a cup of lukewarm water to the flour to "thin out" the mixture.
6. Stir well until the mixture is smooth.
7. Add the yogurt and beat to a firm batter.
8. Set it aside for an hour.
9. Stir vigorously again before beginning to fry.
10. Heat the vegetable oil in a deep frying pan till a high temperature.
11. Using a funnel, pour in the batter making figures of eight.
12. Fry, turning occasionally until crisp and golden on both sides.
13. Lift out, drain for a few seconds, then soak jalebi in the syrup for a minute.
14. Remove the jalebi and place it on a plate to drain.

To make the syrup:

1. Heat the sugar and water over low heat and stir until the sugar dissolves.
2. Turn up the heat and leave the mixture to boil for several minutes until the syrup is fairly thick in consistency.
3. Remove from heat, add the rose essence and orange colouring and set aside until lukewarm.

Serving

Jalebis should be served as soon as possible after making as they don't remain crisp for very long.

Lassi

NYONYA

The Chinese have always excelled historically as travellers. Centuries before Marco Polo made his famous journey halfway across the world, Chinese traders, scholars and monks had voyaged as far west as Afghanistan and as far south as Sumatra. And when Melaka was established as one of the world's great trading centres in the fifteenth century, even more Chinese flocked to the city. Some of the Chinese traders decided to move there permanently and took Malay wives.

The descendants of these Sino-Malay marriages became known as Straits Chinese or **Peranakan** and their way of life, language, food, customs and dressing have become an amalgamation of Chinese and Malay and developed a style uniquely their own.

The basic essentials in Nyonya cooking are lemon grass (*serai*), galangal (*lengkuas*), coconut milk (*santan*), chillies and limes as well as palm sugar (*gula melaka*), glutinous rice flour and screwpine (*pandan*) leaves.

There are three variations of Nyonya cooking — Pulau Pinang, Melaka and Singapore. The Pulau Pinang style of Nyonya cooking has been influenced in part by Thailand because of its proximity to the country while the Melaka and Singapore styles are more Indonesian in influence.

ACCOMPANIMENTS

Poh Piah *(Spring Rolls)*

Ingredients:

24 sheets spring roll wrappers

150 gms prawns
150 gms chicken meat } Minced

150 gms yam bean — peeled and grated and boiled till tender

1 medium carrot — grated and cooked for 2 minutes

1 small cucumber — shredded

2 eggs — beaten, made into omelette and shredded

2 pieces beancurd — fried and shredded

6 stalks spring onions — shredded

20 lettuce leaves

4 cloves garlic — crushed

3 green chillies — sliced

3 tbsps sweet bean paste

3 tbsps oil

Salt, pepper and sugar to taste

Sauce:

2 cloves garlic
2 red chillies } Minced

1 tsp salt

1½ tsps sugar

½ cup vinegar

1½ tsps water

Serves 6 — 8

Method:

1. Prepare sauce. Mix all the ingredients together, stirring until sugar dissolves.
2. Prepare filling. Heat oil and fry minced chicken meat and prawns.
3. Add garlic and fry until meat changes colour. Add chillies and spring onions and cook for 2-3 minutes, stirring occasionally.
4. Add strained vegetables, sugar and bean paste. Cook for 5 minutes, then add shredded cucumber and bean curd.
5. Moisten the filling with sufficient water.
6. Spread a lettuce leaf on each spring roll wrapper and top with a spoonful of filling. Garnish with shredded omelette.
7. Roll up and wet the edges to stick them down.
8. You can serve the poh piah raw or deep fried. Serve with sauce.
   Note: If there are any Popiah skins left over, wrap in cling cellophane wrap and refrigerate.

Otak-Otak

(Spicy Fish Cakes in Banana Leaf)

Ingredients:

300 gms white fish flesh

300 gms fresh prawns — shelled and deveined

3 shallots — chopped finely

2 eggs — beaten lightly

3 cups thick coconut milk — extracted from 1 coconut

1 tbsp sugar

1 tsp salt

4 turmeric leaves — shredded

4 lime leaves — shredded

10 tbsps water
1 tsp salt } Stir until dissolved

40 pieces banana leaves — (17 cm × 9cm)

To pound together:

5 cm piece turmeric

2 tbsps chilli powder

5 fresh red chillies — deseeded

10 slices galangal

5 candlenuts

3 stalks lemon grass — sliced

2 cloves garlic

8 shallots

3 cm piece shrimp paste

Serves 6 — 8

Method:

1. Fillet the fish and cut finely. Mince together with prawns until fine. Add in salt and water and mix well.
2. Put in the chopped shallots, pounded ingredients and eggs and mix well.
3. Add the coconut milk, sugar, salt, turmeric and lime leaves. Mix well.
4. Spread the mixture on the banana leaves and wrap well. Secure ends with tooth picks.
5. Grill over a slow charcoal fire for about 15 minutes. Turn occasionally to cook thoroughly on all sides.
6. Serve either as an accompaniment to rice or by itself as a snack.

It is believed that the rhythm of the pounding of the pestle and mortar can tell whether the person is an experienced cook or not. This was the measure used by match makers in the old days.

Popiah

Pickled Onions

Ingredients:

1 kg white onions
3 cups malt vinegar
8 fresh red chillies
1 stalk young ginger root — sliced
10 cloves

Serves 6 — 8

Method:

1. Skin the onions and dry in the sun on a tray for 3 — 4 hours.
2. Boil the vinegar and allow to cool.
3. In a jar, put in 2 chillies, slices of ginger, 3 cloves and then the onions.
4. Repeat until the jar is full and no more ingredients are left. Use another jar if necessary.
5. Mix the cooled vinegar with 1 tbsp dry gin to every jar of pickles. Pour into jars. Shake well.
6. Seal the jars and store for 6 weeks before use.

Egg Sambal

(Hard-Boiled Eggs in a Thick Spicy Gravy)

Ingredients:

4 hard-boiled eggs — shelled
3 — 4 fresh red chillies — slit lengthwise
3 — 4 fresh green chillies — slit lengthwise
6 small red onions — sliced
4 cloves garlic — crushed
2 thin slices galangal or ginger
3 chillies — pounded fine
½ cup thick coconut milk from ½ grated coconut
6 tbsps oil
Salt and sugar to taste

Serves 4 — 6

Method:

1. Heat oil in a pan and fry the galangal, garlic and sliced onions until fragrant.
2. Add both the cut and pounded chillies and stir fry for 5 minutes.
3. Pour in coconut milk and simmer over a low flame until the gravy thickens a little.
4. Season to taste and add eggs, whole or cut in half. Cook for another 5 minutes.
5. Serve with plain boiled rice.

> *Sambals are highlights to the main dishes of a Nyonya meal.*

Stuffed Chilli

Ingredients:

20 red and green chillies

For filling:

10 tbsps dried prawns — pounded	
4 tbsps green papaya — grated, rubbed with salt and dried in the sun	
1 tbsp sugar	
¼ tsp salt	
5 tbsps oil	
2 candlenuts	} **Pounded together**
5 shallots	
Thumb-sized piece shrimp paste	

Serves 4 — 6

Method:

1. Slit the red and green chillies from the centre to the tip. Seed and soak in water for 30 minutes. Rinse well.
2. Heat oil in a pan and stir-fry the pounded ingredients until fragrant. Add the pounded prawns and fry for 5 minutes.
3. Turn off the heat and add sugar, salt and the grated papaya.
4. Stuff the chillies with the filling and serve immediately.

Lime Pickles

Ingredients:

600 gms large limes or lemons salted in a jar for 1 week
2 litres vinegar
½ cup peanuts — blanched and pounded
½ cup cashew nuts — ground
1½ cups corn oil
1 tbsp mustard seeds
3 sprigs curry leaves (optional)
Salt and sugar to taste

Serves 6 — 8

Method:

1. Put limes in a jar and cover with ½ of the vinegar. Keep aside for a week. Shake the jar occasionally so that the limes are well-soaked with vinegar.
2. Heat corn oil in a pan and fry the mustard seeds and ground peanuts. Lower the flame and fry until fragrant.
3. Pour in the remaining vinegar and stir well. Add salt, sugar and curry leaves. Turn off heat and leave aside to cool completely.
4. When the gravy has cooled, pour over the limes, close the jar tightly and allow the limes to soak in the mixture.
5. The pickles will be ready in a week.

Chicken or Prawn Croquettes

Ingredients:

200 gms prawn or chicken meat
100 gms carrot
6 French beans
100 gms small red onions
2 tbsps butter
5 tbsps plain flour
2 cups milk
2 cups bread crumbs
Salt to taste
½ tsp pepper
2 eggs
3 cups vegetable oil

Serves 6 — 8

Method:

1. If using prawn meat, slit down the back of each prawn and lift off the intestinal vein before washing in salt water. Dry the meat thoroughly on kitchen paper towels so that the meat will be crisp and not soggy after cooking.
2. Scrape the skin off the carrot and dice finely.
3. String the French beans and slice finely.
4. Peel the red onions and slice thinly.
5. Wash the spring onions, discard the white bulbous end and slice the green stalk very finely.
6. Stir the milk into the flour until smooth.
7. Heat a wok over a high flame for about ½ minute then turn the heat down to medium. Put in the butter.
8. When the butter has melted completely, add the sliced onions and stir-fry for 5 minutes until limp.
9. Add the carrots and stir-fry for another 5 minutes before adding in the meat. Stir-fry until the spring onions become limp.
10. Stir the batter once or twice to recombine the ingredients and pour into the wok. Keep stirring over a lower flame.
11. The sauce should be thick and cooked before you turn off the fire.
12. Add in the salt and pepper.
13. Put the white sauce mixture into a bowl and cool at room temperature. Put in the refrigerator for a few hours until cold.
14. When cold and stiff, make the croquette shapes.
15. Break the eggs into a deep plate and beat. Put the breadcrumbs on a large flat plate.
16. Scoop out 1 tablespoonful of the thickened sauce and form into a cylindrical shape. Drop into the breadcrumbs and roll into shape.
17. Lift out the croquette with a spoon and dip into the beaten egg. Make sure you do not spoil the shape.
18. The croquettes should be 5-6 cm long. They can be kept in the refrigerator for a few days.
19. Heat some oil for deep frying. When the oil is hot ease in one croquette at a time. (The oil should be very hot or the crust will bust and the sauce will ooze out.)
20. Turn the croquettes over with chopsticks.
21. Serve with mustard.

Acar Awak *(Mixed Vegetable Pickle)*

Ingredients:

2 kg cucumbers
200 gms long beans
200 gms French beans
2 carrots
300 gms cabbage
100 gms peanuts — roasted and pounded finely
30 dried chillies
300 gms brinjals
2 stalks lemon grass
4 cm piece galangal
4 cm piece turmeric
4 cm piece shrimp paste — toasted
6 candlenuts
Oil
3 tbsps sugar
½ tbsp salt
2 tbsps vinegar

Serves 6 — 8

Method:

1. Grind finely the onions, turmeric, shrimp paste, candlenuts, galangal, lemon grass and dried chillies.
2. Cut cucumber into 4 cm lengths. Soak in salt water for 30 minutes and then squeeze out the water.
3. Cut the rest of the vegetables the same size. Wash well and dry.
4. Heat 1 cup oil in a pan and fry the ground ingredients until fragrant, then add 3 tbsps sugar, salt, ½ tbsp salt and 2 tbsps vinegar.
5. Add in all the vegetables, mix well and mix in the groundnuts.
6. Let the vegetables cook for a few minutes then dish out.
7. Cool well before storing in air-tight jars.

> *Besides being used in cooking, fresh turmeric is also used as a medicine. It is pounded, mixed with salt fish and fried. It is then served with rice to a woman in confinement.*

RICE & NOODLES

Mee Siam *(Spicy Fried Vermicelli)*

Ingredients:

500 gms rice vermicelli — soaked until soft
500 gms beansprouts — tails removed and washed well
600 gms fresh prawns
2 pieces bean curd — sliced thinly and fried
2 tbsps tow cheong
10 dried red chillies
8 shallots
3 cloves garlic — } Ground together
2 large onions — sliced
4 hard boiled eggs — quartered
5 small limes — cut into 2
5 stalks chives
Salt to taste
2 tbsps oil

Serves 4 — 6

Method:

1. Heat oil in a deep pan and fry the ground ingredients until fragrant.
2. Add in the prawns and fry until cooked. Put in the sliced onions and stir.
3. Add in the tow cheong and mix well.
4. Add in the beansprouts and stir-fry but not until too limp.
5. Put in the chives and the fried bean curd.
6. Add in the vermicelli and stir well to mix. Season to taste with salt.
7. Dish out and serve immediately garnished with hard boiled eggs and lime.

Nasi Ulam

Ingredients:

1 grated coconut — dry-fried and pounded
12 shallots — finely sliced and fried until brown and crispy
10 cloves garlic — finely sliced and fried
1 turmeric leaf — finely shredded
1 tbsp lime leaves — finely shredded
600 gms fish — fried and flaked
600 gms small prawns — cleaned and fried in 1 tbsp oil
5 cups cooked rice
1 cucumber — diced
3 red and green chillies — sliced
1 bowl chicken stock
Salt to taste
Oil for frying

Serves 4 — 6

Method:

1. Mix the rice with all the ingredients, adding in a little at a time. Use the chicken stock to moisten the mixture to taste.
2. Serve with a sambal of your choice.

Birthday Mee

Ingredients:

600 gms yellow noodles — scalded and drained
300 gms streaky pork — cut into strips
300 gms prawns — shelled
300 gms beansprouts — tails removed and blanched
5 stalks Chinese chives (kucai) — cut into 3 cm lengths
600 gms pork bones — boiled with 4 litres water to get stock
2 shallots — chopped and fried
1 egg — beaten
Salt to taste
2 tbsps oil
4 cloves garlic — chopped
A little thick and thin soy sauce for seasoning

Serves 4 — 6

Method:

1. Heat oil in a pan and fry the garlic till golden. Add the pork and prawns and fry until cooked.
2. Dish out and keep aside.
3. Put the stock to boil and season to taste.
4. Grease a pan and put in the beaten egg. Swirl the pan around to make a thin omelette. Remove and shred it.
5. Divide the noodles into individual serving bowls. Put in some chives and beansprouts. Top with prawns and pork, a little shredded omelette and fried shallots.
6. Pour the boiling stock over the noodles and serve with sambal belacan.

Nasi Lemak Nyonya

(Rice cooked in Coconut Milk — Nyonya Style)

Ingredients:

1.2 kg rice — soaked overnight
1 cup thick coconut milk ⎫ Extracted from
2 cups thin coconut milk ⎭ 1 grated coconut
4 pieces screwpine leaves
Salt to taste

Serves 4 — 6

Method:

1. Put rice in rice cooker, stir in thin coconut milk and salt.
2. Boil until the rice is dry.
3. Place the screwpine leaves on top and leave the rice for another 30 minutes.
4. Stir rice with a fork, add in the thick coconut milk and stir lightly.
5. Leave rice to absorb the milk for another 20 minutes.
6. Serve hot with prawn sambal, fried peanuts, sliced cucumber and fried fish.

Mee Siam

Pot Laksa

Ingredients:

500 gms laksa noodles — scalded

2 large fried fish cakes

300 gms medium sized prawns — shelled and fried with salt

1 bunch daun kesum

100 gms oysters — boiled

200 gms beansprouts — scalded

1 cucumber — peeled and cut into 4 cm lengths

20 fresh chillies — pounded until fine

For Gravy:

5 candlenuts

100 gms galangal

5 stalks lemon grass

1 thumb length piece fresh turmeric

12 dried chillies

200 gms shallots

Thumb sized piece shrimp paste — toasted

2 cloves garlic

1 tsp peppercorns

20 gms dried prawns

1 tbsp coriander powder

1½ grated coconut

4 cups water

Salt to taste

8 tbsps oil

Serves 4 — 6

Method:

1. Scrape off the skin of the turmeric and galangal. Slice roughly.
2. Slice thinly the white hard part of the lemon grass.
3. Cut off the stalks of the dried chillies and slit down the length of each chilli to remove the seeds. Soak in hot water for 5 minutes. Drain and slice the chillies roughly.
4. Wash and drain the candlenuts.
5. Peel and slice the shallots. Peel the garlic.
6. Wash the dried prawns and soak in hot water for about 5 minutes. Drain.
7. Pound the dried prawns until fine and keep aside.
8. Pound the candlenuts, galangal, lemon grass, turmeric, shrimp paste and shallots until very fine. Keep aside.
9. Squeeze out 1 cup coconut milk. Keep aside. Squeeze out the milk from the rest of the coconut.
10. Heat a wok and add in 8 tbsps oil. Add in the pounded spices and dried prawns.
11. Stir fry until fragrant and add in the coriander powder. Continue frying for 30 seconds before adding in the thin coconut milk.

12. Boil for about 20 minutes. Then add the thick coconut milk and bring to the boil before turning off the heat. Keep aside.
13. To serve. Place some beansprouts in a bowl and top with the laksa noodles. Add oysters and pour the boiling gravy over. Garnish with fish cakes, shredded cucumber, shredded daun kesum and some pounded chilli.

Mah Mee Special

Ingredients:

180 gms streaky pork — boiled in 2 cups water for 20 minutes

¼ tbsp salt

300 gms small prawns — shelled and washed

2 cups water

1 tbsp pounded garlic

1 tbsp tow cheong — pounded

150 gms water convulvulus — cut into 2 cm lengths

500 gms bean sprouts

1 kg fresh yellow noodles — sliced in boiling water for 1 minute. Drain and set aside

½ tsp salt

1 tsp sugar

½ tsp pepper

4 tbsps oil

Garnishing:

1 cucumber — skinned and cut into 3 cm lengths

2 eggs — made into omelette and shredded

3 tbsps fried shallots

3 red chillies — seeded and shredded

1 bunch coriander leaves

Pepper

Serves 4 — 6

Method:

1. Cut pork into thin strips.
2. Pound prawn shells coarsely. Add in water and strain.
3. Heat oil and fry the pounded garlic until light brown and fragrant.
4. Add tow cheong, salt, pepper and sugar. Stir fry for 1 minute.
5. Pour in the prawn liquid, pork stock and bring to boil.
6. Add prawns and pork strips and cook for 1 minute.
7. Add the water convulvulus, bean sprouts and noodles to the boiled mixture. Cook over high heat for a minute, mixing all the ingredients well.
8. Garnish and serve.

Pot Laksa

Penang Laksa

Ingredients:

1 clove garlic	
1 tbsp shrimp paste	
35 dried chillies	Ground to a paste
3 cm piece turmeric	
10 stalks lemon grass	
500 gms shallots	

20 cups water

8 pieces asam gelugur

30 stalks daun kesum

2 stalks bunga kantan

6 tbsps sugar

2 tbsps salt

1 kg fish

2 kg coarse rice vermicelli

6 tbsps shrimp paste — mixed with ¾ cup water

For garnishing:

1 pineapple — sliced

3 cucumbers — thinly shredded

1 bunch mint leaves

250 gms large onions — diced

15 green chillies — sliced

12 red chillies — sliced

120 gms preserved leeks — sliced

Serves 4 — 6

Method:

1. Soak the tamarind in water. Squeeze and strain out the juice. Bring to the boil with ground paste and dried tamarind, daun kesum, bunga kantan, sugar and salt. Boil for 10 minutes.
2. Add the fish and allow gravy to simmer for 15 minutes until the fish is cooked. Remove to cool. Set aside and flake.
3. Let the gravy simmer for 1 hour.
4. Remove the daun kesum and bunga kantan. Return the flaked fish to the gravy and bring to boil.
5. To serve, place the rice vermicelli in individual bowls, put the garnishing on top and pour the gravy over.

> *Nasi Lemak was presented by a Nyonya mother-in-law to the mother of the bride 12 days after the marriage to acknowledge the fact that the bride was a virgin.*

Nasi Kunyit *(Turmeric Rice)*

Ingredients:

340 gms rice — washed and drained well

2 screwpine leaves — washed and tied into a knot

½ cup thick coconut milk	Extracted from
3½ cups thin coconut milk	½ grated coconut

100 gms fresh turmeric — pounded and juice extracted

1 stalk lemon grass — crushed

4 cm piece ginger — crushed

Salt to taste

Serves 4 — 6

Method:

1. Put rice in a pan together with salt, screwpine leaves, thin coconut milk, turmeric juice, crushed ginger and lemon grass. Bring to boil.
2. Cook rice over very low heat until it is completely dry.
3. Pour the thick coconut milk over the top of the cooked rice, cover the pot and cook for another 5 minutes until dry.
4. Remove the screwpine leaves, lemon grass and ginger.
5. Serve with a sambal of your choice.

Nyonya Fried Rice

Ingredients:

350 gms cooked rice

3 eggs — beaten

1 large onion — sliced

4 tbsps pounded dried shrimps

Shredded lettuce for garnishing

Salt to taste

5 tbsps oil

Serves 4 — 6

Method:

1. Heat oil in pan and fry beaten egg until cooked. Shred with ladle and push aside.
2. Fry sliced onion until limp. Lift out the egg and onion.
3. Fry the dried shrimps until fragrant.
4. Add all other ingredients except shredded lettuce and fry well for 3 minutes.
5. Serve garnished with shredded lettuce.

> *This is a wholesome breakfast dish especially if there is any rice left over from the previous night's meal.*

Nyonya Mee

Ingredients:

250 gms belly pork — skin removed and left whole
2 litres water
300 gms prawns — cleaned and washed
5 cloves garlic — crushed finely
3 tbsps soy bean paste — mashed
300 gms fresh yellow noodles
150 gms beansprouts — tails removed
6 tbsps oil
Salt to taste

Garnishing:

10 shallots — sliced finely and fried until golden
1 cucumber — skin removed and shredded very finely
2 eggs — made into thin omelette and shredded
2 red chillies — sliced

Serves 4 — 6

Method:

1. Boil belly pork in water for 10 minutes. Remove and set aside.
2. Dry-fry prawns in a pan until they turn pink. Boil in the pork stock using a sieve with handle for 3 minutes.
3. Fry garlic in hot oil until brown. Remove, leaving 1 tsp garlic in the pan.
4. Add mashed soy bean paste and fry for 2 minutes. Add pork and fry for another minute.
5. Pour in stock and bring to boil. Add noodles and beansprouts and cook for 5 minutes, stirring constantly.
6. Add prawns and season to taste. Add in water if necessary.
7. Garnish and serve with Sambal Belacan.

The Nyonyas distribute Nasi Kunyit (Yellow Glutinous Rice) with hard-boiled eggs dyed red to friends and relatives to celebrate a new baby's first month. This is adopted from the Malay custom.

Sweet Noodles with Hard-boiled Eggs

Ingredients:

3 litres water
300 gms sugar
2 lumps rock sugar
600 gms dry flat noodles
8 hard boiled eggs — dyed red

Serves 4 — 6

Method:

1. Boil both types of sugar in water until completely dissolved. Strain well.
2. Scald noodles and drain under running water.
3. To serve, put one egg in each individual bowl, add in noodles and top with sugar syrup.

This dish was served only at birthdays. One had to finish every drop if one was to grow older. Noodles signified longevity and sugar a sweet life.

Nasi Kunyit *(Yellow Glutinous Rice)*

Ingredients:

600 gms glutinous rice — washed and drained
1½ tbsps freshly ground turmeric
1 tbsp lemon juice
½ cup thick coconut milk } Extracted from
6 cups thin coconut milk } 1½ grated coconuts
Boiling water
1 banana leaf
4 screwpine leaves — washed and knotted

Serves 4 — 6

Method:

1. Add in ground turmeric, lemon juice and water to a level 7.5 cm above the rice. Leave to soak overnight. Drain off the water just before cooking.
2. Line the base of a steamer with banana leaf, pricking holes through the leaf where the steamer holes are to allow the steam through.
3. Place the rice on the banana leaf with the screwpine leaves. Steam for 20 minutes over rapidly boiling water.
4. Scoop the rice into a large bowl and pour in the thin coconut milk.
5. Stir, then cover and steam for another 10 minutes.
6. When rice is almost cooked, stir in the thick coconut milk.
7. Continue steaming until the rice is cooked.
8. Serve with chicken curry and a sambal of your choice.

Chilli Crabs

Ingredients:

1 kg crabs — remove top shell, clean and cut into 2	
1 stalk lemon grass	
10 shallots	
6 cloves garlic	
2 cm piece ginger	Ground together
2 cm piece turmeric	
3 cm piece galangal	
2 cm piece shrimp paste	
15 dried red chillies	
2 tbsps tamarind pulp — mixed with ½ cup water and strained	
Salt and sugar to taste	
½ cup oil	

Serves 4 — 6

Method:

1. Heat oil in a pan and fry the ground ingredients until fragrant.
2. Add in the tamarind juice and salt and sugar to taste.
3. Add in ½ cup water and bring to boil.
4. Add in the crabs and mix well with the ingredients. The gravy should be slightly dry.
5. Dish out and serve with rice.

Sour Fish Soup

Ingredients:

400 gms white fish flesh — cut into medium-sized pieces	
25 gms galangal	
3 stalks lemon grass	Crushed
6 fresh red chillies	
25 gms ginger	
2 galangal leaves	
2 lime leaves	Finely chopped
1 turmeric leaf	
10 gms mint leaves	
5 limes — juice extracted	
Salt and sugar to taste	

Serves 4 — 6

Method:

1. Put all the crushed ingredients into a pan and cover half the pan with water.
2. Bring to boil and simmer for 30 minutes.
3. Add in salt and sugar and also the lime juice. Add the fish and cut leaves. Cook on low heat for a few minutes.
4. Dish out and serve with plain boiled rice and Sambal Belacan.

Fried Salt Fish

Ingredients:

200 gms salt fish — sliced
2 cm piece ginger — sliced
3 shallots — sliced
3 cloves garlic — sliced
4 dried chillies — cut into 2
3 tbsps oil

Serves 4 — 6

Method:

1. Heat the oil and fry the salt fish slices until brown.
2. Remove and place on a steaming tray.
3. Using the same oil, fry the ginger, garlic, shallots and chillies until fragrant.
4. Remove from oil and pour over the salt fish.
5. Steam for 5 minutes and serve immediately.

Stuffed Cuttle Fish With Peanut Sauce

Ingredients:

24 pieces cuttle fish — washed and cleaned but left whole	
500 gms medium prawns — shelled and chopped	
Salt and sugar to taste	
1 sprig parsley — chopped	

Sauce:	
1 cup groundnuts — roasted and roughly pounded	
6 fresh chillies	
12 shallots	
1 stalk lemon grass	Ground together
2 cm piece ginger	
2 cloves garlic	
1 cup thick coconut milk	
2 tsps tamarind juice	
1 tbsp brown sugar	
3 tbsps oil	

Serves 6 — 8

Method:

1. Season the chopped prawns with salt and pepper. Mix in the chopped parsley.
2. Stuff this mixture into the cuttle fish and secure ends with tooth picks.
3. Heat oil in a pan and fry the ground ingredients and peanuts until fragrant.
4. Add coconut milk, tamarind juice and brown sugar.
5. Slowly add in the stuffed cuttle fish and boil until cooked.

Chilli Crabs

Beansprouts with Salt Fish

Ingredients:

350 gms beansprouts — tails removed
1 piece salted threadfin — fried and sliced
1 bunch chives
2 large onions — sliced
3 pips garlic — chopped
2 red chillies — sliced

Serves 4 — 6

Method:

1. Heat oil in a pan and fry garlic until brown.
2. Add chillies and onions and fry for 2 minutes.
3. Add beansprouts and chives and stir-fry until well mixed.
4. Add salt fish, mix well and remove from fire.

Pickled Fish

Ingredients:

1 kg fillets of fish — cut into 2
2 cm piece turmeric
¼ cup garlic
150 gms fresh ginger — sliced finely
2 tbsps sesame seeds
4 fresh red and green chillies — washed, sliced and dried in the sun
18 tbsps sugar
¼ cup vinegar
1 cup oil

Serves 6 — 8

Method:

1. Heat oil and fry the finely sliced ginger until brown. Remove from oil and drain well.
2. Fry the garlic, drain and keep aside.
3. Fry the turmeric until the oil turns yellow and then remove.
4. Strain the oil and cool.
5. In the same pan, roast the sesame seeds until brown and remove.
6. Heat oil and fry the fish until cooked.
7. Prepare the pickle. In a dry jar, sprinkle a layer of sesame seeds, ginger and garlic. Spread the fish slices on top. Add in a few tbsps of the oil and vinegar, followed by more sesame seeds, garlic, ginger and fish. Repeat until all the ingredients have been used. Cover tightly and store for a week.
8. Serve as an accompaniment to rice.

Penang Asam Fish

Ingredients:

1 medium-sized fish — sliced into 3 cm thickness
2 stalks bunga kantan (ginger flower) — cut into fine strips
20 shallots ⎫
10 red chillies ⎪
5 cloves garlic ⎪ Ground together
3 cm piece ginger ⎬
3 cm piece fresh turmeric ⎪
2 cm piece shrimp paste ⎭
7 candle nuts
1 tbsp tamarind pulp — mixed with 2 cups water and strained
Salt and sugar to taste
4 tbsps oil

Serves 4 — 6

Method:

1. Heat oil in a pan and fry ground ingredients until fragrant.
2. Add in the shredded kantan, tamarind water and salt. Bring to boil and add in sugar to taste.
3. Add the fish slices and simmer until the fish is cooked.

Fresh Water Prawns In Curry

Ingredients:

12 fresh water prawns
2 cups coconut milk from 1 grated coconut
10 dried chillies ⎫
1 tsp peppercorns ⎪
10 shallots ⎪
1 tsp coriander seeds ⎬ Ground together
1 tsp cummin ⎪
2 cm piece turmeric ⎪
4 cloves garlic ⎭
Salt to taste
¼ cup oil
Mint leaves for garnishing

Serves 4 — 6

Method:

1. Wash and clean the prawns, trim off the whiskers but leave the shells intact.
2. Heat oil in a pan and fry the ground ingredients until fragrant.
3. Add in the coconut milk and bring to the boil.
4. Add in the prawns, season to taste and simmer until dry.
5. Dish out and serve garnished with mint leaves.

Fish Head Curry

Ingredients:

1 fish head	
100 gms shallots	
6 cloves garlic	Ground together
2 cm piece turmeric	
1 bunch kesum leaves (sweet basil)	
2 cm piece shrimp paste	
10 dried chillies	Ground together
2 stalks lemon grass	
½ cup tamarind pulp — mixed with 1 bowl of water and strained	
2 tomatoes	
Salt to taste	
1 cup oil	

Serves 4 — 6

Method:

1. Heat oil in an earthen pot and fry all the ground ingredients for 10 minutes.
2. Pour the tamarind juice in.
3. Add in the fish head and salt and bring to the boil. Simmer.
4. Add in the tomatoes and kesum leaves. Bring to boil again and remove.

> *Food was traditionally cooked in earthen pots. The food is alleged to taste better as the natural juices of the food are sealed in.*

Cuttlefish With Vegetables

Ingredients:

1 turnip
100 gms streaky pork — sliced thinly
2 big carrots — cut into thin strips
100 gms cabbage — shredded
200 gms fresh cuttle fish — cleaned and cut into thin slices
2 large onions — sliced thinly
1 tbsp soy sauce
3 cloves garlic
3 tbsps oil

Serves 4 — 6

Method:

1. Heat oil in a pan and fry the garlic until brown and fragrant.
2. Add in soy sauce, pork, cuttle fish and vegetable.
3. Stir-fry to mix well. Add in salt and 1 tbsp water.
4. Cook until vegetables are soft.
5. Serve as an accompaniment to rice.

Sour Fish Curry

Ingredients:

400 gms red snapper — cut into thin slices
6 fresh red chillies — sliced
2 stalks lemon grass — finely sliced
½ bunga kantan (ginger flower) — sliced finely
12 dried chillies
2 cm piece shrimp paste — mixed with 2 tsps water
6 shallots — sliced
½ cup tamarind juice — extracted from walnut-sized ball of tamarind
4 tbsps oil
Salt and sugar to taste

Serves 4 — 6

Method:

1. Heat oil in a pan and fry the sliced shallots until transparent and fragrant.
2. Add 3 cups of water and bring to the boil. Add tamarind juice, salt and sugar. Continue boiling.
3. Add sliced chillies, lemon grass and shrimp paste.
4. When the curry begins to boil again, add the fish slices and sliced bunga kantan. Simmer for 5 minutes and remove from heat.

Tenggiri Pedas *(Hot Mackerel)*

Ingredients:

1 piece mackerel — cut into small pieces
16 red chillies
1 cup shallots
2 stalks lemon grass
2 slices galangal
1 cm piece shrimp paste
1½ cups tamarind juice
2 sprigs kesum leaves (sweet basil)
¼ cup oil
Salt to taste

Serves 4 — 6

Method:

1. Season the fish with salt.
2. Heat oil in an earthen pot and fry the ground ingredients until fragrant.
3. Add tamarind juice and kesum leaves. Bring to boil.
4. Lower the heat and simmer for 5 minutes.
5. Add the fish and cook until done.
6. Serve hot with plain boiled rice.

Pais Udang

(Spicy Prawns in Banana Leaves)

Ingredients:

450 gms large prawns — shelled and deveined	
1 tsp turmeric powder	
Salt and pepper to taste	Mixed together
1 tbsp lime juice	

⅔ cup thick coconut milk — extracted from ½ grated coconut

10 shallots	
4 cloves garlic	
4 candlenuts	Pounded together
1 slice galangal	
4 red chillies	

5 cm piece palm sugar (gula Melaka)

2 cm piece shrimp paste

A few pieces banana leaves, 8 cm × 5 cm — steamed until limp

Serves 4 — 6

Method:

1. Season the prawns in turmeric mixture and set aside for 15 minutes.
2. Mix the lime juice with the pounded ingredients, then add in the thick coconut milk and prawns. Mix well.
3. Divide the mixture equally and wrap in the banana leaves.
4. Grill slowly until done.
5. Serve in the wrappers.

Crispy Cuttlefish

Ingredients:

500 gms cuttle fish — cleaned and cut into 2

2 tbsps curry powder

8 shallots — ground finely

60 ml coconut milk — from ½ grated coconut

1 egg

½ tsp salt

4 tbsps cornflour

Oil for deep frying

Serves 4 — 6

Method:

1. Marinate cuttle fish with curry powder, onions, egg, salt and coconut milk for 1 hour.
2. Add in the cornflour and mix well.
3. Heat oil and deep fry the cuttle fish until brown and cooked.
4. Drain well and serve.

Sweet and Sour Cuttle Fish

Ingredients:

300 gms fresh cuttle fish

2 cloves garlic — minced

2 large onions — cut into wedges

1 cup pineapple wedges

2 fresh red chillies — sliced

2 tbsps oil

Sauce:

1 cup water

⅓ cup tomato sauce

3 tbsps sugar

1 tbsp vinegar

1 tbsp chilli sauce

2 tsps cornflour blended with 1 tbsp water

Salt to taste

Serves 4 — 6

Method:

1. Clean the cuttle fish, discarding the skin, ink sac and head. Wash well with salt. Score the outer surface with a criss-cross pattern and cut into bite-sized pieces.
2. Heat oil in a pan, add the cuttle fish and pineapple and stir until almost cooked.
3. Stir in the sauce ingredients and bring to boil. Lower the heat and simmer for 2 minutes.
4. Thicken with the cornflour mixture.
5. Serve garnished with the sliced chillies.

Pineapple Crabs

Ingredients:

1 kg crabs — remove the top shell and cut into 2

½ ripe pineapple

1 stalk lemon grass — crushed

45 cili padi

5 cups coconut milk — extracted from 750 gms grated coconut

5 red chillies	
10 shallots	Ground finely together
1 cm piece turmeric	

Salt to taste

Serves 4 — 6

Method:

1. Skin the pineapple and cut into ½ cm rounds and then into quarters.
2. Combine the crabs with all the other ingredients in a pot. Simmer over medium heat until it boils, stirring for 5 minutes.
3. Add in the cili padi, stir well and remove from heat.

Beef Rendang

Ingredients:

30 dried chillies	
120 gms shallots	
4 red chillies	Ground together
1 clove garlic	
2 cm piece ginger	

3 stalks lemon grass — sliced thinly

4 slices galangal	Ground
5 candlenuts	

1 tsp shrimp paste

1 tsp salt	
1 tbsp sugar	Mixed together
1 tbsp soy sauce	

1 kg rump steak

1 stalk lemon grass

120 gms grated coconut — fried and pounded

2 tbsps curry powder — blended with 2 tbsps water

½ cup thick coconut milk — extracted from ½ grated coconut

8 tbsps oil

Serves 6 — 8

Method:

1. Heat oil and fry ground ingredients and curry powder until fragrant.
2. Add in half of the coconut milk and fry until the oil separates.
3. Add in the soy sauce mixture and steak. Add in also the fried grated coconut and lemon grass. Stir-fry for 10 minutes.
4. Pour in the rest of the coconut milk and simmer until the meat is tender, for about 1 hour.
5. Increase heat to reduce gravy until it is thick and oily.

A bad sore throat can be relieved by drinking tamarind juice mixed with some rock sugar. The juice must first be exposed to the morning dew.

Loh Bah *(Meat Rolls)*

Ingredients:

500 gms lean pork — cut into strips

½ small yam bean — chopped

3 big onions — chopped coarsely

2 eggs

4 tbsps flour

2 tbsps sugar

1 — 2 bean curd sheets

2 pieces bean curd — fried and cut into cubes

1 cucumber — sliced for garnishing

Dash of pepper

Salt to taste

Oil for deep frying

Serves 4 — 6

Method:

1. Sprinkle the bean curd sheets with a little water to soften and then cut into 8 pieces.
2. Mix the pork, onions, yam bean, flour, salt, pepper, eggs and sugar together.
3. Spoon out the mixture onto the bean curd sheets and roll up.
4. Deep fry the rolls in hot oil until dark brown. Drain and slice.
5. Serve together with bean curd cakes, cucumber and chilli sauce.

Pork Fat in Soy Bean Paste and Chillies

Ingredients:

600 gms pork fat — cubed, fried and drained

12 — 15 fresh green chillies

2 — 3 tbsps soy bean paste

1 shallot — sliced

3 — 5 cloves garlic — crushed

200 gms prawns — washed and shelled

2 tbsps oil

A little water

Sugar to taste

Serves 4 — 6

Method:

1. Heat oil in a deep pan and fry the onions and garlic until fragrant.
2. Add in the soy bean paste and stir-fry before putting in the pork fat.
3. Add in the prawns and stir-fry.
4. Add in the green chillies and simmer with a little water. Add sugar to taste and dish out.

Beef Rendang

Beef With Bittergourd

Ingredients:

1 bitter gourd — remove seeds and slice
250 gms beef — sliced thinly
3—4 chillies — cut lengthwise
2 cloves garlic — crushed
3 tbsps oil
Salt to taste

Serves 4 — 6

Method:

1. Heat oil and fry garlic until fragrant. Add in the slices of beef and fry over a low heat until the beef is cooked.
2. Add in the bittergourd and stir-fry.
3. Season to taste and sprinkle a little water to cook the vegetable.
4. Dish out and serve garnished with chillies.

Kidney Soup

Ingredients:

2 kidneys
150 gms minced pork
150 gms pork liver — sliced
7 cloves garlic — pounded
3 cm piece ginger — shredded finely
2 stalks spring onion — cut into 2 cm lengths
2 stalks Chinese celery — cut into 2 cm lengths
2 tbsps soy bean paste — pounded
700 ml water
2 tbsps oil
1 tbsp brandy

Serves 4 — 6

Method:

1. Prepare kidneys. Force running water through kidneys and cut in half lengthwise. Remove and discard centre membrane, slit the outside surface and cut each half into 4. Soak in water for 15 minutes. Discard water and pour boiling water over the kidneys. Soak for another 10 minutes and rinse thoroughly. Add brandy and knead for 5 minutes and then drain.
2. Heat oil and stir-fry garlic until fragrant and golden brown. Remove.
3. Stir fry ginger and soy bean paste. Sprinkle a little water and stir-fry minced pork until cooked.
4. Add water and salt and bring to boil.
5. Add liver and bring to boil again.
6. To serve, place kidneys in a serving bowl, pour in boiling soup and garnish with spring onions, celery and fried garlic.

Bawan Kepeting *(Meatball Soup)*

Ingredients:

350 gms minced pork
350 gms minced fish flesh — from 600 gms fresh fish
200 gms crab meat
75 gms cooked bamboo shoots — finely shredded
6 cloves garlic — fried until golden brown
1 egg
1 tsp thin soy sauce
3 tbsps oil
Salt to taste

Soup:

350 gms cooked bamboo shoots — shredded
1½ litres water
½ tsp sugar
2 tsps salt

Serves 4 — 6

Method:

1. Prepare the soup. Heat oil and stir-fry bamboo shoots for 2 minutes. Remove and set aside.
2. Add water, sugar and salt.
3. Prepare meatballs. Mix the pork and fish together. Add salt, soy sauce, fried garlic, bamboo shoots, egg and crab meat.
4. Mix well and shape into balls. Drop into boiling soup.
5. Add bamboo shoots to soup, simmer for 10 minutes and serve immediately.

> *This is traditionally served at weddings. Just like the Chinese, the Nyonyas too had the tea serving ceremony. The bride served the tea to the groom's family and if they accepted the tea, it meant that they accepted her.*

Chicken Curry

Ingredients:

1 large chicken
600 gms potatoes — peeled
8 tbsps curry powder (for meat and poultry — see glossary) — blended with 8 tbsps water
3 cups water
1 cup thick coconut milk — extracted from ½ grated coconut
3 cups thin coconut milk
7 cloves garlic
10 shallots
1 cm piece ginger
Salt to taste
5 tbsps oil

Serves 6 — 8

Method:

1. Cut the chicken into 20 pieces, leaving the feet and neck aside.
2. Pound the ginger, 6 cloves of garlic and 5 shallots until fine.
3. Mix half of the curry paste with the pounded ingredients and rub all over the chicken pieces. Leave aside for 30 minutes.
4. Slice the remaining garlic and shallots.
5. Heat oil and stir-fry the curry paste until fragrant.
6. Add in the chicken pieces and stir constantly for 10 minutes.
7. Add in the coconut milk and bring to boil. Season to taste with salt.
8. Lower the heat, cover the pot and continue cooking for 30 minutes.
9. Add the potatoes and the thick coconut milk. Boil for another 30 minutes or until the chicken is tender and the potatoes done.

> *Coriander was used in early Hindu medicine to treat constipation and insomnia, and also to aid child-bearing. Large amounts of coriander are not recommended as it has a narcotic effect. To relieve flatulence, drink a concoction of coriander seeds infused in hot water and lemon juice before a meal.*

Chicken Tempra

Ingredients:

1 chicken — cut into small pieces
4 shallots — sliced thinly
4 red chillies — sliced
4 tbsps lime juice
2 tbsps sugar
4 tbsps thick soy sauce
6 tbsps oil
Salt to taste

Serves 6 — 8

Method:

1. Heat oil in a pan and fry the shallots until brown.
2. Add in the chillies immediately, followed by the chicken.
3. When the chicken is half-cooked, add in sugar.
4. Lower the heat and add the thick soy sauce, lime juice and salt.
5. Simmer for 2 minutes.
6. Serve immediately.

Grilled Chicken

Ingredients:

1.6 kg chicken drumstick — cut into halves
1 tsp ground coriander seeds
½ tsp aniseeds — ground
½ tsp cummin seeds — ground
1 tsp turmeric powder
2 tbsps chopped onions
½ cup thick coconut milk
3 tbsps oil
Salt to taste

Serves 6 — 8

Method:

1. Heat oil in a pan and fry the chopped onions until golden brown. Add in the ground spices.
2. Fry until fragrant, put in the chicken, stir well, and add enough water to cook it. Put in salt to taste.
3. Cook over a medium flame until the gravy has dried then add the coconut milk. Bring to boil.
4. When the chicken is tender, remove it from the pan and grill till brown.

Chicken Curry

Chicken Pongteh *(Stewed Chicken)*

Ingredients:

1 chicken — cut into bite-sized pieces
2 medium potatoes — cut into wedges
10 small red onions
4 pips garlic
2 tbsps preserved soy bean paste
½ cup cooking oil
2 cups hot water
1 tbsp sugar
2 tsps thick soy sauce
Salt to taste

Serves 6 — 8

Method:

1. Pound onions and garlic until fine, add in soya-bean paste and mash well.
2. Fry potato wedges in hot oil until lightly browned. Drain and leave about ¼ cup oil in pan.
3. Add in the pounded paste and stir-fry until fragrant. Add in chicken pieces and stir-fry for another 5 minutes.
4. Add in 2 cups water, sugar and thick soy sauce and bring to boil. Lower the flame and continue to cook until chicken is tender.
5. Stir in potatoes and add in salt to taste.

Chicken With Red Sauce

Ingredients:

1 chicken
25 red chillies
1½ cups coconut milk — extracted from ½ grated coconut
Thumb-sized piece shrimp paste — roasted
1 tsp tamarind
Salt and sugar to taste
½ cup oil

Serves 6 — 8

Method:

1. Clean the chicken and cut into 4. Rub salt all over and grill until brown and cooked.
2. Boil the red chillies. Remove seeds and pound chillies into a paste. Add in the shrimp paste and tamarind and pound together.
3. Heat oil in a pan. Put in the pounded ingredients, salt and coconut milk. Simmer until the gravy thickens.
4. Add in sugar to taste.
5. To serve, pour the sauce over the grilled chicken.

Enche Kebin

Ingredients:

1 tsp pepper	
4 tsps thin soy sauce	
2 tbsps ginger juice	To marinate chicken
1 tbsp curry powder	
1 tbsp evaporated milk	
1 chicken — cut into bite sized pieces	
2 tbsps sugar	
Oil for deep frying	
1 cucumber	Sliced for garnishing
2 tomatoes	

Serves 6 — 8

Method:

1. Marinate the chicken for 1 hour. Dry thoroughly in the sun.
2. Heat oil and deep fry the chicken for 2 minutes.
3. Lower the heat and fry to golden brown.
4. Garnish and serve hot.

Cekor Ayam

Ingredients:

400 gms chicken meat
25 gms cekor root
50 gms small red onions
25 gms fresh ginger
Salt and sugar to taste

Serves 6 — 8

Method:

1. Cut the chicken into 2 cm cubes.
2. Grind finely the cekor root, small onions and ginger.
3. Heat oil in a wok and fry the ground ingredients until fragrant.
4. Add in the chicken meat and enough water to cook it. Simmer until dry and add salt to taste. Mix well and serve hot with rice.

> *Cekor root is a small fragrant white ginger. It is used only in nyonya cooking. The leaves, which are just as fragrant, are used in certain Nyonya dishes. The Malays use the root as a herb for a new-born baby during the first 44 days of its life, which is also the confinement period for the mother. The root is mixed with some other herbs, wrapped in a cloth, heated and used to warm the baby's body after his morning bath. This is supposed to prevent wind or colic.*

Fried Chicken, Nyonya Style

Ingredients:

1 chicken — cut into 14 serving pieces (the legs and neck are to be used for stock)
1 tbsp coriander seeds
4 candlenuts
1 fresh red chilli
3 cm piece galangal
2 cm piece fresh turmeric or ½ tsp powdered turmeric
½ cup shallots
4 bay leaves
1 stalk lemon grass
¼ grated coconut
3 tbsps tamarind pulp mixed with 1½ litres water
1 tsp salt
1 tsp sugar
3 cups oil

Serves 6 — 8

Method:

1. Pound the coriander seeds, galangal, chilli, turmeric, candlenuts in that order until finely mashed. Add in the onions bit by bit but the onions need not be too fine.
2. Squeeze out the tamarind juice, strain and keep aside.
3. Clean and crush the lemon grass and add to the tamarind juice together with bay leaves, the pounded ingredients, chicken pieces, salt and sugar to taste.
4. Bring to boil in a pot and simmer for 45 minutes or until the chicken is tender.
5. Add the grated coconut and bring to boil again. Allow to cool before storing in the refrigerator overnight.
6. The next day, 2 hours before serving, take out chicken from the refrigerator and bring to boil again.
7. Drain the gravy from the grated coconut, taking care not to have the coconut clinging on to the meat. Drain till dry.
8. Drain the gravy from the grated coconut over a sieve and press down hard with the back of a spoon to remove all liquid. Let the grated coconut dry too.
9. Heat oil in a pan and fry the chicken pieces one by one. Turn the chicken pieces occasionally until they are golden brown. Drain.
10. Lower the flame and add in the grated coconut and stir-fry constantly for 5 minutes until golden brown. Sprinkle over chicken and serve.

Ayam Sioh

Ingredients:

1 large chicken — cut into 4
10 shallots — pounded finely
1 tsp pepper
2 tbsps thick soy sauce
1 tbsp salt
10 tbsps sugar
3 tbsps coriander powder — roasted
250 gms tamarind — mixed with 1 cup water and strained
2 tbsps salt dissolved in water

Serves 6 — 8

Method:

1. Combine coriander powder, sugar, salt, soy sauce, pepper and shallots with the tamarind juice and stir well.
2. Wash the chicken in the salt water. Drain and add to the mixture. Cover and leave overnight.
3. Boil the chicken in the marinade for 20 minutes over moderate heat.
4. Turn the chicken over, reduce heat and boil for another 20 minutes.
5. Remove and serve.

Variation:

1. Heat enough oil for deep frying in pan and fry the chicken until brown on both sides.
2. Pour tamarind juice over the chicken and fry until fragrant and almost dry.

This traditional Nyonya recipe was a favourite at Chinese New Year. All the shops and markets were closed, and this dish could be prepared in advance and kept unrefrigerated for a few days because the tamarind prevented it from going bad.

Lemon grass (serai) resembles a spring onion and is commonly grown in the back gardens of most Malaysian homes. It is either pounded with other ingredients or used whole. If used whole, crush it first before putting in the pot. If it is to be pounded, use only the white tender portion as the rest is fibrous. Substitute with lemon peel.

Shredded Chicken with Pandan Leaves

Ingredients:

3 chicken drumsticks — shredded
3 screwpine leaves (pandan)
1 large piece ginger
½ tsp coriander seeds — ground
½ tsp aniseeds — ground
½ tsp sugar
1 tsp salt
1 tsp ground pepper
2 tbsps thick coconut milk
3 tbsps oil

Serves 4 — 6

Method:

1. Grind or pound the ginger and extract the juice.
2. Season chicken with ginger juice, ground coriander, aniseed, salt, sugar and pepper for half an hour.
3. In a pan, heat the oil and fry the screwpine leaves until fragrant.
4. Add in the seasoned chicken and cook until it is tender.
5. Add in the thick coconut milk and stir-fry till gravy thickens.
6. Serve hot with plain boiled rice.

Ark Siew *(Coriander Duck)*

Ingredients:

1 duck	
3½ tbsps coriander — dry fried and finely gound	
3 tbsps sugar	
½ cup tamarind juice	
6 shallots	Pounded together
1 tbsp black peppercorns	finely
Salt to taste	
Oil for deep frying	

Serves 4 — 6

Method:

1. Clean the duck, rub salt all over and cut into big pieces.
2. Heat oil and fry the duck pieces until brown on both sides.
3. Remove the duck from the oil and drain. Place in a pot.
4. Mix the ingredients thoroughly and pour over the duck.
5. Cook over low heat until the gravy is almost dry and the duck is cooked through.

Ayam Buah Keluak

Ingredients:

1 chicken — cut into 16 pieces
20 buah keluak — soaked overnight and scrubbed with a brush
50 gms minced pork
4 tbsps tamarind — soaked in 1 litre water and strained
20 gms galangal
4 cm piece fresh turmeric
6 candlenuts — washed well
30 shallots — pounded
10 fresh red chillies — sliced
20 gms shrimp paste
1 stalk lemon grass — bruised
2 tbsps sugar
1 tsp salt

Serves 6 — 8

Method:

1. Chip off the smooth part of the buah keluak at the thicker end of the nut with a pestle and mortar. Using a fork, dig out the whole of the black pulpy nut. Put aside the empty shell but discard if it smells rotten.
2. Pound the nut pulp until it is all mashed up.
3. Add in the minced pork, 2 tsps sugar and ¼ tsp salt. Pound again until well mixed.
4. Fill the shells with the buah keluak mixture and keep aside.
5. Pound the candlenuts, galangal, turmeric, chillies, shrimp paste in that order. Add in the shallots and pound to bind the ingredients.
6. Heat oil in a wok and fry the pounded ingredients until fragrant.
7. Stir-fry for 2-4 minutes until the spices are cooked.
8. Add in the tamarind juice, chicken, buah keluak and lemon grass. Season to taste.
9. Bring to boil and simmer for 30 minutes until the chicken is tender.
10. Serve with plain boiled rice.

> *The tamarind fruit is believed to be able to get rid of the yellow discolouration on the teeth. First, the fruit is fried without oil until crispy, then pounded finely and brushed on the teeth.*

SWEETS

Kuih Lapis *(Steamed Layer Pudding)*

Ingredients:

750 gms grated coconut
600 mls water
360 gms wet rice flour
250 gms sago flour
½ tsp salt
500 gms granulated sugar
300 mls water
8 screwpine leaves
Food colouring

Serves 6 — 8

Method:

1. Squeeze out the coconut milk with 600 mls water (See glossary). Add water to the coconut milk, bringing it to 900 mls.
2. Mix the rice flour, sago flour and salt in a bowl. Add in coconut milk, a little at a time and blend in until smooth.
3. Boil the sugar with the water and screwpine leaves for 10 minutes. Strain the syrup and add hot water if necessary to bring it to 450 mls.
4. Pour the syrup into the flour mixture, stirring all the time until it is well blended.
5. Divide the mixture into 4 portions. Set aside one portion to remain uncoloured and drop a few drops of different food colouring to the other portions. Set aside ¾ cup of the uncoloured mixture to be coloured dark red for the top layer.
6. Grease an 18 cm diameter, 5 cm deep round cake tin. Place the tin in a steamer of rapidly boiling water.
7. Pour ½ cup of a coloured mixture into the tin, and steam for 5 minutes until set. Pour over ½ cup of the uncoloured portion and steam until set. Do the same for the third and fourth portions, using ½ cup of batter and steaming till set each time. Keep alternating the colours until all the mixture has been used up.
8. For the final uppermost layer, use the dark red mixture. Remove from steamer and leave cake to cool for at least 7-8 hours.

Coconut water is usually thrown away but the water of a young coconut has medicinal properties. A child down with measles is given a drink of this water so that the spots will emerge quicker and the child will recover faster.

Pulut Kukus

Ingredients:

For the dough:

2 cups glutinous rice flour
1 cup coconut milk — from ½ grated coconut
A few drops of green food colouring
A pinch of salt

For the filling

1 cup grated coconut
½ cup palm sugar syrup (Dissolve ½ cup brown sugar)
8 cm rounds of greased banana leaves or greased steaming tray

Serves 6 — 8

Method:

1. Mix together all the indredients for the filling and cook until dry.
2. Combine the glutinous flour, salt, coconut milk and food colouring thoroughly into a soft dough. Knead well.
3. Divide the dough into 5 cm diameter balls.
4. Flatten each ball and put some filling into the centre. Seal and roll back into a ball.
5. Flatten slightly and shape into a heart and place on a greased banana leaf.
6. Make designs on the cakes using a fork or sharp object. Steam until cooked for about 45 minutes.

Jemput Jemput Pisang
(Golden Banana Croquettes)

Ingredients:

360 gms self-raising flour
120 gms grated coconut
10 — 12 bananas
4 eggs
250 gms sugar
½ tsp salt
2 cups thick coconut milk — extracted from ½ grated coconut
Oil for deep frying

Serves 6 — 8

Method:

1. Beat eggs and sugar until thick and creamy. Put in salt.
2. Stir in flour gradually.
3. Add in the coconut, mashed bananas and coconut milk. Mix very lightly.
4. Heat oil and when it is hot, drop a few spoonsful of the batter and fry until golden brown. Turn over only when one side has browned.

Pulut Tai-Tai

Ingredients:

350 gms glutinous rice	
1 cup thick coconut milk	Extracted from ½
2 cups thin coconut milk	grated coconut
30 clitoria flowers (bunga telang) — wash and pound and extract the juice	
Few drops blue colouring — to add to the clitoria juice if the colour is not deep enough	
¼ tsp salt	
2 screwpine leaves	
Banana leaves	

Serves 6 — 8

Method:

1. Wash and soak the rice for 3 hours.
2. Put the rice in a pan with the thin milk and screwpine leaves. Steam over rapidly boiling water for 20 minutes.
3. Remove the pan from the steamer and add the thick milk and salt. Mix well using a pair of chopsticks or a fork.
4. Colour 1/3 of the rice blue and return to the steamer to cook for another 10 minutes.
5. When the rice is well cooked, remove from the steamer.
6. Rinse a loaf tin and spoon in the cooked rice, alternating the blue with the white rice.
7. Press the rice down with the banana leaf. Cover the top of the rice with the banana leaf and weigh it down with a heavy object.
8. When the rice is cooled, cut into pieces and serve.

> *Clitoria flowers are believed to help thicken a new-born baby's hair. The flowers are soaked, pounded and the juice extracted. The juice is then rubbed over the baby's scalp.*

Santan Pudding *(Coconut Pudding)*

Ingredients:

1 dsp gelatine
½ cup hot water
¾ cup thick coconut milk
Salt to taste
100 gms pure thick cream
3 egg whites
½ cup castor sugar

Serves 6 — 8

Method:

1. Dissolve the gelatine in hot water. Cool it.
2. Add coconut milk and salt.
3. In a separate bowl, beat the cream for 5 minutes. Add gelatine and thick coconut milk a little at a time.
4. Let it cool in the refrigerator till half set.
5. In another bowl, beat the egg whites until fluffy.
6. Add in sugar and beat again.
7. Put in all the mixture and stir well.
8. Pour the mixture into the mould and let it cool in the refrigerator.
9. When serving, pour over palm sugar syrup or treacle, and garnish with slices of fruits.

Kuih Talam Berempah

(Steamed pudding with spices)

Ingredients:

3 glasses coconut milk (santan) from 1 grated coconut (see glossary)	
½ grated coconut fry without oil and pound	
1 egg	
2 dsps honey	
3 dsps coriander	
3 dsps aniseed	fry and pound until fine
2 dsps cummin	

Serves 6 — 8

Method:

1. Sieve flour and knead with a little bit of coconut milk.
2. Boil the remainder of the milk, pour into the flour mixture and stir well.
3. Beat eggs and honey until white. Add in the fried coconut, sugar, brown sugar and spices.
5. Mix thoroughly into the kneaded flour.
6. Boil water in a steamer.
7. Grease a square dish, pour in mixture and steam until cooked for approximately 30 minutes.

Kuih Ang-Koo

Ingredients:

For the dough

625 gms glutinous rice — soaked overnight

1 tbsp cornflour

A few drops red colouring

For the filling:

250 gms green peas — soak for 4 hours and remove the skin

270 gms sugar

Vegetable cooking oil

1 or 2 ang-koo moulds

Banana leaves to line the moulds

Serves 6 — 8

Method:

1. Steam green peas for 40-50 minutes, then mash finely. Mix with sugar and dry-fry over a low flame until quite dry.
2. Drain the glutinous rice and grind finely. Wrap in cheese-cloth and squeeze out excessive water.
3. Mix the ground glutinous rice, cornflour and colouring. Knead into a dough.
4. Divide dough into small equal portions.
5. Roll out each portion and place 1 tbsp filling on it. Draw up the edges to enclose filling and press with ang-koo mould.
6. Place on a banana leaf which should be cut slightly larger than the ang-koo mould. Steam for 10-20 minutes until the cakes are cooked.
7. Brush with oil, remove from the steamer and cool before serving.

This tea-time treat, because of its red colour, is usually included in festive spreads. Red is favoured as it depicts good luck and prosperity.

Kuih Koci
(Glutinous Rice Flour Cake With Filling)

Ingredients:

For the dough

500 gms glutinous rice flour

270 gms grated coconut, squeeze out enough milk to mix into a soft dough

For the filling:

3 tbsps castor sugar

5 tbsps palm sugar (or demerara sugar)

3 tbsps water

270 gms grated coconut

1 screwpine leaf

Serves 6 — 8

Method:

1. Put castor sugar, palm sugar, water and screwpine leaf in a pan. Cook until the sugar dissolves.
2. Add in the grated coconut and mix well. Remove from heat and cool.
3. Mix flour and coconut milk into a smooth dough and divide the dough into 20-25 portions. Flatten each portion slightly.
4. Put in 2 teaspoons of filling and seal the cake.
5. Prepare some banana leaves, enough for 20-25 rounds of 20 cm in diameter.
6. Fold the banana leaf into a cone shape, put in the dough portions and tuck in the ends.
7. Place the wrapped cakes on a steaming tray and steam over a high flame for 10 — 15 minutes. Remove and cool before serving.

The banana leaves give the cake a special flavour. However, if you cannot get banana leaves, you can place the cakes on a tray a few centimetres apart to allow to rise and then steam as above.

EURASIAN

Eurasian food is an exotic blend of East and West. They have spiced up much of their food with both fresh and dried chillies, and given many of their dishes a typical piquancy by adding tamarind or vinegar. Their curries are adaptations of both the Malay and Indian versions.

Curry debal or devil curry and vindaloo are very popular — both cooked in a racy blend of spices and chillies and flavoured with vinegar.

There are a relatively small number of Eurasian recipes available, due partly to their reluctance to pass on information and culinary 'secrets', which are usually handed down through the generations from mother to daughter.

ACCOMPANIMENTS

Devilled Eggs

Ingredients:

5 hard boiled eggs

1 tsp butter

Pepper and mustard to taste

Serves 4 — 6

Method:

1. Cut the eggs in half and scoop out the yolks.
2. Rub yolks into a paste with a little butter seasoned with pepper and mustard but this paste must not be too moist.
3. Fill in the egg whites and sprinkle paprika liberally before serving.

Mango Chutney

Ingredients:

12 green mangoes — sliced fine or in cubes

750 gms brown sugar

5—6 pods garlic — washed and peeled

1 bottle vinegar

30 dried chilies

1 large piece ginger

Serves 6 — 8

Method:

1. Put mangoes in a saucepan, cover with vinegar and boil till soft.
2. Grind fine the chillies, ginger and garlic and add to the saucepan.
3. Mix in the sugar and salt to taste and simmer on low heat till mangoes are soft. Adjust seasoning if necessary. If you want it more sour add more vinegar.
4. When done, cool before storing in airtight jars.

Pickled Green Tomatoes

Ingredients:

½ kg green tomatoes — cut into quarters

2 cups vinegar

2 cups water

2 cloves

500 gms brown sugar

Serves 6 — 8

Method:

1. Boil the tomatoes in 2 cups water and one cup vinegar and cloves for 5 minutes.
2. Then drop into cold water and drain.
3. Boil tomatoes again with remaining 1 cup vinegar and brown sugar until tender. Cool and store in jars. Let stand for 2 weeks before serving.

Cucumbers in Chilli Paste

Ingredients:

1 large cucumber — seeded and cut into 3 cm lengths

1 tbsp dried shrimps — soaked in hot water, drained and ground fine

4 fresh red chillies

¼ tsp shrimp paste — toasted

Salt to taste

Juice of one lime

Serves 4 — 6

Method:

1. Mix cucumber pieces with salt and leave to soak for 10 minutes. Then squeeze out the water.
2. Pound the chillies and shrimp paste until fine and mix with the cucumbers. Add salt if necessary.
3. Sprinkle pounded dried shrimps over cucumbers and mix in the lime juice. Let stand for 10 minutes before serving.

Papaya Chutney

Ingredients:

½ kg papayas — cut into big cubes

2 apples — cut into cubes

2 cloves garlic

15 gms ground black pepper

3 onions cut into half

15 gms white pepper

½ litre vinegar

60 gms ground ginger

Salt to taste

Pinch of mixed spices

300 gms brown sugar

Serves 6 — 8

Method:

1. In a saucepan, boil the papaya, apples and sugar on low heat until very soft then mix well.
2. Add all the remaining ingredients except vinegar and cook for 10 minutes.
3. Remove from heat and add the vinegar and salt to taste. Cool before storing in airtight jars.

SEAFOOD

Prawn Fritters

Ingredients:

500 gms prawns
350 gms plain flour
3 tbsps cornflour
2 egg whites — beaten until stiff
1 cup water
Salt to taste
Oil for deep frying

Serves 4 — 6

Method:

1. Shell the prawns, leaving tails intact. Wash and drain well.
2. Sift flour into a bowl and mix with cornflour.
3. Make a hole in the centre and gradually pour in water to make a thick batter.
4. Add salt and fold in egg whites gently.
5. Heat oil. Dip prawns into batter and fry the prawns until golden.
6. Serve with lettuce, tomatoes and chilli sauce.

Fish Chowder

Ingredients:

1 kg any white fish
125 gms pork rubbed in salt and left to dry
2 cups milk
1 kg potatoes — cut into cubes
1 onion — sliced
2 tbsps flour
Salt and pepper to taste
4 tbsps oil

Serves 6 — 8

Method:

1. Parboil potatoes and drain.
2. Cut pork into small pieces.
3. Heat a deep saucepan with oil and fry the onions until brown.
4. Add in the pork, sliced fish and potatoes. Mix well.
5. Pour in hot water, cover saucepan and leave to cook gently for 30 minutes.
6. Heat milk in a separate pan and add in the flour. Mix to form a thick sauce. Pour this sauce into the boiling mixture.
7. Add salt and pepper and when gravy thickens dish out.

Turmeric eaten raw is believed to be able to get rid of body odour.

Asam Fish Head Curry
(Sour Fish Head Curry)

Ingredients:

1 fish head (Kurau or Ikan Merah)
6 ladies' fingers
10 shallots
10 — 15 dried chillies
10 fresh red chillies
2.5 cm piece belacan — toasted (optional)
6 cloves garlic ⎫
2 stalks lemon grass ⎬ Ground fine
2.5 cm fresh turmeric ⎭
A walnut-sized ball of tamarind — mix with 1 cup water and extract juice
Salt to taste
4 tbsps oil

Serves 4 — 6

Method:

1. Heat oil in a pan and fry ground ingredients till fragrant.
2. Add tamarind water, ladies' fingers and fish head, and simmer over low heat till fish and vegetables are tender.
3. Add salt to taste and serve hot.

Curry Pementa

Ingredients:

500 gms fish (Ikan Pari) or prawns
10 — 15 dried chillies ⎫
10 shallots
4 cloves garlic
2.5 cm piece fresh turmeric
1 tsp cummin ⎬ Ground fine
3 candlenuts
1 tsp white pepper
1 tsp black pepper
¼ cup tamarind juice ⎭
4 ladies' fingers — cut into 2.5 cm lengths
Salt to taste
4 tbsps oil

Serves 4 — 6

Method:

1. Heat oil in a pan and fry ground ingredients till fragrant.
2. Add fish slices or prawns, ladies' fingers, tamarind juice and salt to taste.
3. Simmer till fish or prawns, ladies' fingers are done and gravy thickens.
   Note: If using fish, tamarind juice should be of thicker consistency.

Prawn Fritters

205

Prawn Pepper Fry

Ingredients:

500 gms prawns

1 tsp black peppercorns } Ground together
3 cloves garlic

2 pieces beancurd — fried and cubed

1 capsicum — sliced

1 tsp thick soy sauce

2 tbsps oil

Salt to taste

Serves 4 — 6

Method:

1. Marinate prawns with ground ingredients and soy sauce.
2. Heat oil in pan, add prawns and fry for 5 minutes.
3. Add 2 tbsps water and simmer over low heat.
4. Add capsicum and beancurd and stir-fry to mix well for 2 minutes.
5. Serve hot with rice.

Brinjal With Salt Fish Curry

Ingredients:

300 gms salt fish — cut into serving portions

3 brinjals — cut into approximately 7 cm lengths

5 candlenuts

2 stalks lemon grass

2 tsps peppercorns

2 cm piece fresh turmeric (or ½ tsp powdered turmeric)

¾ cup small onions

2.5 cm piece shrimp paste

3 cups tamarind juice (from 2 tsps tamarind pulp)

2 tbsps oil

Serves 4 — 6

Method:

1. Heat the saucepan with oil and fry the ground ingredients until fragrant.
2. Put in the salt fish and tamarind juice and cook for 5 minutes.
3. Turn down the heat and allow to simmer for a while.
4. When the gravy boils over, add the brinjals and cook until the brinjals are soft.
5. Serve as a main dish with rice.
   Note: If you can't find tamarind, use 3 cups water and at the last stage of cooking, add a few teaspoons of lime juice to taste.

Fried Fish

Ingredients:

500 gms fish fillets

2.5 cm piece ginger — pounded fine

4 cloves garlic

½ tsp powdered turmeric

2 tsps chilli powder

Salt to taste

Black pepper to taste

A little vinegar or lime juice

Oil for frying

Serves 4 — 6

Method:

1. Marinate the fish pieces in a little vinegar or lime juice mixed with all the rest of the ground spices and seasoning.
2. Leave aside for an hour or more.
3. Heat oil in a pan, and fry the fish fillets, a few at a time.
4. Serve hot.

Goanese Fish Curry

Ingredients:

1 large pomfret — cleaned and sliced

4 cloves garlic — crushed

1 tsp chilli powder

½ tsp turmeric powder

A walnut-sized ball of tamarind — soak in ½ cup water and extract juice

2 green chillies

A small bunch coriander leaves — chopped

Salt to taste

3 tbsps oil

½ grated coconut
1 tbsp coriander } Ground fine
10 black peppercorns
1 onion — chopped

Serves 4 — 6

Method:

1. Rub garlic, chilli and turmeric powder and salt into fish slices and set aside.
2. Heat oil in a pan and fry whole green chillies.
3. Pour in ground ingredients, tamarind juice and 1½ cups water and bring to boil.
4. Add fish slices and salt to taste, and cook for a few minutes more or until fish is done.

Baked Fish

Ingredients:

1 whole ikan senangin
1 tbsp bread curmbs
1 tbsp grated cheese
1 lime
1 tsp salt

Serves 4 — 6

Method:

1. Season the fish with salt and lime juice.
2. Sprinkle bread crumbs and grated cheese over the fish and bake in moderate oven for 20 minutes.

Fish Moolie

Ingredients:

600 gms red snapper — sliced
1 stalk lemon grass
3 slices galangal (Substitute ginger if unavailable)
4 candlenuts or 8 brazil nuts
2.5 cm fresh turmeric (or ½ tsp powdered turmeric)
2 large onions — sliced coarsely
10 cm piece ginger — cut into thin strips
3 cups coconut milk (from ¾ grated coconut, extract 1 cup thick milk and 2 cups thin milk)
Vinegar, sugar and salt to taste
Cornflour for thickening
2 tbsps oil

Serves 4 — 6

Method:

1. Grind the lemon grass, galangal, candlenuts and turmeric together into a fine paste.
2. Shallow fry the fish slices until golden brown.
3. Drain and set aside.
4. Heat the saucepan with oil and fry the onion and ginger until fragrant.
5. Add the ground ingredients and fry until cooked.
6. Pour in the 2 cups of thin coconut milk and leave to simmer until the gravy boils over.
7. Add in the fish and the thick coconut milk, vinegar, sugar and salt.
8. Cook for a few minutes and thicken the gravy with a little cornflour mixed to a fine paste with water.
9. Turn down the heat and cook until the gravy thickens further.
10. Remove from heat.
11. Serve as a main dish garnished with fried onion rings, fried garlic rings, sliced ginger and sliced chillies.

Pineapple And Prawn Curry

Ingredients:

1 pineapple — sliced thick	
10 — 20 dried chillies	
10 shallots	
4 cloves garlic	
2.5 cm piece turmeric	Ground fine
4 candlenuts	
2 stalks lemon grass	
Small piece shrimp paste (belacan) — (Optional)	
Salt and sugar to taste	
200 gms large prawns	
4 tbsps oil	

Serves 4 — 6

Method:

1. Heat oil in a pan, and when smoking, add the ground ingredients and fry till fragrant.
2. Add the prawns and pineapple, and salt and sugar to taste. Stir well and simmer over medium heat till prawns are done and pineapple is tender.

   Note: You can substitute saltfish (ikan sepat) for the prawns in this recipe. If you use the saltfish, it must first be fried.

Prawn Curry

Ingredients:

600 gms large prawns	
15 dried chillies	
1 tsp cummin	
1 tsp aniseed	Ground fine
2 tbsps grated coconut	
½ cup thick coconut milk — from ½ grated coconut	
2 onions — sliced	
1 tsp mustard seeds	
2 stalks curry leaves	
Salt to taste	
3 tbsps oil	

Serves 4 — 6

Method:

1. Heat oil in a pan and fry the mustard seeds till they crackle.
2. Add curry leaves and sliced onions and fry till golden.
3. Add ground ingredients and fry till well browned and oil separates.
4. Add salt to taste and stir well.
5. Add prawns and thick coconut milk and cook over medium heat till gravy is thick and dry.

Crab Cutlets

Ingredients:

120 gms cooked crab meat

1 tbsp cream

1 tsp lemon juice

Salt and pepper to taste

1 egg yolk

Batter:

30 gms butter ⎫

30 gms flour ⎬ Mix to form a thick batter

Milk to bind ⎭

Egg and breadcrumbs

Serves 4 — 6

Method:

1. Remove any shells from the crab meat then mix with butter.
2. In a bowl add the crab meat, the batter, lemon juice, egg yolk, salt and pepper.
3. Pour into a saucepan and heat till mixture binds.
4. Add the cream and mix well.
5. Turn out mixture onto a damp plate and leave until cold.
6. Form into cutlets, dip in egg and rub in breadcrumbs.
7. Fry in deep fat till golden. Arrange on a bed of lettuce and serve with chilli sauce.

Baked Crab

Ingredients:

3 large crabs — remove top shells and wash well

1 tbsp butter

Pinch parsley, dried herbs

Salt and cayenne pepper to taste

4 tbsps breadcrumbs

½ tsp grated lemon rind

Serves 4 — 6

Method:

1. Boil crabs then scoop out all the meat.
2. Chop meat finely then mix with all the other ingredients.
3. Pack filling into the shells and sprinkle with a little more breadcrumbs. Put a small blob of butter on top and bake in a hot oven for 20 minutes.

Fish Roe Sambal

Ingredients:

3 — 4 fish roe — wash and drain well

Salt and pepper to taste

2 tbsps ground chillies

2 tbsps lemon juice

3 tbsps oil

½ cup chopped onions

2 cloves garlic — chopped

Serves 4 — 6

Method:

1. Rub the fish roe with salt and shallow fry until light brown both sides. Remove roe from pan and place in a dish.
2. Pour off excess oil from the pan leaving 3 tbsps and fry the onion and garlic until fragrant.
3. Add in the ground chillies and fry till oil surfaces. Add ½ cup water and bring to the boil.
4. When gravy begins to dry slightly remove from fire. Add in lemon juice and pour gravy over fish roe. Serve hot with rice.

Cold Crab Salad

Ingredients:

400 gms cooked crabmeat

1 large green pepper — seeded and chopped finely

1 tbsp chopped parsley

2 large tomatoes — chopped finely

1 pimento — chopped finely

Mayonnaise

Lemon slices for garnishing

Lettuce

Serves 4 — 6

Method:

1. Mix all the chopped vegetables together in a bowl.
2. Add the crabmeat then mix in the mayonnaise. Add enough mayonnaise to make the salad moist.
3. Arrange lettuce leaves in small salad bowls and spoon the salad mixture in. Garnish with lemon slices. Serve cold.

> *St. Francis Xavier was said to have dropped his rosary in the Malacca Straits and it was retrieved by a crab. He blessed the crab and from then on all species of that crab had a cross sign on their shells. It was forbidden to eat such crabs.*

MEAT

Mutton With Cabbage Curry

Ingredients:

500 gms mutton — cut into medium pieces
¼ cabbage — cut leaves in half and wash well
2 tbsps meat curry powder
2.5 cm piece ginger — sliced fine
3 cloves garlic — crushed
2.5 cm piece cinnamon
1 onion — sliced
2 cups coconut milk — from ½ grated coconut
¼ cup tamarind juice
3 cardamoms
1 sprig curry leaves
2 tbsps oil
Salt to taste

Serves 4 — 6

Method:

1. Put mutton pieces in a saucepan with garlic and ginger. Add water to cover meat and boil until tender.
2. Heat oil in a wok and fry the curry leaves, cinnamon, cardamoms and onions till fragrant.
3. Add curry powder and cooked mutton, mix well and simmer for 10 to 15 minutes.
4. Add cabbage leaves and pour in coconut milk and tamarind juice. Season to taste and bring curry to the boil.
5. When cabbage has softened and gravy is thick, remove from fire and serve hot.

Beef Semur

Ingredients:

1.5 kg beef — diced
30 shallots — ground
2 pods garlic — ground
2 large onions — quartered
2 pieces star anise
5 cm piece cinnamon
5 cloves
2 tbsps thick soy sauce
1 tsp black peppercorns — ground
½ tbsp vinegar
1 tbsp brandy
4 large potatoes — quartered

Serves 6 — 8

Method:

1. Marinate beef in black sauce for about 20 minutes.
2. Heat oil in a deep pan and fry ground shallots and garlic till brown and crisp.
3. Add marinated beef and cook till meat changes colour.
4. Add spices, stir well.
5. Add ½ cup water and simmer till meat is tender.
6. Add potatoes, pepper and salt.
7. Add brandy and vinegar, and cook over a slow fire till potatoes are done.

Spicy Mutton Curry

Ingredients:

500 gms mutton or lamb — cut into large pieces
2 cups coconut milk — from ½ grated coconut
2 tsps cummin ⎫
2 tbsps aniseed ⎪ Fry for a few minutes
8 dried chillies ⎬ without oil then
1 dsp coriander ⎭ grind fine with ginger
1 sprig curry leaves
2.5 cm piece ginger
3 large onions — sliced
5 cloves garlic — chopped
1 tsp mustard seeds
2.5 cm stick cinnamon
3 cardamoms
2 tsps turmeric powder
1 tbsp tamarind juice
Salt to taste
A little water

Serves 4 — 6

Method:

1. Put mutton in a saucepan, add 1 cup coconut milk, half the onions and garlic, turmeric powder and a little water. Cover and cook till mutton is tender.
2. Add the ground spices, tamarind juice and remaining coconut milk. Bring to the boil, and when gravy thickens, remove from heat.
3. Heat oil in a pan and fry mustard seeds, remaining garlic, onions, curry leaves, cinnamon and cardamoms, and fry until fragrant.
4. Add cooked mutton and bring to the boil; simmer till spices are well blended.

Beef Ambila

Ingredients:

1 kg beef — cut into 2.5 cm strips
400 gms long beans — cut into 2.5 cm lengths
10 candlenuts ⎫
1 stalk lemon grass ⎪
2.5 cm piece galangal ⎬ Ground
2.5 cm piece fresh turmeric ⎪
30 dried chillies ⎭
1 walnut sized ball tamarind — soak in 1 cup water and remove juice
3 tbsps oil

Serves 6 — 8

Method:

1. Heat oil in a deep pan and fry the ground ingredients until brown and fragrant.
2. Add the beef and tamarind water and simmer gently till beef is tender. (Add more water if necessary).
3. Add long beans and cook till gravy thickens.
4. Add salt to taste, stir well and dish out.

211

Mince And Vegetables

Ingredients:

| 1 large onion — diced |
| 1 stick of cinnamon |
| 2 pieces beancurd — fried and cubed |
| 500 gms minced beef |
| French beans, cabbage — sliced |
| Water |
| 1 tbsp cornflour |
| 1 tbsp thick soy sauce |
| 1 tbsp light soy sauce |
| 1 tsp pepper |
| 1 tsp mustard |
| Sugar and salt to taste |
| 1 tbsp oil |

Water through Sugar and salt to taste — *Blend into a thin paste*

Serves 4 — 6

Method:

1. In a saucepan, heat 1 tbsp of oil and fry the diced onion and cinnamon stick until fragrant.
2. Add the vegetables and enough water to cover.
3. Put in the mince and boil until the meat is cooked.
4. Add the blended ingredients and beancurd and leave to simmer until the gravy thickens.
5. Serve as a main dish with rice.

Pongtay

Ingredients:

| 300 gms pork (there should be both lean meat and fat) — cut into bite-sized pieces |
| ½ chicken — cut into bite-sized pieces |
| 15 shallots — sliced |
| 4 cloves garlic — sliced |
| 1 tbsp tow cheong — mashed |
| 2 cups water |
| 1 tbsp thick soy sauce |
| Salt to taste |
| 2 tbsps oil |

Serves 4 — 6

Method:

1. Heat oil in a pan and fry onions and garlic till golden.
2. Add pork and chicken and fry for a few minutes.
3. Add the preserved bean paste and soy sauce and just enough water to cover and cook meat. Simmer over low heat till meat is tender.
4. Add salt to taste and stir well. Serve hot.

Beef Curry

Ingredients:

| 750 gms beef |
| 10—15 dried chillies |
| 10—15 cili padi (optional) |
| 2 stalks lemon grass |
| 2 tsps raw rice |
| 10 shallots |
| 6 cloves garlic |
| 1 tsp black peppercorns |
| 2 green chillies — sliced lengthwise |
| A few limau perut leaves |
| 4 tbsps oil |
| Salt to taste |
| 1 tbsp thin soy sauce |
| 1 tsp sugar |
| ½ cup water |

2 tsps raw rice, 10 shallots, 6 cloves garlic, 1 tsp black peppercorns — *Ground fine*

Serves 6 — 8

Method:

1. Heat oil in a pan and fry ground ingredients till fragrant.
2. Add limau perut leaves, beef, salt, soy sauce, sugar, chillies and water, stir well and simmer till meat is tender and gravy thick.

Beef In Tamarind Sauce

Ingredients:

| 750 gms beef — cut into pieces |
| 10 dried chillies |
| 15 shallots |
| 2.5 cm piece fresh turmeric |
| 2.5 cm piece galangal |
| 4 candlenuts |
| 2.5 cm piece belacan — toasted |
| 2 stalks lemon grass |
| 4 dsps oil |
| Salt to taste |
| 2½ cups tamarind juice — from walnut-sized ball of tamarind |

10 dried chillies through 2 stalks lemon grass — *Grind together*

Serves 6 — 8

Method:

1. Heat oil in a pan and fry the ground ingredients till fragrant.
2. Add the meat and fry for 10 minutes.
3. Pour in tamarind juice and bring to the boil.
4. Season to taste and simmer over low heat until meat is cooked and gravy has thickened.
   Note: Pork can be substituted for beef.

Spicy Beef Stew

Ingredients:

500 gms stewing steak
8 potatoes — quartered
½ cabbage — sliced
300 gms french beans — sliced
2 large onions — quartered
2 carrots — sliced
1 tbsp cornflour
1 tsp mustard seeds
½ tsp pepper
Stick of cinnamon
A pinch of salt

Serves 4 — 6

Method:

1. In a saucepan of water, boil the stewing steak with a stick of cinnamon and a pinch of salt until the meat is half-cooked.
2. Add the carrots and potatoes and cook until tender.
3. Put in the cabbage, french beans and onions.
4. Blend the cornflour, mustard seeds and pepper into a fine paste with a little water and add it to the stew.
5. Boil on medium heat until the meat is tender.
6. Serve with garlic bread.

Liver Curry

Ingredients:

500 gms beef liver — cut into small pieces
1½ cups coconut milk — from 1 grated coconut
1 tbsp coriander
½ tsp cummin
½ tsp aniseed
1 stalk lemon grass   } Ground fine
6 dried chillies
1 clove garlic
2.5 cm square piece of burnt coconut
10 shallots — sliced
Salt to taste
2 tbsps oil

Serves 4 — 6

Method:

1. Heat oil in a pan and when hot fry sliced onions till golden.
2. Add ground ingredients and fry till fragrant.
3. Add liver and stir well. Fry for a few minutes.
4. Add coconut milk and salt to taste. Simmer till liver is tender. (The amount of gravy depends on individual taste.)

Devil Pork Curry

Ingredients:

500 gms pork — cubed
2 tbsps chilli powder (more if required)
2 tbsps turmeric powder
2 tbsps mustard   } Mix together
3—4 tbsps vinegar
2 cucumbers — cut into 4 cm lengths
2 big onions — halved
12 shallots — sliced
4 tbsps oil
7 cloves garlic — sliced
2.5 cm piece ginger — sliced
Sugar and salt to taste
A little water

Serves 4 — 6

Method:

1. Take half the ginger, garlic and shallots and grind fine.
2. Heat oil in a pan and fry the ground ingredients till fragrant.
3. Add sliced ginger, pork and salt to taste, and fry for a few minutes.
4. Mix chilli powder and turmeric with a little water to form a smooth paste, then add to the meat. Stir well and add a little water to cook the pork, and simmer over low heat.
5. Meanwhile mix the mustard, sugar and vinegar in a bowl and keep aside.
6. Add onions to the meat and stir well.
7. After 10 minutes add cucumbers and lastly the mustard and vinegar mixture.
8. Stir well and simmer for 10 minutes.

Pork and Pineapple Soup

Ingredients:

400 gms pork with a little fat — slice thinly
10 shallots   } Pound together roughly
1 tbsp black peppercorns
2 cm piece belacan — toasted
Salt and sugar to taste
Pineapple — diced
1 tbsp oil
3 cups water

Serves 4 — 6

Method:

1. Heat oil in a deep pan and fry pounded ingredients, pork and pineapple.
2. Fry for a few minutes, then add water, and salt and sugar to taste.
3. If you like the soup a little sour, add a piece of asam gelugur (see glossary), and simmer till pork is tender.
4. Serve piping hot with rice.

Mutton and Cabbage Curry

Ingredients:

600 gms mutton — cut into bite-sized pieces
¼ cabbage — leaves halved
2 tbsps meat curry powder
1 small piece ginger — sliced
3 cloves garlic — crushed
2.5 cm piece cinnamon
1 onion — sliced
2 tbsps oil
3 curry leaves
2 cups coconut milk
¼ cup tamarind juice or 4 tsps lime juice
3 cardamoms
Salt to taste
Water

Serves 4 — 6

Method:

1. Put the mutton in a saucepan together with the garlic and ginger.
2. Add enough water to cover and boil until tender.
3. Heat a wok with oil and fry the curry leaves, cinnamon, cardamoms and onions until fragrant.
4. Add the curry powder and cooked mutton.
5. Stir well and allow to simmer for a few minutes.
6. Add the cabbage leaves and pour in the coconut and tamarind juice.
7. Add salt to taste.
8. Bring to the boil, ensuring that the cabbage softens and the gravy becomes thick.

Pork Chop Curry With Onions

Ingredients:

8 pork chops	
15 fresh red chillies	Ground fine
2 pods garlic	
1 large onion — sliced into thick rings	
2 tbsps vinegar	
Salt to taste	
4 tbsps oil	

Serves 6 — 8

Method:

1. Marinate the pork in a mixture of the ground ingredients, vinegar and salt for 30 minutes.
2. Heat oil in a large, heavy-bottomed pan, and fry the chops till brown on both sides.
3. Add enough water to cover, cover the pan and simmer over low heat till chops are tender and liquid absorbed.
4. Add the onion rings and fry for a few more minutes till transparent. Serve piping hot with rice and vegetables.

Dry Beef Curry

Ingredients:

1000 gms beef — cut into bite-sized pieces
2 large onions — diced
15 dried chillies — ground fine
½ tsp ground fresh ginger
3.5 cm piece cinnamon
4 cloves
4 tomatoes — quartered
2 tbsps ghee
Salt to taste
Water

Serves 6 — 8

Method:

1. Heat the ghee in a pan and fry the onions until golden brown.
2. Add the ground chillies, ginger, cinnamon and cloves, and fry well.
3. Put in the beef and stir well.
4. Add the tomatoes and enough water to cook.
5. Simmer the curry until the meat is tender and the gravy dries completely.
6. Add salt to taste and remove from heat.
7. Serve as a main dish with rice or bread.

Beef Ball Curry

Ingredients:

750 gms minced beef	
1 dsp finely chopped onions	
1 tsp finely chopped ginger	Mix together thoroughly
2 dsps meat curry powder	
4 dsps sliced onions	
3 cloves garlic — chopped	
1 tsp chopped ginger	
2 cups thin coconut milk	From 1 grated coconut
1 cup thick coconut milk	
4 dsps meat curry powder — mixed to a paste with a little water	
Salt to taste	
A few curry leaves	
4 tbsps oil	

Serves 6 — 8

Method:

1. Shape meat into balls and keep aside.
2. Heat oil in a pan and fry garlic till golden.
3. Add onions, ginger and curry leaves and fry till fragrant.
4. Add curry paste and stir well.
5. Pour in 2 cups thin coconut milk and salt and bring to the boil.
6. Gently add in meatballs and simmer on low heat until firm.
7. Pour in thick milk and cook till gravy thickens.

Pork Feng

Ingredients:

| 1 kg lean pork |
| 1 kg bacon |
| ½ kg liver |
| 3 tbsps coriander seeds |
| 1 tsp aniseed |
| 3 small pieces turmeric } Ground fine |
| 1 pod garlic — ground |
| 2.5 cm piece ginger — shredded fine |
| 1 tbsp vinegar |
| Salt to taste |
| 3 tbsps oil |

Serves 6 — 8

Method:

1. Boil the meat till tender, then cut into cubes.
2. Heat oil in a pan and fry the ground ingredients and garlic.
3. When cooked and fragrant, add meat and stir thoroughly.
4. Add enough water to make a thick gravy.
5. Add shredded ginger, and simmer till gravy thickens.
6. Add salt and vinegar to taste.

Beef Pepper Curry

Ingredients:

| 300 gms beef — slice thinly |
| 1 tsp black peppercorns |
| 10 — 15 cili padi } Grind to a fine paste |
| 3 cloves garlic |
| 2 green chillies — sliced lengthwise |
| 1 tsp thick soy sauce |
| 2 tbsps oil |
| Salt to taste |

Serves 4 — 6

Method:

1. Mix the ground ingredients with the meat and the soy sauce. Set aside to marinate for 15 minutes.
2. Heat oil in a heavy-bottomed frying pan, add meat and fry quickly for a few minutes.
3. Add a little water and simmer over low heat till meat is tender.
4. Just before serving, add in the sliced green chillies. Serve hot.
   Note: You can increase the amount of peppercorns if you like your food really hot and spicy.

Beef Balls In Curry

Ingredients:

| For beef balls: |
| 750 gms minced beef |
| 2 tsps finely chopped onions |
| 2 thin slices ginger — finely chopped |
| 1 tbsp curry powder |

| For the curry: |
| 2 tsps sliced onions |
| 3 cloves garlic — crushed |
| 2 slices ginger — cut into strips |
| 4 tbsps oil |
| 1½ cups coconut milk (½ cup thick milk, 1 cup thin) |
| 2 tbsps curry powder mixed into a paste with a little water |
| 4 curry leaves |

Serves 6 — 8

Method:

1. Mix together all the ingredients for the beef balls.
2. Shape into balls and set aside.

1. Heat a saucepan with oil and fry the garlic until golden brown.
2. Add the sliced onions, ginger and curry leaves, and continue to fry until fragrant.
3. Add the curry paste and fry over medium heat for 4-5 minutes.
4. Pour in the cup of thin coconut milk and bring to the boil.
5. Gradually add in the meatballs and cook on low heat until firm.
6. Pour in the half-cup of thick coconut milk and cook until the gravy thickens.
7. Serve as a main dish with rice or dunked with French bread.

Pork Ribs And Tomato Curry

Ingredients:

| 1 kg pork ribs |
| 25 — 30 dried chillies — ground |
| 6 tomatoes — chopped |
| 2.5 cm stick cinnamon |
| 6 cardamoms |
| ½ cup water |
| Salt to taste |

Serves 6 — 8

Method:

1. Heat oil in a pan and fry ground ingredients and sliced onions for 5 minutes.
2. Add ribs, stir well and simmer for 5 minutes.
3. Add tomatoes, salt to taste, cinnamon, cardamoms and water, and simmer over low heat till ribs are tender.

Chilli Con Carne

Ingredients:

500 gms minced meat
1 large onion
1 medium sized tin tomato soup
1 medium sized tin kidney beans
1 tbsp curry powder
Salt, pepper to taste
1 clove garlic — chopped
½ tsp ginger — crushed

Serves 4 — 6

Method:

1. Fry meat, onions and garlic together until brown.
2. Add in tomato soup, kidney beans, curry powder, salt and ginger. Simmer for 20-30 minutes.
3. Serve hot with French Loaf.

Beef With Long Beans

Ingredients:

750 gms beef — cut into bite-sized pieces
15 dried chillies
4 candlenuts
15 shallots
5 cm piece galangal } Grind fine
4 cloves garlic
Small piece dried shrimp paste (belacan — optional)
4—5 tbsps tamarind pulp — soaked in 5 cups water and juice extracted
250 gms long beans — cut into 2.5 cm pieces
Salt to taste
3 tbsps oil

Serves 6 — 8

Method:

1. Heat oil in a pan and when hot, add ground ingredients. Fry till fragrant.
2. Add beef and fry for 10 minutes.
3. Add tamarind juice and boil till meat is tender.
4. Add salt to taste and simmer till gravy is thick.
5. Add long beans. Cook for a few minutes more till beans are done but still crisp. Serve hot.
   Note: You can substitute pork ribs for the beef in this recipe.

Curry Seku

Ingredients:

1 kg beef — diced
3 tbsps coriander
20 dried chillies
1 tsp cummin
1 tsp aniseed   } Grind to a paste
1 tsp khus khus
1 tsp black peppercorns
½ tsp turmeric powder
2.5 cm piece ginger — sliced
5 cloves garlic — chopped
1 large onion — sliced
1 large tomato — quartered
2.5 cm piece cinnamon
4 cloves
2 star anise
1 sprig curry leaves
5 tbsps oil
Salt to taste

Serves 6 — 8

Method:

1. Boil beef till half-cooked.
2. Heat oil in a deep pan, fry onions, cinnamon, cloves, star anise and curry leaves.
3. When onions are brown, add tomatoes and fry for two minutes.
4. Add ginger and garlic, fry for a minute.
5. Add ground spices and turmeric powder and fry well.
6. Add meat and salt to taste, cover and simmer for five minutes.
7. Add enough water for a thick gravy, cover and cook till meat is tender.

The effects of the common cold can be reduced by adding ground cinnamon to hot milk, strengthened with whisky or sweetened with honey, or stirred into a mixture of lemon juice, honey and hot water. The mixture is to be taken at bedtime.

Devilled Chicken Wings

Ingredients:

750 gms chicken wings

Flour

1 tsp ground ginger

4 stalks celery

2 tbsps thick soy sauce

1 tsp black peppercorns — ground fine

6 cloves garlic

½ cup vinegar

Salt to taste

1 cup brown sugar — loosely packed

½ cup water

Serves 6 — 8

Method:

1. Coat chicken wings in flour seasoned with salt, pepper and ginger.
2. Heat oil in a pan and saute chicken wings until well browned, reduce heat and continue cooking till tender.
3. Heat a little oil in a saucepan and fry garlic till golden.
4. Add celery which has been sliced, soy sauce, vinegar, cornflour, brown sugar and ½ cup water.
5. Stir over gentle heat till sugar dissolves, then bring to the boil.
6. Reduce heat and simmer for 2 minutes.
7. Add chicken wings and heat through before serving.

Dry Chicken Curry

Ingredients:

1 medium-sized chicken — cut into bite-sized pieces

2 large onions — diced

16—20 dried chillies — grind fine

2.5 cm piece ginger — grind

4 cm piece stick cinnamon

4 cloves

2 dsps oil

3—4 tomatoes — quartered

Salt to taste

Water to cook chicken

Serves 6 — 8

Method:

1. Heat oil in a pan and fry onions till golden.
2. Add ground chillies, sugar, cinnamon and cloves and fry a minute or two.
3. Put in chicken and stir well.
4. Add tomatoes and enough water to cook. Simmer till chicken is tender and gravy is thick and dry.
5. Season to taste and serve hot.

Devilled Chicken Wings

Curry Kapitan

Ingredients:

1 medium-sized chicken

2 cucumbers — sliced thickly

12 dried chillies

2 tsps black peppercorns

1½ tbsp tow cheong

2 stalks lemon grass

4 tbsps oil

1 clove garlic — crushed

15 small onions

2 tsps tamarind juice (or 1 tsp lime juice or white vinegar)

Salt to taste

Serves 6 — 8

Method:

1. Cut the chicken into bite-sized pieces.
2. Grind the dried chillies, peppercorns, lemon grass and small onions into a fine paste, and mix with the tow cheong.
3. Blend the paste with the crushed garlic.
4. Rub the paste into the chicken pieces and allow to marinate for half an hour.
5. Heat the oil in a wok and fry the chicken until well-coated with the spices.
6. Add tamarind juice and salt to taste.
7. Cook on low heat until tender.
8. Add cucumber slices and simmer until the cucumbers are soft, stirring constantly.

Old Hindu medicine recommended chillies as an aid to digestion and as a cure for paralysis. Chillies stimulate the flow of saliva and gastric juices so they help to overcome loss of appetite.

Sour and Spicy Chicken

Ingredients:

1 medium chicken (cut into bite-sized pieces)
120 gms butter
4 medium onions (minced)
2 cloves garlic (minced)
1 cm piece ginger (minced)
½ tsp ground black pepper
½ tsp turmeric powder
3 green chillies (sliced)
1 dsp vinegar
1 dsp tamarind pulp (mixed in ½ cup water and juice extracted)
Salt to taste

Serves 6 — 8

Method:

1. Heat deep saucepan with butter and fry the onions till light brown.
2. Then add the ginger and garlic and the chicken pieces. Stir-fry for a few minutes, then cover saucepan and let chicken on low heat, stirring occasionally, until brown.
3. When chicken is almost tender add the pepper, turmeric, green chillies and tamarind juice and bring to the boil.
4. Mix in vinegar, cover saucepan and cook until gravy thickens.
   Dish out and serve hot with rice.

Tomato Chicken

Ingredients:

1 medium chicken (cut into big pieces)
3 tbsps chilli powder
1 tsp turmeric powder
¼ cup water
2 medium onions (sliced)
5 star anise
1 cm piece cinnamon
1 cm piece ginger (minced)
¼ cup oil
½ cup tomato puree (mixed with ¼ cup water)
Salt to taste

Serves 6 — 8

Method:

1. Mix together the chilli powder and turmeric powder with ¼ cup water to form a paste.
2. Heat a saucepan with oil and fry the onions, star anise, ginger and cinnamon till fragrant.
3. Add in chicken pieces and stir-fry until chicken changes colour.
4. Add in the tomato puree mixture and bring to the boil. Then reduce heat and cook gently until chicken is tender. Season to taste and dish out.

Chicken Pie

Ingredients:

400 gms chicken meat (cut into large cubes)
1 carrot (cubed)
½ cup green peas
2 potatoes (quartered)
2 hard-boiled eggs (quartered)
Salt and pepper to taste
1 tsp cornflour (mixed with a little water to form a paste)
2 tbsps oil

Short-Crust pastry:

400 gms flour
250 gms cold butter or margarine
Pinch of salt
Cold water to mix

Serves 4 — 6

Method:

1. In a bowl sieve the flour and salt together.
2. Add butter and cut into little cubes. Then rub in butter lightly.
3. Mix in a little cold water at a time to form a pliable dough. Knead lightly and leave to rest in the refrigerator for a few minutes.
4. Heat a pan with oil and fry the chicken, carrot and potatoes for a few minutes.
5. Then add salt and pepper to taste and cornflour mixture. Leave to cook on low heat until chicken and vegetables are tender.
6. Then add in the green peas, stir-fry and dish out. Leave to cool.
7. Roll out pastry on a lightly floured board.
8. Grease a 20-cm round pie dish and place cooled chicken filling in.
9. Arrange quartered boiled eggs on top and then cover with pastry.
10. Trim pastry edges and flute with a fork. Prick two holes in the centre of the pastry.
11. Bake in moderate oven for 20-30 minutes or until pastry is done.
12. Remove from oven and cool slightly, before serving.

Roast Chicken

Ingredients:

1 large chicken	
3—4 pieces cinnamon stick 1 star anise 5 cloves ¼ piece fresh nutmeg 10 black peppercorns	**Grind together**
Butter	
2 tbsps dark soy sauce	
1 tbsp light soy sauce	
1 tbsp castor sugar	
Juice of two lemons	
½ tsp salt	
1 tsp flour	

Serves 6 — 8

Method:

1. Wash and clean chicken and pat dry.
2. Rub chicken in and out with the ground spices, flour, salt, sugar, dark and light soy sauce and lemon juice.
3. Prick chicken with a fork and leave to marinate for an hour or more.
4. Grease a roasting pan with butter and place chicken in it. Dot chicken with butter and roast in moderate oven for an hour or until done, basting occasionally with pan juices.
5. When cooked dish out and cut chicken into serving pieces.
6. Heat pan juice adding a little water and serve with chicken.

Chicken Stew Eurasian Style

Ingredients:

1 medium chicken (cut into bite-sized pieces)
Salt and ground black pepper to taste
1 tsp light soy souce
Dash of msg
Dash of red wine
2 large onions (quartered)
4 tbsps oil
3—4 cloves
10 black peppercorns
½ star anise
3 large potatoes (quartered)
1 medium carrot (cut into rounds)
2 tbsps green peas

Serves 6 — 8

Method:

1. Season chicken with salt, pepper, soy sauce, wine and msg. Leave aside for half an hour.
2. Heat oil in a deep saucepan and fry the onions till fragrant then add cloves, black peppercorns, cinnamon stick and star anise, and fry well.
3. Add in chicken pieces and stir-fry over high heat till meat changes colour.
4. Then add the potatoes and carrot and continue frying. Add enough water to cover chicken and cook on low heat until vegetables and chicken are tender. Add in peas and cook for a further two minutes. Dish out and serve hot.

Chicken Pot Roast

Ingredients:

1 medium chicken	
A few cloves	
Salt and pepper to taste	
120 gms butter	
2 medium carrots (cut into chunks)	
4 potatoes (cut into half)	
2 Bombay onions (cut into half)	
200 gms french beans (cut into half)	
2 tbsps dark soy sauce	
2 tbsps light soy sauce	
2 tsps allspice	
6 cloves garlic 2 cm piece ginger	**Pounded**

Serves 6 — 8

Method:

1. Wash and clean chicken well then rub salt, pepper, allspice, ground garlic and ginger and dark and light soy sauce inside and out.
2. Press cloves all over chicken and marinate for 30 minutes.
3. Heat a deep saucepan with butter and fry the onions until transparent.
4. Put in the whole chicken and brown all over in the butter.
5. Add carrots and potatoes and add enough water to cook the chicken. Bring to the boil, then simmer gently until chicken is almost tender.
6. Add in the french beans and simmer covered until french beans are cooked.
7. Dish out and cut chicken into serving pieces and serve together with all the vegetables and gravy.

Chicken Vindaloo

Ingredients:

1 medium chicken — cleaned and cut into pieces	
1 large onion — sliced	
10 shallots 1 tbsp cummin 20 dried chillies 1 small piece turmeric 6 cloves garlic 2.5 cm piece ginger	Grind fine
2 sprigs curry leaves	
Vinegar to taste	
Salt to taste	
2 tbsps oil	

Serves 6 — 8

Method:

1. Heat oil in a deep pan and put in mustard seeds.
2. When seeds crackle add the sliced onions and fry till golden.
3. Add ground spices and fry for a few minutes.
4. Add chicken and curry leaves and stir well, frying till the chicken is well coated with the spices.
5. Reduce heat and simmer till chicken is tender.
6. Add vinegar and salt to taste, and cook for a few more minutes over low heat before dishing out.

Chicken With Cabbage And Potatoes

Ingredients:

1 medium chicken — cleaned and cut into pieces	
10—15 fresh red chillies 10 shallots 3 cloves garlic 5 cm stalk lemon grass 5 candlenuts	Grind fine
½ cup thick coconut milk 1 cup thin coconut milk	From 1 grated coconut
Lime juice to taste	
Salt to taste	
A few cabbage leaves — left whole	
2 cm piece fresh turmeric — ground (Or 1 tsp turmeric powder)	
4 tbsps oil	

Serves 6 — 8

Method:

1. Heat oil in a large, heavy-bottomed pan and put in ground ingredients and chicken and stir well for 5 minutes.
2. Add thin coconut milk and potatoes and simmer till chicken and potatoes are tender.
3. Add cabbage and thick coconut milk and continue cooking for a few more minutes till cabbage is tender.
4. Add lime juice and salt to taste. Serve hot.

Curry Dea-Bal *(Devil Curry)*

Ingredients:

1 large chicken — cut into pieces	
20 shallots — grind	
½ pod garlic 6 candlenuts 20 dried chillies 5 stalks lemon grass 2.5 cm piece galangal 1 tsp mustard seeds 1 tsp turmeric powder 2.5 cm piece ginger — shredded	A
2 large onions — quartered	
4 fresh red chillies — slit lengthwise	
1 kg potatoes — quartered	
1 cucumber — deseeded then cut into 5 cm lengths	
1 tbsp vinegar	
Oil	
Salt to taste	

Serves 6 — 8

Method:

1. Heat oil in a pan and fry the shredded ginger till brown.
2. Add ground ingredients (A) and fry till brown and crispy.
3. Add shallots and fry for 2 minutes.
4. Add chicken and mix well, then add enough water to cook chicken, and let it simmer on medium heat till tender.
5. Add quartered onions, potatoes, salt, vinegar, fresh chillies and cucumber, and cook over low heat till potatoes are soft.

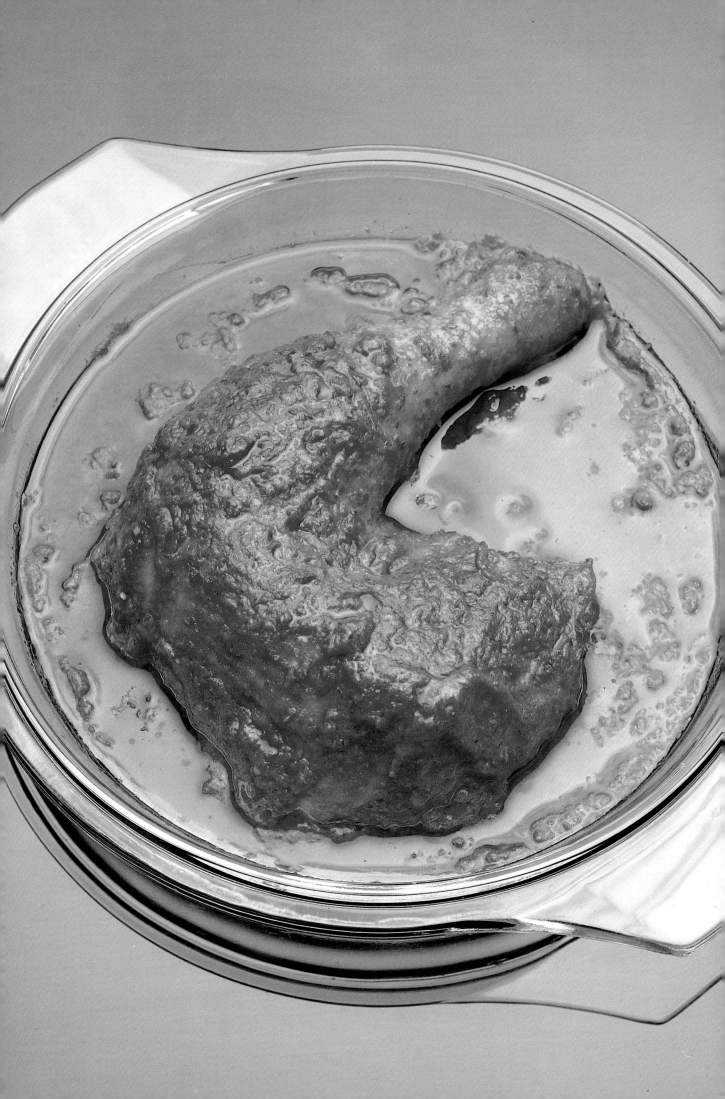

SWEETS

Caramel Custard

Ingredients:

For Caramel:

2 cups sugar

6 tbsps boiling water

For custard:

3⅓ cups cream

2 cups milk

4 tbsps sugar

2 tsps vanila

8 eggs

Serves 4 — 6

Method:

1. Melt sugar in a pan over low heat until a light brown syrup forms. Stir occasionally to get rid of lumps.
2. Add boiling water slowly until smooth.
3. Pour into bottom of mould.
4. Make custard. Boil cream, milk and sugar in pan.
5. Remove from pan and add vanilla.
6. Beat eggs in a bowl and pour mixture over, beating vigorously.
7. Pour into caramel-coated mould and bake or steam until custard sets.

Stewed Prunes

Ingredients:

500 gms prunes

A piece of cinnamon or orange rind

Cold water

Custard or whipped cream for topping

Serves 6 — 8

Method:

1. Put the prunes in a saucepan, cinnamon or orange rind and cover with water.
2. Bring to the boil, then simmer for 1 hour until soft.
3. Spoon prunes with juice into individual dessert bowls, top with custard or whipped cream and serve hot or cold.

Banana Bread

Ingredients:

250 gms sugar

500 gms flour

2 eggs

1 tbsp milk

½ tsp salt

1 cup mashed bananas — bananas should be ripe

1 tsp baking soda

1 tsp baking powder

½ cup butter

Serves 4 — 6

Method:

1. Cream the butter and sugar till light and fluffy.
2. Add eggs slightly beaten then add the milk and mashed bananas.
3. Stir in the flour, soda, baking powder and salt. Fold in well and pour into a prepared loaf tin.
4. Bake in moderate oven for about 1 hour.
5. Serve hot or cold with ice cream or custard.

Semolina Cake

Ingredients:

250 gms semolina

250 gms plain flour

300 gms sugar

200 gms butter

6 eggs

3 tsps baking powder

120 mls milk

¼ cup almond — chopped fine

1 tsp vanilla essence

Serves 6 — 8

Method:

1. Sift dry ingredients.
2. Separate the eggs and beat the yolks.
3. Cream the butter and sugar then slowly add the yolks.
4. Stir in the plain flour, baking powder and semolina alternately with milk. Then fold in the almonds.
5. Whisk egg whites till stiff then fold into the mixture.
6. Add vanilla essence and pour mixture into a greased baking tin (18-20 cm square).
7. Bake in moderate oven for 40 minutes till cooked.

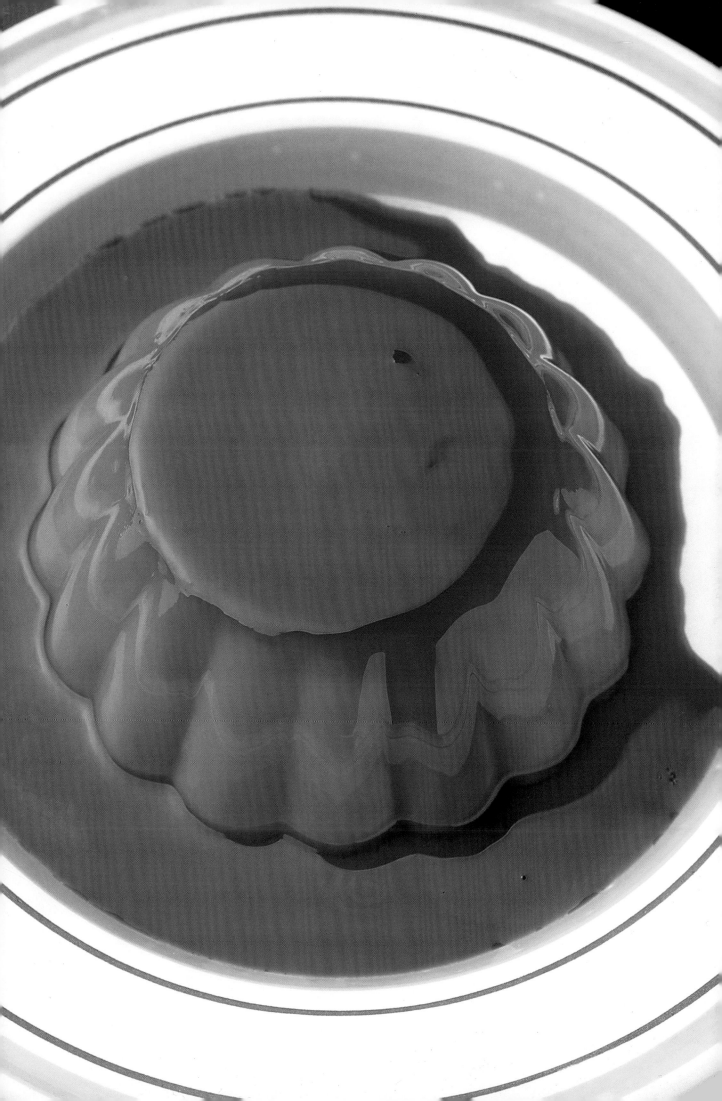

GLOSSARY

(M — Malay • C — Chinese • T — Tamil • H — Hindu)

Agar-agar *(M)*
Seaweed jelly. It is used like gelatine mainly in desserts. It is sold in strips which have to be boiled and dissolved in water, but the powdered variety is also available.

Aniseed
(M) Jintan manis
(T) Peeru jeeragam
(H) Saunf
This spice is very similar in shape to cummin, though it is larger and plumper. Popularly used in Malay and Indian cooking, it has a light, licorice flavour.

Asafoetida
(T) Perunkayam
(H) Heeng
Dried gum, used to flavour some North Indian dishes.

Asam gelugor *(M)*
(Asam keping)
Dried tamarind slices used mainly in Malay, Indian and Nyonya recipes to give the dish a little sourness. Substitute with tamarind pulp if not available.

Atta flour
Fine wholemeal flour used in making Indian breads. Ordinary wholemeal flour can be substituted.

Beancurd
There are several types of fresh and dried soya beancurd used in Malaysian cooking. They are highly nutritious and being a good source of protein, are extensively used in Chinese vegetarian cooking.
Soft beancurd (C) *Taufu*: used in soups, some claypot dishes and vegetarian food. Available in the market at most vegetable stalls, as well as in supermarkets. Is sold canned overseas.
Hard beancurd (C) *Taukwa*: made by compressing beancurd to remove most of the water. Sold in squares at markets and supermarkets. Used in a variety of dishes.
Dried beancurd 'skins' (C) *Foo chok:* sold in sheets and used as wrappers and stuffed with minced meat or seafood in Chinese cooking. Wipe with a damp cloth to clean, then cut with scissors.

Bee hoon
Dried rice vermicelli is sold in packets at most provision shops and supermarkets. It must be soaked in boiling water for 2-3 minutes before using.

Belacan *(M)*
(belachan)
Dried shrimp paste used to flavour Malay and Nyonya food. When uncooked, it has a highly unpleasant smell, but it is delicious when toasted and ground with fresh chillies for a sambal to accompany a meal. It is also roasted and ground along with other herbs and spices in many recipes.
Most local cooks prefer to use the little brown squares sold in packets in most provision shops. It should be stored in a container and kept tightly covered, and must always be cooked before being eaten.

Belimbing
Carambola — A small, sour, green fruit available in most local markets and supermarkets. Used whole in sambals and certain other Nyonya and Malay dishes.

Candlenut
(M) Buah keras
(C) Saik ku chai
Very popularly used finely ground, in Malaysian cooking to thicken and enrich curries. It is actually the oily kernel of a round nut, about 3 cm in diameter, with a very hard furrowed shell. The shell must be broken. To test for freshness, shake the fruit. The sound must be heavy. Substitute with almonds, Brazil nuts or even macadamia nuts.

Capsicum
Also known as bell pepper, capsicum is either red or green. Used extensively by Chinese, Indians and Eurasians. It has a very mild and sweet flavour.

Cardamom
(M) Buah pelaga
(H) Illaichi
(T) Elakai
There are 2 varieties of cardamom, the large dark brown and the small, pale green variety. The one popularly used here is the smaller variety which is bleached to appear almost white. Available also in powdered form.

Cashew nuts
(M) Kacang gajus
(Kachang)
(H) Kaju
A kidney shaped nut which is popularly used in Indian cooking and also in Indian-influenced Malay dishes. Cashew nuts are sold either roasted or raw.

Bunga kantan; lemon grass; galangal; turmeric

Chick pea flour
(H) *Besan*
(baysun)

This flour is mainly used in Indian cooking. If chick pea flour is not available, roast yellow split peas in a heavy pan and take care they are not burnt. Cool, then pound or grind. Sift the flour and keep in an air-tight container. Wheat flour cannot be substituted as chick pea flour has a distinctive flavour.

Chillies
(M) *Lada/cabai*
(chabai)
(H) *Mirich*

The varieties available are red chillies, green chillies and the small chillies known locally as *cili padi* (chilli padi). Of the three, cili padi is the hottest. Some people have also called it *cili api* (chilli api), literally meaning fire chillies because of its fiery taste. Red chillies are mainly used for sambals, and together with green chillies are used for garnishing. The hottest parts of the chillies are the seeds so remove them to reduce the sting.

Chilli powder

This red, fiery powder is made from ground dried chillies. Use sparingly if you do not like your dishes too hot.

Chinese cabbage

A common vegetable in Malaysian dishes, this vegetable has long, pale-green thick stems with light green leaves. Also known as Tientsin cabbage or celery cabbage.

Chinese rice wine

Very popularly used in Chinese dishes. Comes in bottles. Substitute with dry sherry if unavailable.

Chinese sausages
(C) *Lap cheong*
(Larp-chee-yong)

Used mainly in Chinese cooking, these are thin sausages filled with raw, lean and fat pork. Steam or fry and cut into diagonal slices before adding to claypot rice or fried rice or other rice dishes.

Chinese vinegar

This fermented brown rice vinegar is used mainly in Chinese dishes. It has a mild but pungent flavour. Substitute with white vinegar or malt vinegar.

Cinnamon
(M) *Kayu manis*
(H) *Dalchini*

The bark of the cinnamon plant which is a native of Sri Lanka. Usually sold in sticks and although available in powdered form, the sticks are preferred as they can be stored longer. Only when the recipes call for ground cinnamon do you use the powdered form. Popularly used in Malay and Indian cooking.

Cloud ear fungus
(C) *Mok yee*

This dark-brown, almost black fungus is used extensively in Chinese cooking. Sold dried, they look like greyish-black pieces of paper. To use, soak in hot water for about 10 minutes after which they will swell into cloud or ear shapes. Has no taste of its own but takes on the flavours of other foods.

Cloves
(M) *Bunga cengkih*
(chengkay)
(C) *Ting heong*
(H) *Laung (Long)*
(T) *Karambu*

These are the dried flower buds of an ever-green tropical tree native to South East Asia. Used in all Malaysian cooking.

Coconut milk
(M) *Santan*

Very popularly used in Malaysian cooking, especially in Malay and Nyonya cakes and also in Malay and Indian curries. This white, creamy liquid is extracted from the grated flesh of mature coconuts. Also available in cream form in cans. Substitute with evaporated milk. See 'Cooking Tips' on how to extract coconut milk.

Coriander
(M) *Ketumbar*
(C) *Yim sai*
(H) *Dhania*
(T) *Kotamalee*

These dried, brown seeds of the coriander plant are highly pungent and have a narcotic effect. Use sparingly. It is also one of the main ingredients in curry powder. The leaves are used in Malay and Indian cooking for garnishing.

GLOSSARY

Cummin
(M) *Jintan putih.*
     (pootay)
(C) *Sai kook*
(H) *Zeera*
(T) *Jeeragam*

An essential ingredient in making curry powder. Cummin and caraway seeds are similar in appearance but one cannot replace the other. Also available in powdered form.

Curry leaves
(M) *Daun kari*
(C) *Kali yip*
(I) *Karipattar*

An essential item in Indian and Malay curries. The plant is found in abundance in Malaysia — almost every home has at least one plant. Although they are available dried, Malaysians prefer to use them fresh.

Curry powder

Used in making curries, it is best to grind your own if you are using a lot. Commercially prepared curry powder does not keep fresh for long so always buy in small amounts. There are two types available, one for meat and poultry, the other for seafood dishes.

Daun kesum *(M)*

A very fragrant leaf used to flavour certain dishes like Nyonya or Chinese laksa. The plant rarely grows taller than 25 cms and the leaves are pointed, thin and narrow measuring 4 cm long and 1 cm wide.

**Daun limau
purut** *(M)*

Also a very fragrant leaf used mostly in Nyonya dishes. The leaves are that of a rough-skinned lime which is not used in cooking but as a hair rinse.

**Dried egg
noodles**
(C) *Wonton mee*

Made from wheat flour and eggs and are widely available in packets or loose in round 'cakes'. They must be cooked in boiling water for a few minutes before using as directed in the recipe.

Dried shrimps

The shrimps are shelled, steamed and dried in the sun. The flavour is very different from fresh prawns but if fresh prawns are not available, these can be used but must be cooked for about 25 minutes.

Drumsticks
(I) *Murungakai*

A vegetable used in Indian cooking. It is delicious both cooked in dhall as well as with prawns in a hot, spicy dry curry.

Fennel
(M) *Jintan manis*
(T) *Peeru
     jeeragam*
(H) *Saunf*

Often used in place of aniseed. In fact the two have become known as one and the same, though this is not correct.

Fenugreek
(M) *Alba*
(H) *Methi
     (Maythee)*
(T) *Ventayam*

A native of Western Asia, it has a slightly bitter flavour. Should be used only in the stated quantities. Used mainly in fish dishes, the seeds which are small, flat, squarish and light brown, are believed to have medicinal properties.

**Five-spice
powder**
(C) *Ng heong
     fun*

A blend of ground star anise, fennel, cloves, cinnamon and Szechuan pepper, it is sold in tiny packets in Chinese stores. Buy in small quantities as it loses its flavour very rapidly.

Fish balls

Popular in Chinese dishes, fish balls are made from minced fish flesh. The fish flesh is mixed with cornflour and then made into balls. Ready-made ones are easily available at markets and supermarkets, but are not as tasty as those prepared at home.

Fish sauce

This thin, salty, brown sauce is the liquid obtained from fish packed in wooden barrels with salt. Available in bottles and mainly used in Chinese dishes. Substitute with light soy sauce; to each cup add 1 tsp dried shrimp paste which has been grilled for 5 minutes and powdered.

Galangal
(M) *Lengkuas*

A member of the ginger family and is often called aromatic ginger. It cannot be substituted for fresh ginger nor vice versa. It gives a distinct aromatic flavour and is used together with lemon grass in certain Malay and Nyonya dishes. It is sold dried outside Asia and must be pounded or pulverised. It can also be found in powdered form — *laos (layos)*, and half a teaspoon is approximately equivalent to one fresh slice.

Salted Eggs

GLOSSARY

Garam Masala *(H)*
A blend of spices used only in Indian cooking. Unlike the commercially prepared curry powder, this does not contain powdered turmeric or chilli powder. Can keep up to a month if stored in an air-tight container.
See 'Cooking Tips' on how to make garam masala.

Garoupa
A very tender and fine textured fish excellent for steaming. This is a tropical fish found from the estuaries to the deep waters and usually in the vicinity of rock and coral reefs. Substitute with trout.

Ghee
Clarified butter used in Indian cooking. It has a lovely flavour, and is preferred to butter because there is no residue which can burn or stick to the pan. It can be bought tinned.

Ginger
(M) Halia
(T) Injee
(H) Adrak
(Uthrak)
(C) Keong
Fresh root ginger is used in almost all Malaysian dishes, either sliced fine or pounded with other herbs and spices.
Ginger juice is made from very young roots which can be pounded or put in a blender, and the juice squeezed out through a piece of fine muslin.

Ginger bud
(M) Bunga kantan
This pink bud with its delicate fragrance is used to garnish some dishes, such as Penang Laksa. There is no substitute.

Gluten balls
Brown, light, round balls of deep-fried wheat gluten. To use, scald and squeeze out all the water. Used mainly in Chinese vegetarian dishes. Store in freezer.

Glutinous rice
A short-grained rice that becomes very sticky when cooked. Used in sweets and certain savoury dishes. Also known as sticky rice.

Glutinous rice flour
(M) Tepung pulut
More elastic than ordinary flour. Used in making local cakes and batters, it becomes almost clear and sticky when cooked.

Hoi Sin sauce
A very thick, sweet red sauce which looks very much like tomato paste. Made from soy beans, garlic and spices and used to marinate certain foods as well as an accompanying sauce. Available in bottles or tins. Store in a refrigerator.

Hot bean paste
Sometimes known as 'chilli bean sauce', this is a mixture of fermented soy beans and ground hot chillies. Substitute with mashed black beans mixed with Chinese chilli sauce.

Ikan bilis *(M)*
(Eekan)
(Anchovies)
Small dried fish used mainly in Malay and Nyonya cooking. The head and black intestinal tract are discarded, and fried crisp in a little oil, they make a tasty and nutritious snack or accompaniment to a meal. Available in most provision shops. Many Malaysian pubs serve a delicious concoction of ikan bilis fried with onion and dried chilli, and a squeeze of lime.

Kai lan *(C)*
Used in Chinese cooking, it is also known as Chinese broccoli.

Kangkung *(M)*
Water convulvulus. A green leafy vegetable which, when fried in *belacan (belachan)* pounded with chillies and other herbs, makes a delicious accompaniment to a meal.

Kway teow *(C)*
White, flat, fresh noodles made from rice flour. Are available in flat sheets which are cut into strips and used mainly in Chinese cooking.

Laksa noodles
Made from rice flour and available fresh at most markets and supermarkets. They should be scalded in boiling water for a minute or so before use. Substitute with dried rice vermicelli if necessary.

Lemon grass
(M) Serai
(H) Sera
(T) Vasanelalang
Used for flavouring food, especially curries. Very similar to grass but it has a very fleshy base. Use only 10 cm to 12 cm of the white bulbous base. Also available in dried or powdered form. Use 12 strips of the dried variety as equivalent to one fresh stem. Substitute with 2 strips very thinly peeled lemon rind.

Large onions, garlic; shallots

Lentils

Known as dhall, used extensively in Indian cooking, especially for vegetarian dishes. High content of protein. Lentils are the seeds of leguminous plants and there are many varieties available. Among the ones commonly used are red lentils, green lentils and brown lentils.

Limes

There are several varieties. The large, ordinary lime — (M) *limau nipis* — is round, and the juice is strong and sour.
The (M) *limau kesturi* is a smaller, milder-flavoured variety, and more generally used to flavour curries, sambals and noodle soups.

Lotus seeds

Round, brown coloured seeds of about 1 cm in diameter. To use, soak and boil to remove skins. Remove also the bitter green centre core. Available dry and used in Chinese cooking.

Mee

Fresh yellow noodles made from egg and flour used mainly in Chinese cooking and to a limited extent by Malay and Indian cooks as well. Substitute with dried wheat noodles or spaghetti.

Mushrooms

Used extensively in Chinese cooking. The types available are:
(a) dried, black mushrooms which are the most tasty. To use, soak in hot water first and cut or shred as specified in the recipe.
(b) straw mushrooms, which are tiny, cultivated mushrooms consisting of a sheath within which is the mushroom. Available canned or dried and can be substituted with champignons.
(c) button mushrooms which are available canned or fresh.

Mustard seeds
(M) Biji sawi
(T) Kardugu

Used mainly in Indian cooking, this spice is a little dark brown seed.

Nutmeg
(M) Buah pala
(T) Jathika
(H) Jaiphal

Used to flavour some sweets and cakes and sometimes in garam masala. Always grate finely before use for maximum flavour. Too much (more than one nut) can be poisonous, so use sparingly.

Onion

Comes in many varieties. The small red ones, known as shallots, taste very sweet if put whole in pickles. For garnishing, slice finely and fry until golden brown. The bigger onions, known as Bombay onions are usually ringed if used for garnishing.

Oyster sauce

A very popular sauce in Chinese cooking. This thick sauce is made from oysters cooked in soy sauce and brine, and can be kept indefinitely without refrigeration.

Palm sugar
(M) Gula melaka
(I) Jaggery

Obtained from the sap of coconut palms. The sap is boiled until it crystallises. Comes in flat, round cakes wrapped in dried leaves.

Panch phora *(H)*

A combination of 5 different aromatic seeds (Panch in Hindi means five). To prepare, combine 2 tablespoons each of mustard seeds, cummin seeds, kalonji (onion seeds) to 1 tablespoon each of fenugreek seeds and fennel seeds. Put in an air-tight container and shake well for even distribution.

Pomfret
(M) Bawal Putih
  (Pootay)
(M) Bawal Hitam

Two species commonly used are (a) white pomfret which is silvery white and usually steamed and (b) black pomfret which is a dark grey fish which is usually cooked in curries, fried or other highly-spiced dishes.

Poppy seeds
(I) Kas Kas
(Khus Khus)

These white seeds are used in Indian cooking for thickening gravies. Black poppy seed cannot be substituted as it has a different flavour. Substitute with ground almonds.

Dried Cuttlefish

GLOSSARY

Preserved cabbage
(C) *Ham Choy*

Made by soaking in brine. To use, first soak and then rinse in clear water to remove most of the salt before using.

Preserved radish

Used in Chinese cooking, two types are available.
(a) *Tai tou choy* is radish cut into slices lengthwise and salted and dried
(b) *Choy poh* is cut into even-sized pieces and preserved with spices and salt.

Rice
(M) *Beras*

Staple food of Malaysia. Eaten just plain boiled or as a one-dish meal e.g. Indian biryani.

Rice flour
(M) *Tepung beras·*

Made from rice and used in making batters and certain local cakes. You can also grind your own rice flour but the rice must be soaked first.

Rice wine

Sold bottled in most provision shops. Substitute with dry sherry.

Red beans
(M) *Kacang merah (Kachang)*

Used mainly for Malay and Chinese sweets, these are small, dried beans. Soak before use.

Saffron
(M) *Koma-koma*
(H) *Zaffran*
(T) *Kesari*

King of the spices and the most expensive spice in the world. It appears as thread-like strands and is dark orange in colour. Gives off a beautiful fragrance when mixed with cooked food. Used mostly in Indian cooking. Saffron is often wrongly confused with powdered turmeric.

Salt fish

Many types of fish are salted and dried, the best tasting being thread-fin. Can be simply fried and eaten with rice or cooked in a curry.

Screwpine leaves
(M) *Daun pandan*

Very fragrant and gives food a nice flavour. The leaves are bright green, stiff and long with a distinctive furrow down the centre. Used in most Malaya and Nyonya (cakes) the leaves are pounded and the juice extracted and added to the kuihs for colour as well as for flavour.

Sesame oil
(M) *Minyak bijan*
(C) *Mah yow*
(H) *Til-ka-tel*

Used extensively in Chinese cooking. A nutty dark-brown oil obtained from toasted sesame seeds. Use in small amounts as it is very strong. It retains the colour in boiled vegetables and adds more flavour to steamed food. Indians also use sesame oil, but it is lighter with a different flavour. If light sesame oil is not available, use 1 teaspoon dark sesame oil to 1 tablespoon vegetable oil.

Sesame seeds
(M) *Bijan*
(C) *Tse mah (See-ma)*

Highly regarded for their nutritional value, these seeds are lightly toasted before crushing, or sprinkled whole in some Chinese desserts. The white variety is generally preferred.

Shark's fin

Dried gelatinous fin of shark, which when soaked in water, looks like clear noodles. Available in packets and must be soaked before use. A speciality of the Chinese.

Silver paper
(H) *Varak*

An edible decoration made from pure silver used widely in Indian dishes. It is a very light tissue-like paper. To use, just turn it over the dish as it is too fragile to cut with scissors or a knife.

So hoon

Fine transparent noodles made from dried mung pea flour. Must be soaked in boiling water for 2-3 minutes before using.

Soy bean paste
(M) *Tauco (Taucho)*
(C) *Tow cheong*

A brown paste made from preserved soy beans and popularly used in Chinese cooking. Use amounts specified in recipe as too much would make the dish too salty. Available both bottled and canned.

Soy sauce
(M) *Kicap (Kichap)*

Two types are available. One is a thin, watery liquid and is very salty. This is the type most often used in Chinese cooking. The other type is thicker and sweet. It is used when sauces or meats need additional colour.

Beans

GLOSSARY

Spiced salt
Used as a condiment in Chinese dishes, especially dry-cooked food. Made with finely ground white salt, slightly roasted, cooled and then mixed with finely ground pepper powder.

Spring onion
(M) Daun bawang
(C) Choong
A very popular garnish. Just cut into 3 cm lengths or as the recipe requires.

Spring roll skin
(C) Popiah skin
Sold frozen as thin white sheets of pastry in packets. Thaw when using, peeling off one piece at a time. Unused skins can be kept in refrigerator.

Star anise
(M) Bunga lawang
(C) Baht ghok
This spice, which resembles a star, is also known as Chinese anise and is used a lot in Chinese cooking.

Sweet bean paste
(C) Tausa
Used in Chinese sweet steamed buns or moon cakes. Made from red beans which are cooked and mashed with sugar. Available canned. The Japanese version is called 'yokan'.

Tamarind pulp
(M) Asam jawa
(C) Pulee
(H) Imlee
Known locally as *asam jawa*, it is used in most Malaysian dishes. To use, take the amount of pulp called for in the recipe, add some water and strain the juice. Repeat squeezing until all the juice has been strained.

Tapioca
A plant that grows well in Malaysia. The edible parts are the leaves and the roots. The leaves are scalded and served with *sambal belacan* (*belachan*) or peanut sauce. They can also be cooked in coconut gravy and served with rice. The root is boiled and eaten with grated coconut and also made into a number of sweets.

Threadfin
A very tasty but expensive fish. Substitute with snapper.

Turmeric
(M) Kunyit
(H) Haldi
(T) Manjal
This is another one of the rhizome family and is yellow in colour with a slight fragrance. Also available in powdered form and can last if kept in an air-tight container. However, if the recipe calls for fresh turmeric, do not substitute with the powdered form. Do not confuse with saffron.

Wonton skin
Paper thin squares of egg noodle dough sold in packets. Used exclusively in Chinese cooking.

Yam bean
(M) Sengkuang/ bangkuang
(C) Sar gott
Tuberous root with brown skin which when peeled reveals white flesh. This sweet flesh is eaten raw.

Yoghurt
(T) Tairu
(H) Dahi (Thahee)
Used extensively in Indian cooking. Home-made yoghurt is preferred, but when using commercial variety, be careful to use unflavoured yoghurt. Substitute with evaporated milk mixed with a little vinegar.

Lentils

COOKING TIPS

HOW TO COOK RICE

Weigh the amount of rice needed. Allow 50-75 gms rice per serving. Wash the rice well to remove husk and stones, then drain well. Put the rice in a pot and cover with double the amount of water and a pinch of salt.

Bring to the boil then reduce heat and cook gently covered until all the water has been absorbed. Stir with a fork or chopsticks just before serving so that the rice will not be lumpy.

HOW TO EXTRACT COCONUT MILK

To obtain thick milk or first santan, just add a little water (½ cup to 1 grated coconut) to the grated coconut. Then knead coconut well and squeeze out the milk. The coconut can be put into a muslin cloth and squeezed. For thin milk or second santan add more water (about 2 cups) to the grated coconut, knead well and squeeze.

HOW TO MAKE GARAM MASALA

Garam Masala is a mixture of ground spices. The spices include black pepper, cummin, cinnamon, cardamon, cloves, nutmeg and coriander seeds.

In a small pan roast separately the following: 4 tbsps coriander seeds; 2 tbsps cummin, 1 tbsp whole black peppercorns; 2 tsps cardamom seeds; 4 cinnamon sticks measuring 7 cm; 1 tsp whole cloves; 1 whole nutmeg.

As each spice starts to smell fragrant turn on to a plate to cool. After roasting cardamoms, peel pods and use the seeds. Put all the ingredients into an electric blender and blend to a fine powder. Then grate nutmeg and add in. Store in glass jar with airtight lid.

HOW TO MAKE TAMARIND JUICE

Soak tamarind pulp (1 heaped teaspoon) in half cup water. Knead well and strain the water. Discard seeds and skin.

HOW TO MAKE CURRY POWDER

For meat and poultry: 400 gms coriander seeds
150 gms aniseeds
150 gms cummin
150 gms dried chillies
30 gms cinnamon
30 gms black peppercorns
1 tsp cloves
70 gms turmeric

Roast the ingredients separately except the turmeric, then grind in a blender. Grind the turmeric and mix all the spices together. Store in airtight containers.

For fish and seafood: 400 gms coriander seeds
150 gms aniseeds
150 gms cummin
100 gms peppercorns
150 gms dried chillies
70 gms turmeric powder
50 gms cardamoms
90 gms fenugreek

Roast all the ingredients except the turmeric powder. Blend the roasted ingredients in a blender till fine. Sift the ground ingredients then mix in the turmeric powder. Store in airtight containers.

POPULAR METHODS OF MALAYSIAN COOKING

STIR-FRYING: The most popular method in Chinese cooking is stir-frying and the best utensil for this is the kuali or wok. Stir-frying is very easy; it is important to remember that the oil must be very hot and the ingredients to be cooked must be in small quantities. This is to allow the food to be cooked quickly.

To stir-fry vegetables in a wok, just add a few tablespoons of oil and when it is hot, toss in the vegetables and stir using a long-handled ladle. You must stir the vegetables fast to seal in their juices and to keep the vegetables crisp. Then dish out and serve hot. If you allow the juices of the vegetables to escape, the vegetables will turn yellow and become overcooked.

STEAMING: This is another popular method of cooking and here the wok comes in handy. If you don't have a steamer, just add water to the wok and put it on the fire. Then put in a steaming rack or just a pair of chopsticks across and place your steaming tray on. Cover and cook. When the dish is ready, remove from the wok and serve at once. Steamed food should not be reheated as it will change the texture of the food.

DEEP-FRYING: Here the wok is used again and a pair of long wooden chopsticks are useful to turn the pieces of food over. Remember to use enough oil.

POUNDING OR GRINDING:

Malaysians like to use the traditional methods of pounding or grinding. They believe that spices, especially for curries, taste better if ground this way than in an electric blender. A pestle and mortar made of heavy stone is used for pounding. And it is "seasoned" before use by pounding roasted grated coconut until coconut becomes soft and granite dust from the pestle and mortar is removed. Then remove the coconut, rub in a little cooking oil and leave for a day or two then wash out thoroughly. The same method is used to "season" a grinding stone. The grinding stone, though more difficult to use, is preferred when spices have to be ground really fine and smooth.

HANDY HINTS

1. To clean the inside of aluminium kettle fill it with water and put a little tamarind pulp inside. Leave for a while then rinse.
2. To season earthen or clay pots: (i) fill the pot with used grated coconut and leave it over dying embers on a charcoal stove. Repeat the process a few times.

OR
(ii) Pour boiling water into the clay pot and leave to stand for 48 hours.
3. Substitute tapioca if potatoes are not available. Just peel and boil the tapioca for 25 minutes and then use according to recipe.
4. Lentils and pulses will cook faster if soaked in water for a few hours.
5. Dried foodstuff e.g. dried prawns, shrimp paste and salted fish will last longer if stored in airtight containers and kept in the fridge. Will not attract insects and worms.
6. Lemon juice added to rice makes it more fluffy.
7. When boiling pulses, put in a porcelain spoon; it will hasten the cooking time.
8. Yoghurt is an excellent meat tenderizer. Just marinate the meat to be roasted or grilled in yoghurt and leave for a few hours before cooking.
9. To rid hands of smell after washing prawns and fish, wash hands with lime juice or tamarind juice.
10. Bamboo shoots should be washed with rice water to get rid of the smell.
11. Meat wrapped in unripe papaya slices or papaya leaves will help to tenderize it.
12. To keep bean sprouts fresh if they are to be used later, soak them in water with lime juice.
13. Rice should be stored in bins without lids so that air can get in. Rice in closed bins will become mouldy. Cover bins with light netting to keep out mice and other pests.

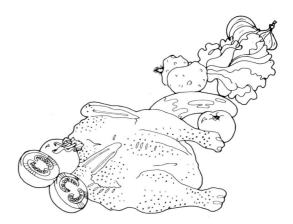

WEIGHTS AND MEASURES

MASS (WEIGHT)

Imperial		Metric
½ oz	———————————	15 gms
1 oz	———————————	30 gms
2 oz	———————————	60 gms
3 oz	———————————	90 gms
4 oz (¼ lb)	———————————	125 gms
6 oz	———————————	185 gms
8 oz (½ lb)	———————————	250 gms
12 oz (¾ lb)	———————————	375 gms
16 oz (1 lb)	———————————	500 gms (0.5 kg)
24 oz (1½ lb)	———————————	750 gms
32 oz (2 lb)	———————————	1,000 gms (1 kg)

LIQUID MEASURES

2 oz	¼ metric cup	30 ml
4 oz	½ metric cup	100 ml
5 oz (¼ pint)	⅔ metric cup	150 ml
6 oz	¾ metric cup	200 ml
8 oz	1 metric cup	250 ml
10 oz (½ pint)	1¼ metric cups	300 ml

4 metric cups	———————————	1 litre

1 metric teaspoon	———————————	5 ml
1 metric tablespoon	———————————	20 ml
1 metric cup	———————————	250 ml

"LOCAL" MEASUREMENTS

1 tahil	———————————	approximately 38 gms
1 kati	———————————	approximately 600 gms
100 gms	———————————	approximately 3 tahils

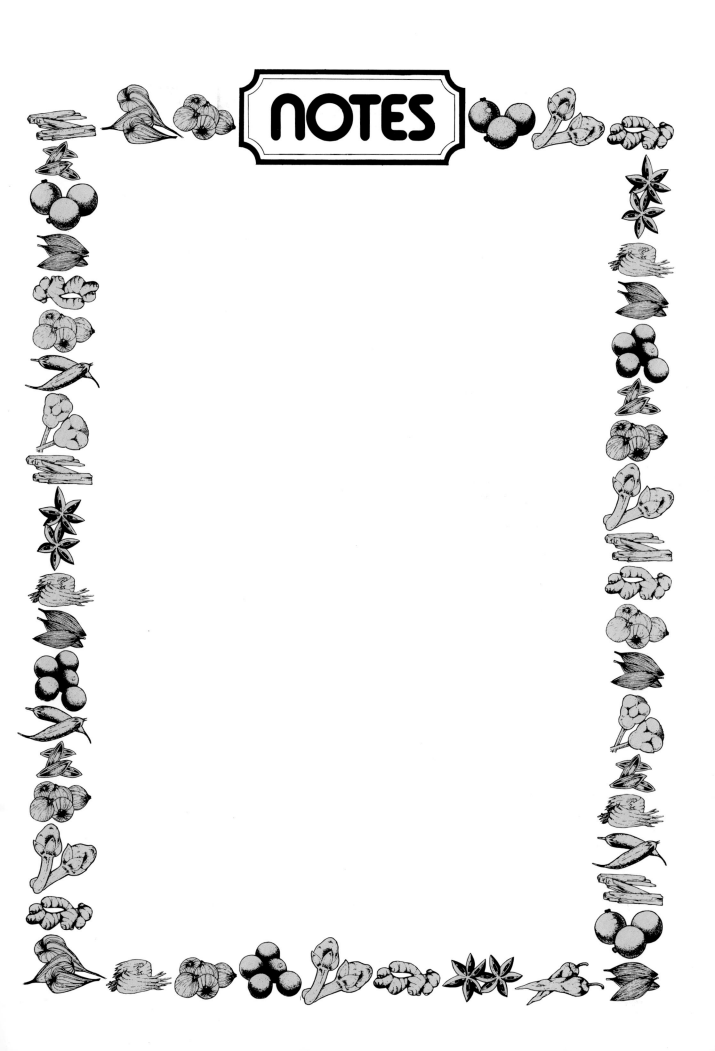

NOTES

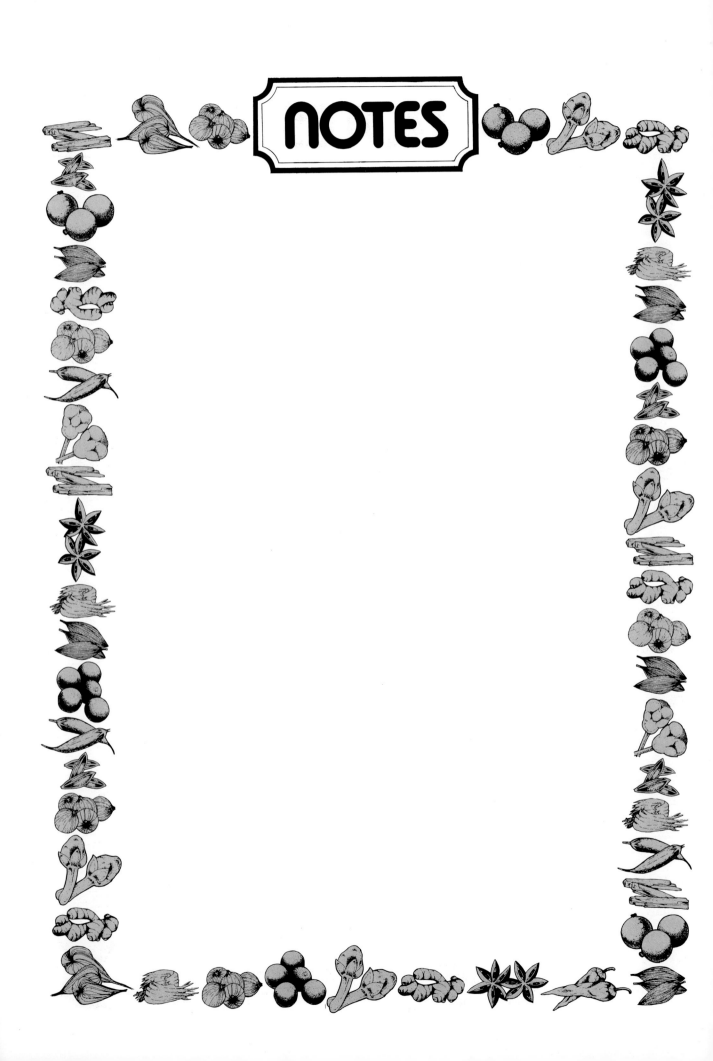

NOTES

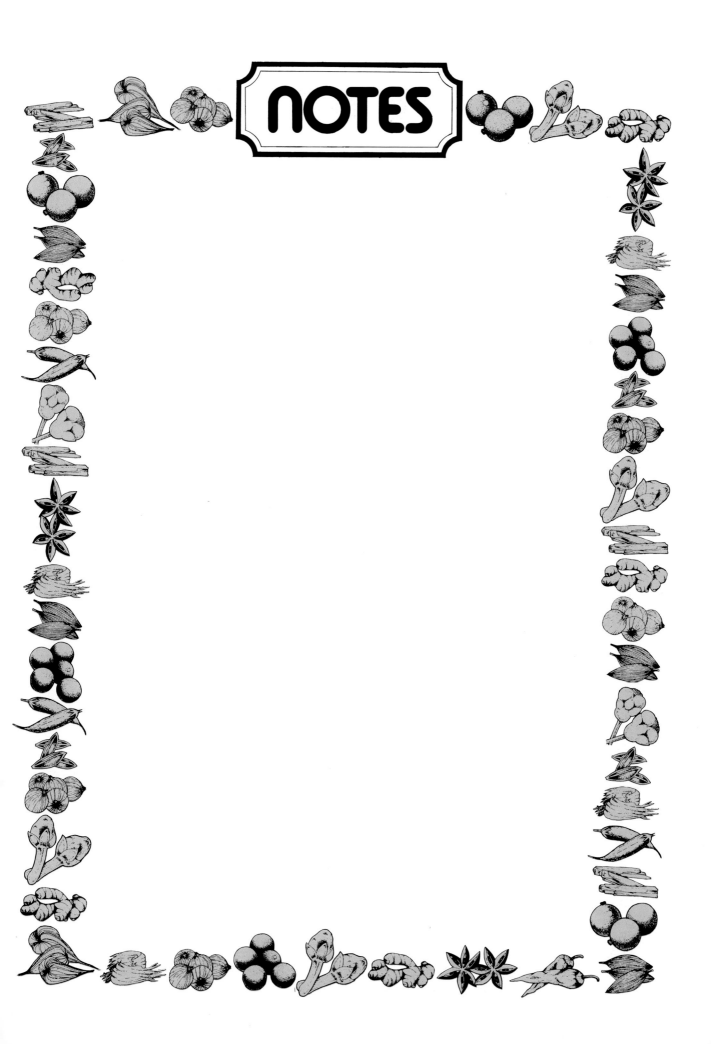

NOTES